Literacy, Technology, and Diversity

Teaching for Success in Changing Times

Jim Cummins

University of Toronto

Kristin Brown

San Diego State University

Dennis Sayers

California State University, Stanislaus

PEARSON

Boston   New York   San Francisco
Mexico City   Montreal   Toronto   London   Madrid   Munich   Paris
Hong Kong   Singapore   Tokyo   Cape Town   Sydney

Executive Editor: Aurora Martínez Ramos
Series Editorial Assistant: Lynda Giles
Marketing Manager: Danae April
Production Editor: Paula Carroll
Editorial Production Service: Lynda Griffiths
Composition Buyer: Linda Cox
Manufacturing Buyer: Linda Morris
Interior Design and Electronic Composition: Deborah Schneck
Cover Administrator: Linda Knowles

For related titles and support materials, visit our online catalog at www.ablongman.com.

Between the time website information is gathered and then published, it is not unusual for some sites to have closed. Also, the transcription of URLs can result in typographical errors. The publisher would appreciate notification where these errors occur so that they may be corrected in subsequent editions.

Cataloging-in-Publication data is not available at this time.
ISBN 0-205-38935-X

Printed in the United States of America

10 9 8 7 6 5 4 3 2 1   10 09 08 07 06

CONTENTS

"Media Assassins" at the 99th St. Elementary School ■ The Algebra Project ■ California Students Use Technology to Connect with Tsunami Survivors ■ Student-Generated Databases Using Knowledge Forum® in the Eastern Arctic ■ Educational Video Center ■ Authors in the Classroom: "The Early Authors Program" ■ Virtual Pre-K ■ Write the Truth ■ DiaLogos: A Sister Class Exchange between Greece and Canada ■ Dual-Language Bookmaking

PREFACE

According to politicians, media warriors, boardroom chief executive officers, and some members of the public, American education is in crisis. This is nothing new. The rise and fall of "literacy crisis" rhetoric has been as regular as the ebb and flow of the stock market throughout the history of public schooling. However, the current educational bear market is a little different, if only in its longevity. The crisis was first proclaimed to the public in 1983 in the report of the National Commission on Educational Excellence entitled *A Nation at Risk*. This report posited a direct causal link between the alleged underachievement of U.S. schools and the economic performance of American business. In the words of the Commission, "Our once unchallenged pre-eminence in commerce, industry, science and technological innovations is being overtaken by competitors throughout the world."

The education panic button has been stuck in the "on" position for the past 20-plus years. Radical reforms have been implemented to develop standards for all content areas, improve literacy and numeracy skills, and hold schools and individual teachers accountable for student progress. Remarkably, the "literacy crisis" rhetoric has persisted in good economic times as well as bad and has been immune to the fact that the United States has led the world in economic productivity during the latter part of the twentieth century. In fact, there is no evidence whatsoever of any overall decline in literacy attainment during the past 30 years. As documented by many researchers, the "literacy crisis" has been manufactured (e.g., Berliner & Biddle, 1995).

Despite the fact that there has been no general decline in literacy standards, we argue that there *is* an ongoing literacy crisis: Low literacy levels and academic underachievement are concentrated among students who grow up in impoverished conditions and among groups such as African American, Latino/Latina, and Native American students whose identities have been devalued in the wider society for generations. The myriad educational reforms of the past 20 years have had minimal success in closing the achievement gap between economically advantaged and economically disadvantaged students. Historical patterns of discrimination contribute to the fact that many students of color are also living in poverty. Students from these groups continue to attend schools that are grossly inferior in both material and human resources to those attended by students from more affluent backgrounds (Barndt & McNally, 2001; Biddle & Berliner, 2002; Kozol, 1991). Thus, low-income students have been denied access to effective instruction and have not been supported in harvesting the language of academic success.

Current reform efforts in the United States rest on three pillars: (1) rigorous reading instruction, (2) technology as a means of improving instructional delivery, and (3) high-stakes testing to monitor instructional effectiveness. Unfortunately, in many contexts, these potent tools are being applied in crude and scientifically ill-informed ways. For students from low-income backgrounds in inner-city and rural schools, instruction and curriculum have been hijacked to focus primarily on rote memorization of content unconnected to students' experiences or life aspirations. Teacher initiative and imagination are frequently seen as dysfunctional—a threat to the efficient implementation of the one-size-fits-all, teacher-proof, standardized curriculum required by "disadvantaged" students in underachieving schools. By contrast, powerful learning, amplified by technology, can readily be found in suburban schools attended by advantaged students. The digital divide has become a pedagogical divide. Until this situation is reversed, we should expect to see no significant reduction in the achievement gap between social groups nor any overall rise in literacy attainments.

Our goal in this book is to sketch a pedagogical blueprint for implementing literacy instruction appropriate for an increasingly diverse Information Age society. We focus in particular on the role that technology can play in promoting both the linear text-based literacy that has traditionally dominated school curricula as well as the multiple forms of literacy that are increasingly relevant within the new economy. We see the pursuit of traditional and multiple forms of literacy as complementary rather than competing goals.

Our previous book on this topic, *Brave New Schools: Challenging Cultural Illiteracy Through Global Learning Networks* (Cummins & Sayers, 1995) showed the potential of linking schools through the Internet in sister class networks to pursue collaborative critical inquiry into issues of both curricular and social significance. Here we expand the focus to consider how a range of technological tools can be harnessed for powerful pedagogical purposes. We contrast the anemic instructional vision embedded in current literacy reforms with the much more ambitious vision of teachers whose technology-supported practice we document through a wide range of case studies. Working with low-income and linguistically-diverse students, these teachers consistently build on the cultural and social capital that students bring to the classroom; they also focus their instruction on expanding students' intelligence, imagination, and multilingual talents, using technological tools as powerful amplifiers. Their rationale is simple: When instruction focuses on topics of relevance to students' lives and when it engages them cognitively, students will read more, think more, write more, and ultimately learn more. Furthermore, teachers argue that society funds education in order to expand students' social capital rather than constrict it, and clearly our society can use all the intelligence, imagination, and multilingual talent our schools can produce.

In the chapters that follow, we analyze the nature of the literacy crisis faced by our schools (Chapters 1 through 4) and then document technology-supported examples of the kinds of pedagogy that will resolve this crisis (Chapters 5 through 10); we go on to synthesize the pedagogical framework implied by these powerful examples (Chapter 11), and discuss how we can implement the instructional changes required to close the achievement gap (Chapter 12). Throughout, we emphasize that educators, both individually and collectively, have *choices*. Despite the attempt to expel imagination and empower human relationships from the "scientifically-correct" instructional mandates that are being enacted, educators who strive to develop their students' critical literacy, and expand their social capital by harnessing technological tools, will always be able to find cracks in the system of top-down control. There will always be some degrees of freedom with respect to the *content* of instruction, the levels of *cognitive engagement* our instruction can evoke, and the kinds of *tools* we can use to expand our students' literacy development. Far from being lost for words, students in the classes we document articulate their realities and analyze social issues with strong and clear voices. Imaginative use of technology, integrated with expanded notions of what it means to be literate, has enabled them to generate knowledge, take ownership of their own learning, and achieve academically.

Our perspective on technology use in schools differs from a number of other treatments of the issue. Often there has been a tendency to focus on technological tools in isolation from an analysis of what it means to be literate and what pedagogical options are available to promote different forms of literacy. For example, it is clearly relevant and valuable for teachers and students to know how to make web pages or create PowerPoint presentations. But a focus on these technical skills in isolation ignores fundamental issues of what *content* is worth presenting by means of these tools, for what purpose, and to which audiences. Also frequently ignored is the level of *cognition* or problem-solving we want our students to exercise as they pursue these projects. In the absence of a clearly articulated pedagogical rationale with respect to both *content* and *cognition*, the potential power of technological tools is frequently dissipated in trivial pursuit. Intrinsic motivation and sustained personal investment in learning require content that is challenging, socially meaningful, and that evokes higher-order thinking and critical literacy.

We have grounded our analysis of technological innovation explicitly in a conception of education that is not neutral with respect to what forms of literacy are worth promoting. In our Information Age twenty-first century society, knowledge is the coin of the realm and the ability to think critically is a prerequisite for democratic participation. When schools abdicate responsibility to develop their students' critical literacy, democracy risks becoming little more than the expression of internalized sound-bites pre-packaged for the masses by powerful media conglomerates.

Within this social and educational context, we argue that technology will improve student outcomes and resolve the real "literacy crisis" only when it is grounded in a pedagogy of collaborative critical inquiry that seeks to expand rather than constrict human possibilities.

We would like to let our readers know that authorship of this book is equally shared among the authors and the order of authorship will rotate in future editions.

The discussion questions at the end of each chapter can be used in study groups at those schools that participate in book clubs.

There is also a CD that accompanies *Literacy, Technology, and Diversity* and it includes:

1. ***A 20+ minute film of Jim Cummins explaining the Academic Expertise framework in Chapter 11.*** This framework highlights the importance of instruction that generates cognitive engagement and identity investment on the part of learners and represents a powerful tool for the development of school-based language policies.

2. ***The PowerPoint presentation used in the video.*** This presentation relates the Academic Expertise framework to the broader research literature on how people learn and draws on classroom practice to show how even recently arrived ELL students can be supported in creating dual language books that affirm their identities as engaged learners.

3. ***Science, math, dual language, and social studies monographs authored by Jim Cummins.*** These monographs include helpful information about how ELL students develop academic language proficiency and how teachers can promote students' academic learning across the curriculum.

4. ***A template for the school-based literacy planning framework that is discussed in Chapter 12.*** This can be used by teachers in electronic form to plan change in their school sites.

ACKNOWLEDGMENTS

This book is the result of multiple collaborations that we have been fortunate to be part of during the past 25 years. In the early 1980s, Kristin Brown and Dennis Sayers, together with Enid Figueroa, initiated the sister class network, *De Orilla a Orilla (From Shore to Shore)*, that was among the first efforts to explore the potential of digital technologies for literacy development and intercultural exchange in culturally and linguistically diverse contexts. In the mid-1990s, in their book, *Brave New Schools*, Dennis Sayers and Jim Cummins attempted to draw out the implications of global networking for educational reform initiatives in the United States and elsewhere. We are indebted to all our colleagues, friends, and critics who contributed significantly to these precursors of the present book.

Many people have also contributed in important ways to the writing of this book. We would first like to thank the educators who generously shared the teaching practices and innovations that are featured in the portraits (Chapters 5–10) and vignettes (Appendix). As documented in the book, the narratives that are featured here are not isolated examples that appear "out of thin air" but rather reflect long-term organizational and professional development efforts to implement theoretically grounded and empirically supported classroom practices that use technology in powerful ways to promote literacy engagement. We chose project examples that employ a range of easily accessible and relatively inexpensive technologies that will continue to be applicable over time in order to show how technology can support the powerful learning that occurs when students engage in exploring oral histories, community research, collaborative publishing, and digital storytelling. Among those who contributed generously of their time and expertise are Michelle Singer and Amada Pérez, who initiated Project FRESA, as well as their students who also shared their experiences; James Green, and Stanley and Yolanda Lucero, in the context of the Oral History project; and Patti Purcell McLain and Diane Rosen in the Biographies project. Enid Figueroa, a long-time friend and collaborator, coauthored the Biographies project. For the Student Lexicography portrait, Ruth Bennett shared her pioneering work in this area among Native American communities and Jacek Iwanski provided invaluable information on the development of his computer program *Verbs & Nouns*.

The vignettes that appear in the Appendix also reflect multiple forms of collaboration and sharing of experiences and insights. Salina Gray and Jeff Duncan-Andrade documented the Media Assassins project at the 99th St. School. Information on the Tsunami project was provided by Joana de Sena and Carla B. Herrera. Sandy McAuley shared his observations on the use of Knowledge Forum® in the Eastern Arctic. Judith Bernhard, Alma Flor Ada, F. Isabel Campoy, and Cheryl Winkley discussed with us at length their experiences in implementing and evaluating the Authors in the Classroom project, as did Alicia Narvaez, Jenny Ramos, Jan Gustafson, and María Huizar for the Virtual Pre-K project. The description of the DiaLogos sister class project is based on the doctoral dissertation of Vasilia Kourtis Kazoullis at the University of Rhodes, Greece, and also reflects numerous discussions among Vasilia Kourtis Kazoullis, Eleni Skourtou, and Jim Cummins. The Dual-Language Bookmaking vignette reflects several ongoing collaborative research projects initiated by Sandra Schechter in the Toronto area and Margaret Early in several urban sites across Canada that has involved (in the Toronto area)Vicki Bismilla, Louis Chen, Patricia Chow, Sarah Cohen, Sameena Eidoo, Suchi Garg, Frances Giampapa, Diane Knowlton, Lisa Leoni, Jacqueline Ng, Perminder Sandhu, Padma Sastri, Lynda Sutherland, and Tassos Theodoridis. In the vignettes, we have also drawn on the published work of Robert Moses (the Algebra Project), Steven Goodman (The Educational Video Center) and *Rethinking Schools* editor, Bob Peterson (Write the Truth). All of these brilliant and socially committed educators have inspired us; their voices are the heart and soul of this book.

It has been a challenging task to integrate this classroom practice with the empirical and theoretical literature and transform the resulting fusion into a coherent whole. We are particularly indebted to Aurora Martínez Ramos, executive editor at Pearson Allyn & Bacon, who supported and encouraged us through the initial drafting, reviews, and subsequent revision of the book. Further editorial support was provided by Lynda Giles and Lynda Griffiths, who ushered the manuscript into final production. Four anonymous reviewers provided insightful comments that improved the manuscript in important ways. Other colleagues and "critical friends" who read various parts of the manuscript and provided useful feedback include Alma Flor Ada, Rachel Adelson, Donal Brown, Carla B. Herrera, Magaly Lavadenz, Laura Parks-Sierra, and Stefan Rosensweig. Finally, Louis Chen and Leanne Hagglund checked the manuscript and helped generate the discussion questions that appear at the end of chapters.

Others who shared ideas, projects, and resources with us include Sarah Alam, Marsha Alibrandi, Andy Alm, Judith Baker, Tim Byers, Karen Cadiero Kaplan, Patrick Camangian, Bob Carter, Ruty Chotzen, Gladys Abu Elezam, Judi Freeman, Lorena Garcia, Andrew Greene, Camille Hall, Jay Holmes, Raymond Isola, Mohammed Jabreen, Jove Jankulovski, Lisa Jobson, Kaye King, Virginia King, Ben Ashour Kingsbury, Michael Lach, Marguerite Lukes, Mark McCann, Dorothy Menosky, Peggy Morrison, Mardi Musick, KimOanh Nguyen-Lam, Walter Paul, Carolyn Redendo, Nataki Reynolds, Kevin Rocap, Yolanda Ronquillo, Raymond Rose, Susan Santone, Nancy Jean Smith, Udara Soysa, Rosemary Tejada, Zoiner Tejada, Anna Vásquez, Jim Wallace, Rose Wooten, and Sheli Wortis. Organizations and projects with which these educators are affiliated include *Rethinking Schools,* iEARN, and CLMER under the leadership of J. David Ramírez.

Finally, we would like to thank our families who have lived through and shared in the intensity of the writing of this book. This book could not have been written without the support and encouragement of Neil Joyce and Patricia Brown (Kristin), Robbie Edge (Dennis), and Ioana Cummins (Jim).

Part 1

Changing Times, Changing Schools

Literacy

T he quotation from *Hamlet* appears apt in reviewing the recent history of U.S. federal policy on the teaching of reading. Reading policy documents have insisted that methods of reading instruction be not only "scientifically based" but also "scientifically proven." These policies have resulted in the implementation of dramatically different instructional approaches for poor children as compared to rich children. In the early grades, poor kids increasingly get one-size-fits-all scripted programs that focus primarily on phonics while rich kids are encouraged to get into extensive reading of real books. Rich kids typically have an abundance of books in their homes, whereas poor kids do not. And this *pedagogical divide* is based on scientific research? In fact, there is no scientific research supporting the kinds of drill-and-practice literacy instruction currently being inflicted on many low-income rural and inner-city students. Methinks that ideology is masquerading as science. This chapter looks at the actual scientific basis for literacy policies in schools and finds much to be concerned about in the lack of empirical support for the instructional practices that increasingly characterize low-income schools.

Introduction

Why do some students perform well in school and others perform poorly? It might seem obvious that any attempt to raise academic achievement levels in U.S. schools should be based on a rigorous analysis of the causes of underachievement. Incredibly, this question has received little sustained examination from policymakers during the past 20 years of intensive educational reform efforts. Certainly, the reforms that have been proposed and implemented are based on *assumptions* about the roots of underachievement. Unfortunately, the analysis of causal factors has been selective, unscientific, and ideologically loaded. We argue in this chapter that as a consequence of this inadequate analysis, the current reforms are unlikely to produce any sustained growth in literacy or numeracy attainment. Similarly, as we discuss in subsequent chapters, the current infusion of technology into schools will yield minimal gain in student academic outcomes because the technology is generally not integrated with forms of pedagogy that promote cognitive and affective engagement with learning. This is unfortunate because, as we document throughout this book, technological tools *can* exert a powerful impact on literacy development and overall academic achievement when they are harnessed to a pedagogy that engages students affectively, cognitively, and imaginatively.

In 1983, the National Commission on Excellence in Education proclaimed that U.S. schools suffered from "a rising tide of mediocrity that threatens our very future as a nation and a people." The educational reform effort initiated by this report gathered momentum through the late 1980s and 1990s, and the juggernaut continues to roar along unabated in the new millennium. There is widespread belief that literacy standards are in decline and that the educational system is failing both students and society. A variety of culprits for the apparent precipitous decline in literacy attainment have been identified at different times. These include the lack of rigorous instruction oriented to attainment of specific standards, the lack of effective testing and accountability, and the obduracy of "the education establishment" (e.g., teacher unions) in protecting its own interests at the expense of quality education. Also included in the list of "America's Most Wanted Scapegoats" are the following:

■ Progressive "child-centered" pedagogy together with whole-language approaches to reading instruction that (allegedly) fail to provide students with the basic foundation for academic success (e.g., Levine, 1996);[1]

■ Bilingual education programs that (allegedly) focus on maintaining children's home languages at the expense of achievement in English (e.g., Rossell & Baker, 1996; Schlesinger, 1991); and

■ Multicultural children's literature that (allegedly) deprives children of access to the rich linguistic resources contained in the more traditional canon of Euro-American literature and consequently undermines children's ability to read, write, and reason (Stotsky, 1999).

These themes are regularly invoked by critics of the education system, as illustrated in the following excerpts from a *New York Times* op-ed piece by Diane Ravitch (March 15, 2005):

> It is true that American student performance is appalling. Only a minority of students—whether in 4th, 8th or 12th grade—reach proficiency as measured by the Education Department's National Assessment of Educational Progress. On a scale that has three levels—basic, proficient and advanced—most students score at the basic level or even below basic in every subject. American students also perform poorly when compared with their peers in other developed countries

on tests of mathematics and science, and many other nations now have a higher proportion of their students completing high school. . . .

To really get at the problem, we have to make changes across our educational system. The most important is to stress the importance of academic achievement. Sorry to say, we have a long history of reforms by pedagogues to de-emphasize academic achievement and to make school more "relevant," "fun" and like "real life." These efforts have produced whole-language instruction, where phonics, grammar and spelling are abandoned in favor of "creativity," and fuzzy math, where students are supposed to "construct" their own solutions to math problems instead of finding the right answers.

The subtext of this account reflects several common themes in neo-conservative analyses of what's wrong with the education system and how to fix it. Specifically, although Ravitch's focus on academic achievement is clearly appropriate, her argument would have been more credible had she acknowledged and accounted for the fact that academic achievement has *not* declined over the past 30 years (as measured by National Assessment of Educational Progress [NAEP] reports). She implies that the educational system is in crisis and in need of a radical fix; we agree, but the nature of the "fix" we envisage and outline in this book is very different from that currently being implemented in many low-income school districts. Ravitch also implies (by omission) that social factors associated with wealth and poverty are irrelevant to understanding educational achievement, preferring to focus blame on "pedagogues" who have inflicted a series of misguided instructional fads on the school system. Thus, educational reform requires no social changes (such as funding all schools equally); instead, educators need to discard relevance, fun, creativity, and real life from our classrooms in favor of rigorous direct instruction that will help students find "the right answers."

In line with these assumptions, the central thrust of current reform efforts has been to implement an accountability system based on the specification of content standards in various subject areas of the curriculum together with use of high-stakes tests to monitor students' and schools' attainment of these standards. In this way, underachieving schools (and teachers) can be identified and removed from the system if they fail to respond rapidly to treatment. These reform efforts are ostensibly intended to strengthen the *public* school system, but the private sector is in hot pursuit, ready and eager to absorb any schools that fail to keep up with the pack. For example, in cities such as Baltimore and Philadelphia, Edison International, a for-profit corporation, has been granted control of a significant number of schools. Edison's claims that it can turn around failing schools, and turn a profit at the same time, are yet to be demonstrated (Bracey, 2003).

In this and subsequent chapters, we propose a very different analysis of the nature of the "literacy crisis" and a very different set of directions for educational reform. In this chapter, the focus is on the scientific basis for current literacy policies in schools. We limit our analysis in this chapter to traditional definitions of "literacy," viewed simply as reading and writing skills, but expand this definition in subsequent chapters to include an expanded range of *literacies* that are increasingly relevant to life in contemporary societies. We set the stage for this analysis by examining the ambitious reform agenda ushered in by the Elementary and Secondary Education Act (ESEA), otherwise known as the No Child Left Behind Act, signed into law by President George W. Bush on January 8, 2002.

The No Child Left Behind (NCLB) Act

The NCLB Act rests on four major propositions:

1. There is a crisis in literacy attainment (as well as in math and science attainment).

2. The crisis can be resolved by implementing "scientifically proven" methods of instruction.

3. Yearly testing (initially from grades 3 through 8) will enable failing schools to be identified by monitoring the extent to which schools and school districts are making adequate yearly progress toward the attainment of state standards.

4. Chronically failing schools can be weeded from the educational system by giving parents the right to remove their children from these schools and/or obtain supplementary educational services from private for-profit or religious service providers.

As evidence that there is indeed a crisis of achievement, the federal government's No Child Left Behind website (www.nochildleftbehind.gov/next/overview/overview.html) notes that despite increased federal government spending since 1996

■ Less than one-third of the nation's fourth-graders read proficiently.

■ Reading performance has not improved in more than 15 years.

A major part of the solution involves providing federal dollars only to "curricula and teaching methods that are scientifically proven to work." The notion of "scientifically proven to work" is elaborated on the website as follows:

■ President Bush is confident that if educators use the best materials, scientifically proven instructional methods, and textbooks aligned with state standards, students can succeed.

■ Under No Child Left Behind, the federal government will invest in educational practices that work—that research evidence has shown to be effective in improving student performance.

Schools and school districts are to be held accountable for their students' progress. Making a school system accountable involves several critical steps:

1. States create their own standards for what a child should know and learn for all grades.

2. With standards in place, states must test every student's progress toward those standards by using tests that are aligned with the standards.

3. Each state, school district, and school will be expected to make adequate yearly progress (AYP) toward meeting state standards. This progress will be measured for all subgroups of students by disaggregating test results for students who are economically disadvantaged, are from racial or ethnic minority groups, have disabilities, or have limited English proficiency. Schools are required to demonstrate that all of these groups are making adequate yearly progress.

4. School and district performance will be publicly reported in district and state report cards. Individual school results will be on the district report cards. If the district or school continually fails to make adequate progress toward the standards, then they will be held accountable (www.nochildleftbehind.gov/next/overview/index.html).

The NCLB Act also gives parents options for helping their children if they are enrolled in schools chronically identified as "in need of improvement." Parents will be able to transfer their child to a better-performing public school or public charter school. For the first time, parents with children in a school identified as in need of improvement will be able to use federal education funds (taken from Title I allotments to the school district) for what are called "supplemental education services." These services include tutoring, after-school services, and summer school programs. Schools that are in need of improvement are not eligible to provide supplemental services to their own students, and school districts that are designated as failing are also ineligible to provide such services. It should be noted that if any one identified subgroup (e.g., students with disabilities, students who are English language learners [ELL], etc.) at any grade level within a school fails to make adequate yearly progress (typically about 5 percent gain per year on state test scores), this will result in the entire school being designated as failing.

In addition, the NCLB Act highlights the potential of technology to improve children's educational performance. In 2002, more than $700 million was made available to states and schools through the Enhancing Education through Technology program, along with $2.25 billion through the e-rate initiative that provides low-cost Internet access to schools. In addition, the law provides states and schools with more flexibility to use their federal funds to make better use of technology. Many technology-oriented companies are also offering supplemental services to schools under the provisions of the law (Miner, 2003). Secretary of Education Rod Paige, in a July 12, 2002, speech in Denver, Colorado, highlighted the link between technology and the NCLB Act:

> By harnessing technology, we can expand access to learning and close the achievement gap in America. And that's the critical mission of the No Child Left Behind Act of 2001. These new education reforms say loud and clear: One size does not fit all when it comes to educating our children. We must challenge the old ways. We must be innovative and creative in our thinking. We must do *whatever it takes* to help ensure that every child is educated. (Retrieved from www.nclb.gov/media/news/071202.html)

The goal of NCLB is to have 100 percent of students performing at grade level and attaining state-mandated proficiency standards by 2014. This is clearly an ambitious and admirable goal. No Child Left Behind *has* put underachievement associated with poverty, race/ethnicity, and exceptionality on the accountability map. Unfortunately, however, many provisions of the law are based on a woefully inadequate analysis of current scientific research in education. Furthermore, the act shows minimal appreciation of the implementation challenges that its provisions entail in school systems starved for cash and attempting to educate an increasingly impoverished and linguistically diverse student population. As we argue in subsequent chapters, two critical

> The provisions of NCLB are based on a woefully inadequate analysis of current scientific research in education.

dimensions of learning and literacy—*affect* and *identity*—are totally absent from the scientifically correct prescriptions of NCLB. In other words, few remedies are likely to result from prescriptions about teaching and testing that take no account of how students feel about themselves and about their chances of being successful in the classroom.

Despite the limitations of the current reform agenda, the positive aspects should be emphasized. First, NCLB identifies reading as central to all aspects of educational attainment and places appropriate emphasis on the improvement of reading. Second, it recognizes that overall improvement in achievement must entail improvement among those groups of students who currently experience the most disproportionate school failure. Thus, schools must focus on improving achievement among low-income students, English language learners, and minority group students who, in the past, have typically experienced vastly inferior educational provision. Finally, the law increases Title I funding for poor schools by 20 percent. However, much of this money will be used to pay for supplemental services and/or transfers of students to other schools, if other schools can be found that will accept them. One of the most prominent authorities on educational accountability, Robert L. Linn, has also pointed to positive aspects of NCLB:

> NCLB has much that is worthy of praise. It is particularly praiseworthy for its emphasis on all children and special attention it gives to improving learning for children that have been too often ignored or left behind in the past. The emphasis on closing the achievement gap is certainly praiseworthy. The encouragement that NCLB gives to states to adopt ambitious subject matter standards is also noteworthy. (2004, p. 2)

In assessing the adequacy of the NCLB reform agenda in this and subsequent chapters, we examine:

- The extent to which there is a "literacy crisis" that would justify such radical top-down intervention in the educational system;

- The empirical basis for the literacy instruction mandates that are repeatedly described as "scientifically proven" in press releases concerning NCLB;

- The adequacy of the assumptions underlying the testing provisions of NCLB, including the most basic assumption that standardized testing improves learning; and

- The adequacy of the assumption that technology by itself can improve learning.

Reading Achievement:
A Crisis of Credibility

The orchestrated panic in relation to declining standards has been convincingly debunked as a "manufactured crisis" designed to impose more top-down control over the educational system (Berliner & Biddle, 1995). In international comparisons of literacy achievement, the United States performs well relative to other industrialized countries at the grade 4 level but less well at grade 8 (Elley, 1992; National Center for Educational Statistics, 2004; Organization for Economic Cooperation and Development [OECD], 2001). Comparisons of National Assessment of Educational Progress (NAEP) data from 1971 through 2005 show no drop in reading scores (Allington, 2001; Carroll, Krop, Arkes, Morrison, & Flanagan, 2005; Donahue, Voelkl, Campbell, & Mazzeo, 1999). Graves, Juel, and Graves (2001, pp. 21–22) summarized the NAEP data through 1998 as follows: "For all practical purposes, U.S. students in 1998 read just about like U.S. students in 1971." And in 2005, they read at a similar level to U.S. students in 1998.

As illustrated in Table 1.1, national NAEP data from 1992 through 2005 show a pattern of flatlined reading achievement despite the fact that during this period many states implemented reforms designed to rid schools of any vestiges of "child-centered" and "whole-language" instruction. Additionally, there has been minimal progress in closing the reading achievement gap between different social groups during this period.[2]

TABLE 1.1 U.S. Student Performance on NAEP Reading, Grade 4 and Grade 8

Grade 4

1992	1994	1998	2000	2002	2003	2005
217	214	215	213	219	218	219

Grade 8

1992	1994	1998		2002	2003	2005
260	260	263		264	263	262

Source: www.nces.ed.gov/nationsreportcard/nde/.

As noted, background documentation to the NCLB (as well as commentary such as that by Ravitch [2005]) puts a negative spin on these trends, highlighting the fact that there has been no improvement in reading scores during the past 15 years and that only about one-third of fourth-graders read adequately. Obviously, conceptions of "adequacy" are somewhat arbitrary and there will always be room for improvement no matter what criterion is specified. What is clear from the international comparisons is that if U.S. fourth-graders are reading inadequately, then they are joined by fourth-graders in the vast majority of countries around the world. The real problems in patterns of reading achievement are very different from those identified by NCLB; in fact, as we will argue, NCLB "remedies" are likely to exacerbate the real problems that schools face in helping students attain high levels of literacy.

The consistency in levels of reading performance over a 30-year period incorporates several more disturbing patterns. First, the data suggest that in spite of intensive educational reforms during the 1990s focused on early reading attainment, there has been no reduction in the gap between Euro-American students, on the one hand, and African American and Latino/Latina students on the other (Table 1.2).

TABLE 1.2 U.S. Student Performance on NAEP Reading, Grade 4 and Grade 8 by Race/Ethnicity

Grade 4

	1992	1994	1998	2000	2002	2003	2005
White	224	224	225	224	229	229	229
Black	192	185	193	190	199	198	200
Hispanic	197	188	193	190	201	200	203
Asian/Pacific Islander	216	220	215	225	224	226	229
American Indian					207	202	204

Grade 8

	1992	1994	1998	2002	2003	2005
White	267	267	270	272	272	271
Black	237	236	243	245	244	243
Hispanic	241	243	243	247	245	246
Asian/Pacific Islander	268	265	264	267	270	271
American Indian				250	246	249

Source: www.nces.ed.gov/nationsreportcard/nde/.

These trends are strongly related to socioeconomic status (SES) differentials between these groups. In short, while middle-class children read relatively well, low-income students continue to lag and there is minimal evidence that current instructional reforms have had any impact on improving the literacy attainments of low-income students. The average score gap between low-income and higher-income students changed minimally between 1998 and 2005.

When looking specifically at the period between 2002 and 2005, again one sees minimal evidence of improvement that might be attributed to the provisions of NCLB, which was implemented during this period. Overall performance is unchanged for grade 4 students and declines by 2 points for grade 8 students. Slight improvements for Black and Hispanic students at the grade 4 level are offset by declines in performance at the grade 8 level. American Indian students show a slight decline at both grade levels. No Child Left Behind also appears to have minimal impact on the achievement of students from low-income backgrounds. The gap between grade 4 students eligible for free or reduced lunch (low-income) and other students is unchanged between 2002 and 2005. At the grade 8 level, the scores of students eligible for free or reduced lunch decline by 2 points between 2002 and 2005, as do the scores of those not eligible for free or reduced lunch. Some improvement during this period is evident among grade 4 English language learners (from a score of 183 in 2002 to a score of 187 in 2005, compared to scores of 221 and 222 among non-ELL students) but at the grade 8 level, ELL students' scores are unchanged from 2002 to 2005.

> Reading achievement has remained stable over a period of 30 years. Contrary to the pervasive literacy crisis rhetoric, there has been no decline in achievement.

A second disturbing pattern is that although early literacy attainments have remained stable over time and are comparable to other industrialized countries, as indicated by comparisons of 9-year-olds (discussed later), many U.S. students show gaps in their ability to deal with the more demanding literacy tasks encountered at more advanced grade levels. The summary of trends articulated by Graves and colleagues in 2001 applies equally to the more recent data:

> By fourth grade, the vast majority of students can read easy material and answer simple questions on it. However, once the texts become slightly more difficult—the sorts of things middle-grade students are expected to deal with—a large percentage of middle-grade students cannot read and understand the questions and neither can a sizable percentage of high school seniors. And once both texts and questions become demanding—the sorts of material one would need to read to

understand political and social issues or enjoy relatively sophisticated literature—very few students, even those about to graduate from high school, can deal with them. (2001, pp. 22–23)

Graves and colleagues also note that "the reading proficiency of students attending schools in disadvantaged communities lags very significantly behind that of students attending schools in advantaged communities" (p. 23).

These points assume significance in the present context for two reasons:

1. The impact of poverty on school achievement has been largely ignored in current educational reforms; it is assumed that providing "scientifically proven" reading instruction will enable all children to succeed academically, thereby removing the need for any social interventions (e.g., better prenatal care for low-income pregnant women).

2. The research data from both domestic and international studies show that U.S. students perform relatively well in reading in the early grades of elementary school but show much more varied performance at higher grade levels. The NCLB reforms, however, focus on implementing "scientifically proven" approaches to initial reading instruction (thereby providing a solution to a nonexistent problem), while largely ignoring the real problems that many adolescents face in more advanced forms of reading comprehension.

Recent international comparisons reveal some very clear patterns with respect to these two issues. Two studies of reading achievement conducted by the International Association for the Evaluation of Educational Achievement (IEA) in 1991 and 2001 (Elley, 1992; National Center for Educational Statistics, 2003) demonstrate that younger U.S. students are performing well in comparison to their peers in other industrialized countries. The comparative performance of older (15-year-old) U.S. students is much weaker, how-

> The NCLB emphasis on early reading (phonics and decoding) attempts to solve a nonexistent problem while neglecting the real problems that students experience in reading comprehension beyond the primary grades.

ever, due largely to the highly significant impact of poverty on student performance.

In the 1991 study (Elley, 1992), U.S. 9-year-olds performed at the second highest level (after Finland) in a comparison of almost 30 countries, whereas the reading performance of 14-year-olds placed the United States ninth among participating countries. Elley noted that 9-year-old students in the U.S. sample "are relatively strong in literacy,

International comparisons suggest that U.S. performance is comparatively better at the grade 4 level than at the grade 8 level.

in spite of reading in a language with an irregular orthography" (p. 16). In addition, the U.S. 14-year-olds performed at a level very close to what would be expected based on the level of U.S. economic and social development but "the American students performed considerably better at the 9-year-old level relative to the other participating countries than at the 14-year-old level" (p. 26).

A follow-up study entitled "Progress in International Reading Literacy Study (PIRLS)" (National Center for Education Statistics, 2003) was also conducted by the IEA and released in April 2003. This study examined fourth-graders' ability to comprehend narrative (literary) and expository (informational) text. On the combined score, "U.S. fourth-graders outperform their counterparts in 23 of the 34 other countries participating in PIRLS 2001, although they score [significantly] lower than students in England, the Netherlands, and Sweden" (National Center for Education Statistics, 2003, p. 4).

White and Asian students in the United States scored significantly better than Black and Hispanic students, a finding that reflects the strong impact of poverty on test performance. As illustrated clearly in Figure 1.1, there is a linear relationship between reading performance and the percentage of children in a school eligible for free or reduced-price lunch.

Although different tests were used in the 1991 and 2001 IEA studies, subsamples of students from different countries in the 2001 study were administered items from the earlier research. For the U.S. sample, no significant difference was noted in the performance on these items between 1991 and 2001—evidence again that there has been no general decline in reading performance among elementary school students. Thus, the premise of NCLB that there is a crisis in literacy attainment due to inadequate methods of early reading instruction is refuted over and over again by all of the scientific research. It is worth noting that the strong performance of U.S. fourth-grade students in the 1991 study came at a time when whole-language methods were at the height of their influence in U.S. classrooms.

Among the international comparisons that are of interest in the PIRLS data is the fact that U.S. schools reported a greater curricular emphasis on reading than their international counterparts. For example, 65 percent of U.S. fourth-graders receive more than six hours of reading instruction per week compared to the international average of 28 percent. However, U.S. students engage in reading for enjoyment outside of school to a significantly lesser extent than the international average. For example, 32 percent of U.S. fourth-graders never or almost

FIGURE **1.1**

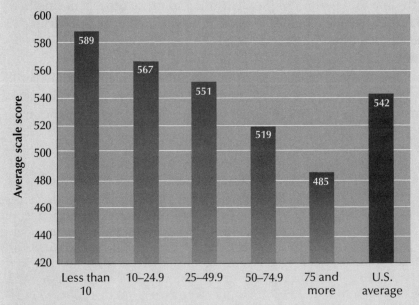

U.S. Fourth Grade Public School Students' Average Scores
on the Combined Reading Literacy Scale by the Percentage
Enrollment Eligible for Free of Reduced-Price Lunch

Percentage of school enrollment eligible for free or reduced-price lunch

Source: National Center for Educational Statistics, 2003, p. 15.

never read for enjoyment outside of school, compared to only 18 percent of students in comparison countries. Only 35 percent of U.S. students reported that they read for fun every day or almost every day, compared to 40 percent of international students.

The international comparisons, together with the NAEP data, suggest that the real problems in reading achievement among U.S. students emerge in the later grades of elementary school (after grade 4) and reflect these students' difficulties with advanced levels of reading comprehension rather than with decoding skills. The pattern can be seen clearly in the results of the Programme for International Student Assessment (PISA), an ongoing international study of academic performance among 15-year-olds conducted by the Organization for Economic Cooperation and Development (OECD) (2001, 2004a, 2004b). In the

2000 survey of 32 countries, the United States ranked fifteenth in reading, considerably lower than other English-speaking countries (e.g., Canada, second; Australia, fourth). The reading results from the 2003 survey again placed the United States at about the average for OECD countries (OECD, 2004a). The overall mediocre performance of U.S. adolescent students in both surveys reflected a much larger gap between high- and low-performing students than in many other industrialized countries. The best U.S. students read as well as students anywhere in the world but less proficient adolescent readers have considerably lower reading skills than their peers in many other countries.

This pattern was strongly related to the social inequalities experienced by low-performing U.S. students. The PISA study found that family income was more strongly related to reading performance in the United States than in any other country. Huge differences were observed in reading performance between affluent and impoverished 15-year-old students:

> Among the participating countries, the United States shows the largest differences, the gap in reading performance between students in the top and bottom quarters of wealth being 85 points (OECD average difference 34 points). Expressed differently, students in the United States are at least twice as likely to be among the 25 percent lowest performers in reading literacy if they are in the bottom quarter of the PISA index of wealth [than] if they are in the top quarter. (OECD, 2001, p. 143)

The PISA data also highlighted the impact of socioeconomic segregation on reading performance:

> Thus, there appears to be an advantage for an individual in attending a school in which other students have more favourable home backgrounds. This advantage may stem from a variety of factors, including peer group influences, differences in the resources of quality of schools attended by different social groups, or differences in teacher expectations. . . . This analysis also suggests that high segregation of students by social background can create an intense disadvantage for students in the least favoured schools. . . . Thus, policies that limit the extent of social segregation across schools appear likely to help more students to achieve their potential. (OECD, 2004b, p. 15)

This finding carries particular weight in light of what Jonathan Kozol (2005) calls "the restoration of apartheid schooling in America." School segregation by race (and socioeconomic status) has increased significantly during the past 15 years.

In short, the NAEP and international data show clearly that there is no general decline in literacy standards within the United States. Rather, the so-called crisis is an ongoing one: Underachievement is concentrated among the approximately 20 percent of American students who grow up in impoverished conditions and among groups such as African American, Latino/Latina, and Native American students. Historical patterns of discrimination contribute to the fact that many of these groups are also living in poverty. Students from these groups continue to attend schools that are grossly inferior in both material and human resources in comparison to those attended by students from more affluent backgrounds (Anyon, 2005; Berliner & Biddle, 1995; Kozol, 1991, 2005; Neuman & Celano, 2001).

The impact of poverty on reading achievement has been noted in some of the research syntheses that contributed to NCLB. For example, Snow, Burns, and Griffin (1998) point to the correlation of .68 between reading achievement and the collective poverty level of students in a school. This correlation is considerably greater than the correlation of approximately .45 between reading achievement and early literacy indicators, such as knowledge of the letters of the alphabet or phonological awareness.

Despite the strong correlation between academic failure and the collective poverty level of children in a school, there has been little political will to push for equality of access to funding as a means of raising achievement in the inner-city and rural schools that serve low-income students. It is much safer to focus on the presumed "deficits" that low-income children bring to school (e.g., lack of phonological awareness) and teachers' alleged lack of competence to remediate these so-called deficits, than to highlight inequities in the distribution of economic and educational resources as causal factors in students' underachievement (Gee, 1999, 2000).[3]

A number of U.S. researchers and commentators have highlighted the "disconnect" between current educational reform initiatives and the demonstrated impact of poverty on academic achievement. Bracey (1999), for example, points to the hypocrisy of the rhetoric of educational reform in light of the fact that politicians and policymakers have shown minimal interest in addressing issues of child poverty, which has a "devastating impact" on school performance:

Poor children get off to a bad start before they are born. Their mothers are likely to get prenatal care late, if at all, which can impair later intellectual functioning. They are more than three times as likely as nonpoor children to have stunted growth. They are about twice as likely to have physical and mental disabilities, and are seven times more likely to be abused or neglected. And they are more than three times more likely to die [early].

What these kids need are high standards, right? (p. 19A)

Payne and Biddle (1999) have demonstrated the independent effects of school funding levels and child poverty on mathematics achievement in the United States. Together these variables accounted for 25 percent of the variance in achievement. Level of curriculum challenge (ranging from remedial to advanced algebra curriculum) was also significantly related to achievement. They suggest a far more likely explanation for the relatively poor showing of U.S. schools in international comparisons than the "declining standards" usually invoked by politicians:

> Since poorly funded schools and communities with high levels of poverty are very rare in other industrialized nations, education in America is uniquely handicapped because of the singular tolerance for large numbers of poorly funded schools and massive amounts of child poverty in our country. And as long as this tolerance continues, *none* of the present programs being touted for "reforming" American education—educational vouchers, "setting high standards," "accountability" schemes, charter schools—are likely to improve America's aggregate math achievement substantially. (1999, p. 12)

Rothstein (2002) reviewed research that compared the cost benefits of school versus nonschool interventions. Nonschool interventions in areas such as increasing family income, ensuring adequate nutrition, prenatal care, maternal smoking, health care, and housing were associated with increased cognitive ability and/or academic achievement among low-income students. For example, research studies have reported significant test score gains as a result of vitamin and mineral supplements given to poor children (reviewed by Neisser et al., 1996). Similarly, Duncan, Brooks-Gunn, and Klebanov (1994) showed that when other family characteristics were controlled, there was a 9-point IQ gap between children from persistently poor families when compared to those from families whose income during the five-year study period never fell below the poverty line. Rothstein concludes that although schools should certainly be improved, attention also must focus on national failures in income distribution, housing, and health care. School improvement efforts that ignore these social problems are unlikely to be successful.

Anyon's (2005) review of the impact of poverty on educational success reaches a similar conclusion. She notes that poverty has been found to exert consistently negative effects on children's cognitive development.

Furthermore, longitudinal studies demonstrate that family income consistently predicts children's academic and cognitive performance, even when other family characteristics, such as educational level, are taken into account. The research also demonstrates that poor children have more health and behavior difficulties than those from more affluent families, which mitigates against educational success. Anyon concludes that "economic access creates the financial and political conditions in families and communities for educational commitment and reward" (2005, p. 83). In calling for a new paradigm for educational policy that takes into account the macroeconomic context, she highlights the futility of educational initiatives, such as NCLB, that ignore the link between economic conditions and educational achievement:

> As education policymakers and practitioners, we can acknowledge and act on the power of urban poverty, low-wage work, and housing segregation to dwarf most curricular, pedagogical, and other educational reforms. The effects of macroeconomic policies continually trump the effects of education policies. (2005, p. 83)

In short, current reform efforts selectively highlight empirical data linking individual student characteristics to underachievement while simultaneously ignoring much stronger empirical relationships between achievement and social and educational inequities. No Child Left Behind does not deny the impact of social and educational inequities on academic achievement; it simply ignores these factors, as have most previous attempts at educational reform. The implicit assumption underlying these (and previous) reform efforts is that instructional interventions by themselves can remediate student "deficits" while ignoring the associated social and educational inequities. There is little evidence of serious inquiry into why decades of reform initiatives, each with its claims to scientific legitimacy, should have yielded such paltry results.

> Scientific research shows that social disparities related to poverty exert a considerably greater influence on reading development than instructional variables and, furthermore, intervention at the social level can significantly improve achievement among low-income students.

The Scientific Research on Reading: An Empirical Reality Check

The No Child Left Behind Act drew on research reviewed by the National Reading Panel (NRP) (2000) that pointed to the role of phonological awareness training and systematic phonics instruction in helping children learn to read. Phonological awareness training helps children understand that words are composed of discrete sounds, and phonics teaching systematically maps these sounds onto the written word. The official view, as expressed by NRP panelists Ehri, Nunes, Stahl, and Willows (2001), is that "systematic phonics instruction helped children learn to read better than all forms of control group instruction, including whole language" (p. 393). The Summary Report of the National Reading Panel went much further by proclaiming, "The meta-analysis revealed that systematic phonics instruction produces significant benefits for students in kindergarten through 6th grade" (NRP Summary, p. 9) (see Garan, 2001, 2004). Lyon and Chhabra (2004) reiterate the NRP claim that systematic phonics instruction benefits students across the elementary schools grades: "Systematic phonics instruction produced significant benefits for K–6 students and for those having difficulty learning to read" (p. 15). However, this spin on the NRP data omits mentioning that systematic phonics instruction produced *no benefits* in reading comprehension for normal-achieving and low-achieving students in grades 2 through 6.

As discussed earlier, in order to receive funds under the No Child Left Behind Act, school systems must implement "scientifically based" reading instruction (which is code for a strong focus on phonological awareness training and systematic phonics teaching). They are also required to test children with appropriate standardized tests every year between grades 3 and 8. Thus, phonological awareness training and systematic phonics instruction have emerged as "scientifically proven" magic bullets to solve the literacy crisis in U.S. education. The major beneficiaries of these policy developments have been scripted reading programs such as Open Court and Direct Instruction (DISTAR) that continue intensive phonics instruction for a significant part of the school day well beyond the primary grades (Cain, 2005; Metcalf, 2002; Meyer, 2002; Newkirk, 2002). Although some teachers appreciate the structure of these programs, others regard them as rigid and inflexible and resent the fact that adherence to the script is mandatory and enforced by school principals or program monitors. Many large urban school districts across the United States have adopted these one-size-fits-all programs as a "quick-fix" to problems of underachievement among low-income children.

The emphasis on systematic phonological awareness and phonics instruction as *the* key elements in effective reading instruction has been incorporated into the criteria whereby school systems qualify for funds under the Reading First initiative, a direct funding outgrowth of the No

Child Left Behind Act. Thus, the NRP literature review has exerted a huge impact on the way reading is taught throughout the United States.

It is a sad irony that this report, produced by well-intentioned academics, appears likely to exacerbate the instructional conditions that have contributed to inadequate reading development among low-income students. The reforms in literacy instruction that the NRP report has spawned are reinforcing the *pedagogical divide* that characterizes instruction for low-income as compared to more affluent students. Low-income students increasingly receive an instructional diet of drill-and-practice while upper- and middle-income students are apprenticed to knowledge construction and critical inquiry, all in the name of scientifically based reading instruction. Ivey and Baker (2004) highlight the impact of recent reading policy initiatives on the instruction that middle school students receive:

> In all our work with older struggling readers, we have not come across a single student who would benefit from phonemic awareness training or phonics instruction. Unfortunately, in the past year or so, we have received a disconcerting number of reports from middle schools and high schools that have adopted reading programs focused on these two basic elements of reading. (p. 35)

Our view (shared by many who have written about recent reading policy in the United States) is that the NRP report is bereft of scientific credibility (see Allington, 2004; Coles, 2001, 2002, 2003; Cummins, 2001; Garan, 2001, 2004; Krashen, 2001, 2004a). This strong statement is based on the fact that there are serious flaws in the analyses and interpretations presented by the NRP; there is also clear evidence within the report of unintentional bias in the interpretation of data, and there are blatant distortions of the actual NRP findings in discussions of the report produced for public consumption. Not surprisingly, policies enacted on the basis of this report and its distortions are far from "scientifically based" and are likely to exacerbate the underachievement of low-income students.

Flaws in the NRP Analyses

The flaws in the National Reading Panel analyses include the fact that the panel considered only experimental and quasi-experimental research as "scientific," they made elementary and puzzling errors in interpreting certain studies, and they failed to examine in any detail the radically different pattern of relationships evident in the research between systematic phonics instruction and decoding as compared to systematic phonics instruction and reading comprehension.

What constitutes "scientifically based" reading instruction?

The National Reading Panel report considered only experimental and quasi-experimental research involving treatment and control groups, thereby ignoring an enormous amount of ethnographic and correlational research on reading development that is just as capable of contributing to scientific knowledge as experimental research (Cummins, 1999; Pressley, Duke, & Boling, 2004). Pressley and colleagues (2004) argue that "the NRP did not include much of the science that can inform beginning reading instruction and . . . a much fuller evidence-based vision of beginning reading is possible simply by considering available scientific evidence that the NRP failed to consider" (p. 40). They review research pointing to the positive influence of high-quality preschool, exposure to educational television, one-on-one tutoring, literature experiences, and reduction of class size. These empirically supported interventions were not considered by the NRP partly because it is difficult to carry out true experiments or quasi-experiments on the influence of these variables.

The insistence on the part of the NRP that only medical model experimental "treatment/control" studies qualify as "scientific" is bizarre in light of the history of scientific discovery and current scientific inquiry in many disciplines. In most scientific disciplines, knowledge is generated by constantly testing and refining theory-based predictions. Experimental research represents only one way of doing this. In many disciplines, experimental treatment/control comparisons are not possible. In meteorology, for example, knowledge is generated by observing weather phenomena, forming hypotheses to account for the observed phenomena, testing these hypotheses against additional data, and gradually refining the hypotheses into more comprehensive theories that have broader explanatory and predictive power (Cummins, 1999).

In real-life educational contexts, it is notoriously difficult to implement the rigorous scientific controls required for experimental studies (e.g., random assignment to treatment and control groups). Therefore, scientific advancement, of necessity, relies to a considerable extent on the accumulation of data from a variety of quantitative and qualitative research approaches. Hypotheses gain considerable credibility when they are supported by a variety of research approaches—for example, experimental, correlational, and ethnographic.

In short, the NRP's conclusions about what constitutes effective reading instruction are seriously compromised by the panel's naïve preconceptions about the nature of scientific inquiry. The problems are compounded by the NRP's failure to acknowledge and interpret what it *actually* found (*systematic phonics instruction has minimal impact on reading comprehension after grade 1*) instead of highlighting a misleading half-truth as fact (*systematic phonics instruction helps children learn to read*). Additionally, the unintentional bias of the panel is evident in its failure to consistently apply its own scientific criteria in interpreting the research.

What did the NRP actually find?

A number of commentators (e.g., Allington, 2004; Coles, 2003; Garan, 2001, 2004; Krashen, 2004a) have pointed out that there is a glaring inconsistency between the conclusions of the National Reading Panel report and the findings that it actually reports. The report concluded that "systematic phonics instruction helps students learn to read" (Ehri et al., 2001) but, at the same time, reported no significant relationship between systematic phonics instruction and reading comprehension for normally progressing and low-achieving readers beyond grade 1. Part of the problem here is the failure of the panel to clearly define the nature of "systematic" phonics instruction and to distinguish decoding from reading comprehension abilities in discussing what constitutes "reading."

The fuzzy nature of what constitutes so-called systematic phonics instruction is evident in the fact that the following very different interventions are given equal billing as representing "systematic phonics instruction":

- A 5- to 6-minute daily word study component of an individual tutoring program for grade 1 students (Santa & Hoien, 1999);

- A 15-minute program for kindergarten students, Jolly Phonics (Lloyd, 1993), involving "playful, creative, flexible teaching" (Ehri et al., 2001, p. 422); and

- Scripted phonics programs such as Open Court and Direct Instruction (DISTAR) that continue intensive phonics instruction for a significant part of the school day well beyond the primary grades.

Few critics of the NRP report would have any problem acknowledging the potential usefulness of the first two interventions noted above because they are clearly compatible with providing ample opportunities for students to engage actively with reading and writing.

Many educators, however, have serious reservations about scripted programs that provide minimal opportunity for teachers to connect with their students "outside the script" and that emphasize phonics and decoding to a greater extent than the promotion of active engagement by students with real books. Yet, the interpretation of the NRP report incorporated into the Reading First initiative views systematic phonics instruction as the teaching of all the major phonics rules in an invariant one-size-fits-all order throughout elementary school. It is clear that this interpretation goes far beyond what the NRP actually reported.

It is ironic that scripted programs with a predominant phonics emphasis have been the main beneficiaries of the NCLB Act in view of the fact that the NRP explicitly pointed to some of the limitations of these programs. While noting the significant impact on *decoding* obtained by some of these programs, the panel expressed caution about the effect of scripted programs on teachers' orientation to instruction: "Although scripts may standardize instruction, they may reduce teachers' interest in the teaching process or their motivation to teach phonics" (National Reading Panel, 2000, pp. 2-135).

The looseness in the kinds of instructional support represented by "systematic phonics" is compounded by a lack of precision in use of the term *reading.* National Reading Panel committee member Joanne Yatvin (2002), in commenting on the Minority Report she submitted as part of the overall NRP report, noted:

> In the various subcommittee reports, "reading" is used to represent many different kinds of operations, from accurate pronunciation of nonsense words to a thorough understanding of a written text. When a subcommittee report asserts that a particular instructional technique "improves children's reading," the public deserves to know whether the authors mean word calling, speed, smoothness, literal comprehension, or the ability to assimilate a subtle and complex set of ideas. (p. 368)

This point is crucial in interpreting the NRP phonics subcommittee report and the Ehri and colleagues' (2001) version of that report. As noted earlier and as will be discussed in more detail, systematic phonics instruction shows a positive impact on decoding skills but a minimal impact on reading comprehension beyond grade 1. However, at crucial rhetorical points (e.g., the title and abstract of the Ehri and colleagues' [2001] article), these documents collapse decoding and comprehension into constructs such as "reading" or "learning to read." In doing so, they ignore the fact that their own data demonstrate that decoding and comprehension show very different developmental patterns in relation to phonics instruction and thus cannot be compacted into any unitary notion of reading.[4]

The NRP report examined the impact of phonics instruction for three separate groups of readers: normally achieving readers, low-achieving readers, and reading-disabled readers. It also separated the findings into those that applied to kindergarten and grade 1 students (K/grade 1) and those that applied to students in grades 2 through 6. Dependent measures varied from one study to another but included Word Identification, Decoding, Spelling, Comprehension, Nonword Reading, Oral Reading, and General Reading.

The comparisons that are of primary interest in the present context are those between decoding and comprehension and between students in K/grade 1 and those in grades 2 through 6. The data show clearly that whereas decoding and comprehension behave similarly in K/grade 1 comparisons, they diverge markedly for older students. Specifically, phonics instruction (of widely varying types) shows a positive impact on both decoding and comprehension for younger students but *no impact on comprehension beyond grade 1 for normally achieving and low-achieving students.* Some impact of phonics instruction on comprehension continues to be observed for the reading-disabled group in grades 2 through 6, probably because, by definition, these students experience longer-term difficulty in decoding than normally developing readers. Thus, phonics instruction may help comprehension because it permits these students to decode words whose meanings they already understand but which they were previously unable to decode. However, students formally designated as "reading disabled" represent only a small fraction of the student body.

> Phonics instruction clearly has an important role in early reading development but as far as reading comprehension is concerned, the NRP report documented that it rapidly reaches a point of diminishing returns for the vast majority of students after grade 1.

In short, for the vast majority of students, systematic phonics instruction ceases to be effective in promoting reading comprehension after grade 1. The minimal relationship found in the NRP analyses between systematic phonics instruction and reading comprehension after grade 1 aligns uneasily with the blanket statement in the title of the Ehri and colleagues' (2001) article ("Systematic Phonics Instruction Helps Students Learn to Read") and even more so with the claim in the Summary Report ("The meta-analysis revealed that systematic phonics instruction produces significant benefits for students in kindergarten through 6th grade") (NRP Summary, p. 9). This latter statement misrepresents the overall trends in the NRP data, and some members of the NRP have distanced themselves from it while still, paradoxically, arguing for a relationship between systematic phonics instruction and reading comprehension (e.g., Shanahan, 2001).[5]

Alternative Analyses and Interpretations of the NRP Report

We focus here on two aspects of the NRP report: (1) the report overstates the impact and relevance of systematic phonics instruction (however defined) for the long-term development of reading proficiency and (2) the report ignores the extensive research highlighting the importance of sustained engagement with actual reading for the development of reading comprehension abilities.

The impact of systematic phonics instruction

As noted earlier, the NRP does show a significant relationship between phonics instruction and the development of early decoding skills. Few, if any, reading theorists dispute that phonics instruction plays an important role in helping to develop decoding skills. However, the report also demonstrates that phonics instruction rapidly reaches a point of diminishing returns when it comes to the development of reading comprehension abilities. The differential pattern of relationships with respect to decoding and comprehension are related to the major differences between these two aspects of reading. These differences and the instructional implications are discussed in the next chapter. Here, it is sufficient to note that the data reviewed by the NRP point to the limitations of scripted programs in developing reading comprehension, even in the early grades. Ehri and colleagues (2001), for example, note the small but negative impact of the scripted Open Court program on both reading comprehension and spelling at the grade 2 level. Similarly, DISTAR showed no significant impact on reading comprehension or spelling in comparison to controls over a three-year period (Garan, 2004). The statistical measure used in these analyses is termed an *effect size* and the NRP viewed an effect size of .20 as significant. The effect size for the relationship between Open Court and reading comprehension at the grade 2 level was minus .19—obviously very close to the statistically significant level.

The claim that the NRP overestimated the impact of systematic phonics instruction is reinforced by the meta-analysis of the same data by Camilli, Vargas, and Yurecko (2003). These authors criticized the analytic methods used in the NRP report and, using a more sophisticated statistical model, reported effect sizes for programs using systematic phonics that were only half as large as those reported by the NRP. Furthermore, these effect sizes were substantially smaller than the effect sizes for one-to-one tutoring. Additionally, a considerably broader range of language and literacy activities was found to be significantly related to reading development than just phonemic awareness and phonics instruction.

Camilli and Wolfe (2004) argue on the basis of these data for differentiation in early reading instruction:

> Using this strategy, the teacher assesses students' needs, determines the appropriate methods to address those needs, and creates individual and group experiences accordingly. Perhaps some students need direct instruction in decoding skills; perhaps none do. . . . Direct instruction in phonics is necessary for certain at-risk kindergartners, but only if embedded in a print-rich, comprehensive literacy program and delivered in brief, individualized lessons. (p. 28)

This recommendation, based on a more adequate analysis of the NRP data, is a far cry from the one-size-fits-all scripted programs that have assumed the mantle of "scientifically proven" on the basis of virtually no empirical evidence.[6]

The impact of extensive reading on reading comprehension

The National Reading Panel report was largely dismissive of claims that extensive reading or sustained silent reading in class was an important factor in promoting reading comprehension. In reaching this conclusion, the panel ignored much of the research data and their interpretation of some studies they included was problematic. Krashen (2004a) critiqued their analyses as follows:

> They were, however, able to find only 14 comparisons, all lasting less than one academic year, between students in in-school free reading programs and comparison children, devoting only six pages of their massive report to this topic (as compared to approximately 120 pages devoted to research on phonemic awareness and phonics).
>
> Interestingly, in-school reading did not fare badly even in the limited analysis done by the NRP, with in-school readers doing better in four cases, and never doing worse. . . . [E]ven a finding of "no difference"

suggests that free reading is just as good as traditional instruction and is therefore preferable, because it is more pleasant and provides benefits other than literacy development. (pp. 45–46)

Suffice it to say that there is massive evidence in both first and second language contexts for the impact of extensive reading on reading comprehension abilities (e.g., Cunningham & Stanovich, 1997; Day & Bamford, 1996; Elley, 1991; Elley & Mangubhai, 1983; Krashen, 2004b; McQuillan, 1998; OECD, 2004b). The data from two large-scale international studies will illustrate the pattern of findings.

Postlethwaite and Ross (1992), using data from the IEA study of reading achievement in 32 systems of education around the world, showed that variables related to reading opportunities and frequency of reading were among the strongest predictors of a school's overall reading performance at the grade 4 level. More than 50 variables were ranked in order of importance for reading comprehension at grades 4 and 8 levels. The first ranked indicator at the grade 4 level was the school's perception of the *degree of parent cooperation*. This variable is probably a reflection of socioeconomic status. The second and third ranked variables were *amount of free voluntary reading* (#2) students reported and *reading in class* (#3). The significance of opportunity and encouragement to read for reading comprehension is further suggested by the high rankings of variables such as *amount of reading materials in the school library* (#8), *having a classroom library* (#11), and *frequency of borrowing books from a library* (#12). With respect to teaching methods, a focus on *comprehension instruction* was ranked #9 and *emphasis on literature* was ranked #17, both considerably higher than whether or not the school engaged in explicit phonics teaching (#41). The ranking of selected variables in this study from home, school, and classroom spheres is outlined in Figure 1.2.

The low ranking of explicit phonics instruction in determining reading comprehension does not, of course, mean that phonics instruction is not important in the early stages of learning to read. Indeed, for some students it may be a crucial component. However, beyond the initial stages of reading development, systematic phonics instruction yields diminishing returns and plays a considerably lesser role in comparison to the amount of reading that students engage in and the amount of instruction they receive that is specifically focused on comprehension.

Obviously, correlation does not imply causality and it is likely that good readers will read more than those for whom reading is challenging. However, this line of reasoning cannot explain the school and instruc-

FIGURE 1.2

Ranked Indicators Predicting Reading Comprehension, Grade 4

Home

02. Amount of free voluntary reading
12. Frequency of borrowing books from library

School Resources

08. Amount of reading materials in school library
14. School resources (school library, reading room for students, student/school newspaper)
19. School library books per student

School Initiatives

16. Sponsoring of reading initiatives

Classroom Conditions and Teacher Practices

03. Reading in class
11. Classroom library
18. Frequency of visiting school library

Teacher Methods

09. Comprehension-focused instruction (deliberate emphasis on text understanding)
17. Emphasis on literature (encouragement of silent reading, listening to student reading, focus on library skills, etc.)
41. Phonics teaching

Source: Adapted from Postlethwaite & Ross (1992).

tional initiatives that emerged as significant predictors in the Postlethwaite and Ross (1992) study. For example, the strong relationship observed between reading comprehension and instructional variables such as *reading in class* (#3) and *comprehension-focused instruction* (#9) cannot easily be attributed to noninstructional factors.

A similar pattern of relationships was observed in the more recent PISA study discussed earlier in this chapter (OECD, 2004b). The report points out:

The PISA results underline the importance of student engagement. For example, students who are habitual readers and who enjoy reading are also more likely than others to have high levels of reading literacy. Greater engagement in literacy can be a consequence, as well as a cause, of higher reading skill, but the evidence suggests that these two factors are mutually reinforcing. . . . Indeed, the level of a student's reading engagement is a better predictor of literacy performance than his or her socioeconomic background, indicating that cultivating a student's interest in reading can help overcome home disadvantages. (2004b, p. 8)

The pattern of relationships between access to print, extensive reading, and reading achievement is reinforced by a number of other analyses. McQuillan (1998), for example, examined the relationship between state rankings on the 1992 NAEP and the amount of print access and frequency of reading by state. The print access index was derived from the three most likely sources of reading matter for children: the home, the school library, and the public library. McQuillan reported that more print access is correlated positively with free reading ($r = .720$), suggesting that the more access to print students have, the more they read. In addition, reading proficiency correlated .852 with *total print access* and .644 with *free reading*. According to McQuillan, "This means that simply knowing how much print access students have in a state can explain 73 percent of the variance in reading test scores; knowing how much free reading takes place accounts for 41 percent of the variance" (1998, p. 74). These results cannot be explained by socioeconomic variables. Poverty indices were also related to reading achievement ($r = -.77$) but when the influence of poverty was controlled statistically, "the effects of print access on reading scores remains strong and positive ($r = .63$), indicating that print access makes a powerful contribution to determining reading achievement in the states independent of socioeconomic factors" (pp. 74–78).

Summary and Conclusions

We believe that the National Reading Panel missed an important opportunity to elucidate the instructional conditions for effective reading development. Because of the panel's failure to inquire further into (or perhaps even accept) the lack of relationship between phonics instruction and reading comprehension beyond grade 1, they overemphasized the long-term importance of systematic and explicit phonics teaching and almost totally neglected the crucial importance of providing students with ample opportunities and encouragement to read extensively.

The core problem with the NRP report, and with subsequent policy initiatives, is that the construct of "reading" is treated as unitary, with little appreciation of the very different instructional conditions that are required to promote sustained reading comprehension development as compared to initial decoding skills. Phonics instruction clearly has an important role in early reading development but as far as reading comprehension is concerned, the NRP report documented that it rapidly reaches a point of diminishing returns for the vast majority of students after grade 1.

The problematic conclusions of the NRP report derive from a number of factors. First, only a narrow band of research was considered "scientific," resulting in the exclusion of an extensive body of relevant research. The NRP also made serious errors in its interpretation of the research it did consider. This was illustrated in the way the NRP and Ehri and colleagues (2001) ignored the multiple confounding of variables in the Santa and Hoien (1998) study, inappropriately attributing effect sizes to a phonics (word study) component rather than to several other competing candidates. This compromised not only the interpretation of this study but also the credibility of the overall effect sizes reported in the phonics subgroup report (see endnote 6).

The overall credibility of the NRP report, and the policies it spawned, is further jeopardized by the inaccuracies in the Summary Report and subsequent discussions (e.g., Lyon & Chhabra, 2004) that claimed scientific support for the implementation of systematic phonics instruction from kindergarten through sixth grade. Inaccurate statements such as this clearly reflect an ideological rather than a scientific perspective.[7]

The empirical research strongly supports the importance of extensive reading (e.g., Krashen, 2004b), together with an instructional focus on comprehension strategies (e.g., Pressley et al., 2004), for sustained growth in reading comprehension. Unfortunately, these instructional initiatives have been largely neglected in the policy directives that have followed the NRP report. Low-income children who are considered "at risk" have overwhelmingly borne the brunt of these misguided policy directions. As we discuss in the next chapter, many low-income children are currently receiving instruction that owes more to 1950s behaviorist-era learning theory than to the scientific consensus regarding how people learn. We examine the research about how people learn and discuss how we can align literacy instruction for low-income children more closely with this scientific foundation.

1 The No Child Left Behind (NCLB) legislation has highlighted the need for educators to be accountable for the achievement of *all* students in a school, including low-income students and English language learners. Do you think this is a realistic goal? What changes would you suggest to NCLB that might increase its effectiveness in meeting its goals?

2 Why do you think NAEP achievement scores have remained largely unchanged over the course of the last 30 years despite massive school reform efforts throughout this period? Identify three promising strategies that might have more success in raising achievement levels than what has been tried up to this point.

3 What is the relationship between decoding and comprehension in the process of learning to read? Can the same approaches be used to teach both decoding and comprehension? What differences in instructional approach would you suggest?

4 Think of young children growing up. Identify at least three things they learn without being explicitly taught. Now try to think of things that students learn in schools without explicit teaching. Discuss with a partner what skills and concepts need to be explicitly taught to students at school and what skills and concepts students might be able to learn without explicit teaching.

Endnotes

1. "Whole-language" approaches to literacy instruction emphasize that reading and writing involve the active construction of meaning by learners. Instruction should therefore be meaning centered rather than skills driven. Krashen (1999) suggests that the "core of whole language is providing children with interesting texts and helping them understand these texts" (p. 26). A common perception of whole-language instruction is that it avoids direct instruction and minimizes the teaching of phonics. Freeman and Freeman (1992) clarify this misconception as follows:

> It is true that whole language teachers are more apt to use real literature than to use basal programs, and they prefer to engage students in authentic activities rather than drilling them on worksheets. They generally avoid the direct teaching of skills as the prerequisite for reading and writing. They prefer to teach skills in the context of real reading and writing activities. (p. 3)

2. The National Assessment of Educational Progress (NAEP), often called "The Nation's Report Card," was authorized by Congress in 1969. It attempts to provide an independent measure of what students across the United States know and can do in reading, mathematics, science, and writing, as well as other core subject areas.

3. Litigation challenging disparities in educational funding is underway in 45 of the 50 states (www.schoolfunding.info/litigation/litigation.php3).

4. Ehri and colleagues (2001) acknowledge this pattern of findings, as the following quotations make clear:

Among the older students in 2nd through 6th grades . . . phonics instruction was not effective for teaching spelling ($d = 0.09$) or teaching reading comprehension ($d = 0.12$). (p. 418)

Readers in 2nd through 6th grades classified as low achieving (LA) revealed no overall effects of phonics instruction. (p. 418)

The . . . effect sizes on the comprehension measure . . . reveal that all the effect sizes were positive for readers with RD [reading disability], whereas effect sizes were negative for normally progressing and LA [low-achieving] readers. These findings reveal that the nonsignificant effect on the comprehension outcome among 2nd through 6th grade students arose primarily from the students without RD. (p. 418)

In other words, phonics instruction helps reading-disabled students in grades 2 through 6 comprehend text but does not help normally achieving and low-achieving students in grades 2 through 6 to comprehend text. A small effect size ($d = 0.27$) was reported for normally achieving students on the overall measure of reading (presumably including both decoding and comprehension components) but this disappeared when reading comprehension was considered alone. For low-achieving students in grades 2 through 6, no impact of phonics instruction was observed on the overall measure of reading ($d = 0.15$).

5. Why would the public relations company hired to publicize the NRP findings misrepresent the actual conclusions of the report? Garan (2004) and Metcalf (2002) document a set of relationships between the Bush administration, certain publishers, and the public relations company that wrote the Summary Report. The reader is referred to this documentation for further insight into the relationships between science and spin.

6. Basic errors in the interpretation of research data contributed to the inflated effect sizes in the NRP report. The manner in which both the NRP and Ehri and colleagues (2001) report, the Santa and Hoien (1999) study on the impact of a tutoring program termed *Early Steps* (Morris, 1992; Morris,

Shaw, & Perney, 1990) stands out as a particularly clear example and we use this to illustrate the broader pattern.

The study is described as follows by Ehri and colleagues:

Santa and Hoien (1999) modified the RR [Reading Recovery] format to include more systematic phonics instruction. In their study, at-risk first graders received tutoring that involved story reading, writing, and phonological skills based on a program developed by Morris (1992). The unique part of this phonics program was that it used word study activities to develop phonological awareness and decoding skill. Word study consumed 5–6 minutes of the 30-minute lesson. Children were given cards to sort into categories. . . .

The control group received small-group guided-reading instruction. Students practiced reading and rereading books in 30-minute lessons but did not receive any word study activities. It is important to note that the control group here was not one that received RR unenriched by phonics. Rather, it received a different form of instruction that did not involve tutoring. Results showed that the phonics word study program produced much better performance in reading than did the guided reading program, $d = 0.76$. The phonics group significantly outperformed the control group in reading comprehension ($d = 0.73$) as well as word reading ($d = 0.93$). These findings demonstrate the effectiveness of larger-unit phonics instruction added to an RR format. (2001, p. 426)

This account of the study is similar to that in the NRP report (p. 2-130) except that the original NRP account made no mention of the fact that the control group "was not one that received RR unenriched by phonics."

Even without consulting the original Santa and Hoien (1999) study, Ehri and colleagues' interpretation of the data appears highly problematic and at variance with normal scientific conventions with respect to research design and elimination of confounding variables. The data certainly suggest that the *Easy Steps* program was more effective than the comparison program but there is no way that the impact of its various components can be disaggregated. The experimental program is described repeatedly in the NRP and by Ehri and colleagues (2001) as a "phonics program" despite the fact that the word study (phonics) component involved only 5 to 6 minutes of the 30-minute intervention. Thus, less than 20 percent of the intervention focused on phonics instruction. This would not pose a problem for interpretation if the comparison group had received an identical intervention program except for the phonics component. The effect of phonics (word study) instruction could then be isolated from the effects of the other 80 percent of the intervention.

However, as Ehri and colleagues acknowledge (but the earlier NRP report did not), the experimental program differed from the comparison program in major respects in addition to the inclusion of phonics in one program but not in the other. According to Santa and Hoien (1999), the experimental program also emphasized real *book reading* with an emphasis on comprehension strategy instruction (8 to 10 minutes), *writing* (5 to 8 minutes), and *introduction of a new book* that the child was expected to read without much help the next day. By contrast, in the comparison group, "practically the entire 30-minute session was spent in reading" (Ehri et al., 2001, p. 64). The obvious question, never addressed by the NRP researchers, is: Why should the positive impact of the *Early Steps* program be attributed to the phonics (word study) component rather than to the writing component or book reading or comprehension strategy component, each of which occupied more time than the phonics component?

As Santa and Hoien (1999) note, "Every aspect of the *Early Steps* lesson undoubtedly promoted word recognition performance" (p. 70). Yet, the NRP authors have no hesitation in attributing the positive impact to the 20 percent of the program that involved word study (phonics) rather than to the 80 percent of the program that involved activities such as book reading and writing.

Another confounding variable in this study is the fact that the experimental *Early Steps* group received one-on-one tutoring, whereas the comparison group received small-group instruction in groups of 2 to 4.

Thus, the effects of the entire *Early Steps* intervention (and within that, the phonics component) are confounded with the potential effects of one-on-one versus small-group tutoring, a variable that some research studies suggest can significantly impact outcomes (Pinnell et al., 1994; Vellutino et al., 1996). Other studies (Evans, 1996; Iversen, 1997) have not reported a significant impact for one-on-one tutoring in comparison to small-group tutoring. However, the conflicting research on this issue does not alter the fact that the only scientifically acceptable procedure is to acknowledge that no inferences regarding the impact of phonics instruction are possible due to the confounding of variables. Santa and Hoien (1999) explicitly note this potential confounding of variables:

> It is also difficult to tease out the effects related to one-to-one tutorials. While we have some evidence that the results of the study cannot be explained solely by the fact that the Early Steps was a one-to-one tutorial, it would be worthwhile to test this question in a cleaner design. (p. 71)

In short, because of the multiple confounding effects within this study, no scientific inferences can legitimately be drawn regarding the specific impact of the word study (phonics) component on any of the dependent variables. The inclusion of the effect sizes for this study into the calculation of the overall effect sizes for the impact of phonics also means that these overall effect sizes are inflated. Thus, the scientific credibility of the entire meta-analysis is called into question.

There is also evidence of going beyond the data in an attempt to make the most persuasive case for the impact of systematic phonics instruction. For example, in contrast to Santa and Hoien's cautious and appropriate discussion of the findings, Ehri and colleagues (2001) reference the confounding variables ("It is important to note ...") but promptly ignore their own caution by interpreting the data as unequivocal support for the positive effect of phonics instruction. The three final sentences in the passage quoted earlier explicitly attribute a *causal* role to the impact of phonics instruction ("... the phonics word study program produced much better performance ..."), ignoring completely the potential impact of the systematic comprehension-focused and meaning-oriented instruction that comprised 80 percent of the intervention. Similarly, no discussion is provided regarding the confounding of one-on-one tutoring with small-group instruction. Instead, the authors misrepresent the findings by repeatedly attributing the effects to the impact of phonics alone (e.g., "... the phonics groups significantly outperformed ...").

7. In a detailed response to critiques of the National Reading Panel (NRP) report, Shanahan (2004) has argued that the critics rarely dispute the findings of the report—for example, that phonemic awareness training and systematic explicit phonics instruction promote reading achievement. However, his response fails to address two crucial issues relevant to interpreting the NRP findings. First, he ignores the fact that the construct of "systematic explicit phonics instruction" is essentially meaningless when it is used to include treatments as divergent as a 5- or 6-minute intervention for grade 1 students (Santa & Hoien, 1999) compared to extensive scripted phonics instruction throughout elementary school. In fairness to Shanahan, this point was not prominent in the critiques he considered.

However, Shanahan (2004) ignores a second issue that *was* explicitly addressed in the critiques—namely, the minimal relationship between sys-tematic explicit phonics instruction and reading comprehension. Instead of acknowledging and trying to explain this finding, Shanahan reverts to the argument that decoding skills "are highly correlated with reading comprehension and have been shown to be causally implicated in reading improvement" (p. 259). Certainly, decoding and comprehension skills are correlated as a result of the fact that both are strongly influenced by access to and opportunity to engage with print (which varies across socioeconomic groups).

Also, there is a quasi-causal relationship between decoding and comprehension insofar as decoding skills are a necessary but not sufficient condition for developing strong reading comprehension skills (if you can't decode written language, you clearly can't comprehend it). However, the fact remains that the NRP found no relationship between systematic phonics instruction and reading comprehension for the vast majority of students beyond grade 1. Appeals to correlations (which the NRP explicitly rejected as nonscientific) and nebulous causal connections (which the NRP did not find) lack credibility, especially in a book entitled *The Voice of Evidence in Reading Research* (McCardle & Chhabra, 2004). Some of the reasons for the very different pattern of relationships between phonics instruction and decoding, and phonics instruction and reading comprehension, are discussed in Chapter 2.

Education is not the filling of a pail, but the lighting of a fire.

William Butler Yeats

Stimulating the imagination is not an alternative educational activity to be argued for in competition with other claims; it is a prerequisite to making any activity educational.

Kieran Egan & Dan Nadaner
Imagination and Education
(1988, p. ix)

CHAPTER 2

Pedagogy

I n this chapter, we review research on both learning and teaching in order to provide a foundation for planning educational change. For decades, educational debates have been characterized by a set of "either-or" dichotomies (e.g., child centered versus teacher centered, phonics versus whole language, etc.) that have frequently degenerated into ideologically loaded slogans. This is not surprising, as education *is* fundamentally ideological. Whether one examines inequities in the way schools are funded or analyzes disparities in the kinds of instruction received by different social groups, it is clear that education is never neutral with respect to societal power structures.

Schools are intended to shape the next generation, and images of students, teachers, and society are inevitably embedded in this process. In planning curriculum and instruction, we ask ourselves what kinds of skills, knowledge, values, and literate competencies students will need when they graduate from school to participate as adults in their societies. What kinds of contributions do we want these students to be able to make to their societies? What kind of society do we want these students to form? How do teachers define their role as educators who shape student identities in the context of societal needs and expectations? What pedagogical choices do teachers make and how do these pedagogical choices reflect their own identities?

We acknowledge that transmission of information and skills is an important component of education. However, if students are to participate effectively in a democratic society and an Information Age economy, they must also be enabled to generate knowledge and to think critically about social issues. Thus, pedagogy entails not only the promotion of learning in a narrow sense but it also entails a process of *negotiating identities* between teachers and students. An image of the society that students will graduate into and the kind of contributions they can make to that society is embedded implicitly in the interactions between educators and students. Pedagogy opens up (or closes down) identity options for students.

Starting from the perspective that a global society needs all the intelligence, creativity, and multilingual talent it can get, we argue that pedagogy will certainly involve "filling pails," but it must also ignite curiosity, imagination, and social commitment.

Introduction

Educational debates on the topic of pedagogy have tended to revolve around dueling dichotomies—alternative approaches that are constructed as antagonistic and mutually irreconcilable. Urszula Clark (2001), for example, points to the polarized debate in many countries between "traditionalists" and "progressivists," the former portrayed as "representing order in the classroom with a defined sense of what was right and wrong, whilst 'progressivists' were represented as child-centered, relativist and presiding over chaotic classrooms" (p. 149). Traditionalists have tended to argue for greater instructional rigor and the need for elevated standards; they emphasize the importance of direct instruction and deride what they see as the absence of rigor and accountability in child-centered approaches to teaching and learning. In reading, phonics is prioritized over pursuit of meaning. By contrast, those who espouse more progressive principles have been influenced by American philosopher John Dewey's (1916) emphasis on the importance of relating instructional content to students' experience and, more recently, by Soviet-era psychologist Lev Vygotsky's (1978) theories on the construction of knowledge through social interaction. Student inquiry and the social construction of knowledge are seen as more pertinent to effective learning than simply the transmission of information and skills.

These orientations to pedagogy do not have to be framed in opposition to each other. We argue that they are more usefully seen as nested within each other. A transmission or traditional pedagogical orientation incorporates a considerably narrower, but still legitimate, focus with respect to means and goals than does a social constructivist orientation. Typically, the goal of transmitting information and skills is pursued by requiring students to engage primarily in memorization and practice. By contrast, the social constructivist goal of enabling students to build knowledge and develop deeper levels of understanding frequently requires dialogue and collaborative inquiry rather than just memorization and practice.

The research on literacy development reviewed in this chapter suggests that although it may be feasible to develop students' knowledge of the rule-based aspects of language (e.g., phonics, spelling, grammar, etc.) by means of a transmission approach, this orientation is ineffective in promoting reading comprehension beyond the early grades of schooling. The nature of reading comprehension, and of academic language proficiency more generally, demands higher-order cognitive processes than simply memorization and practice. These higher-order processes include analysis, synthesis, and evaluation of alternatives.

However, neither transmission nor social constructivist orientations provide an adequate blueprint for pedagogy insofar as they fail to address explicitly the content of the curriculum and the social goals of education. Both orientations are silent on the ways in which power intersects with knowledge. They plead innocence with respect to the sanitization of the curriculum and the erasure of voices other than those of the dominant group. Virtually no country encourages its textbook developers to disturb the glorious myths upon which national identity is founded. The heroic tales of *How the West Was Won* are rarely presented from the perspective of Native Americans who might regard the process as one of ethnic cleansing. Few schools in the United States encourage their students to read Howard Zinn's (1995) *A People's History of the United States* as a fundamental reference work. Canadian history textbooks are silent about the widespread sexual abuse of First Nation's children in residential schools funded by the federal government and operated by religious orders. Similarly, Japanese textbook writers gloss over the atrocities committed by Japanese troops in China in the 1930s and 1940s, just as Chinese textbooks present a very one-sided perspective on the Chinese invasion of Tibet in 1950 and the subsequent repression of Tibetan culture and aspirations.

We argue that education for participation within a democratic society requires that schools explicitly aim to develop critical literacy—the ability to read between the lines rather than just skim over the surface structure of texts. Democracy requires the exercise of informed choice with the goal of promoting the common good. Clearly, the ability to critically analyze social issues is a prerequisite for making informed choices. Pedagogy oriented toward the development of critical literacy can be termed a *transformative* orientation because its goal is to enable students both to understand how power is exercised within society and to use their democratic rights to change aspects of their society that they consider unjust or discriminatory.

> Education within a democratic society requires that schools explicitly aim to develop critical literacy.

Before examining these orientations in more detail and relating them to the research on learning and literacy development, we describe the rapidly changing societal contexts within which schools are operating. If, as we have suggested, an implicit image of society and its future needs is embedded in all teacher–student interactions, then it is important to articulate how our societies are changing and what social realities students who enter kindergarten in 2007 will be expected to face when they graduate in 2020.

The Changing Context of Education

Two trends are particularly relevant in considering the demands being placed on education systems around the world: *globalization* and *technological change*.

Globalization and Diversity

Cultural and linguistic diversity has become the norm in major urban school systems across both North America and Europe. In California, for example, 25 percent of the school population is considered "limited English proficient" and approximately 85 percent of teachers have children in their classes who are in the process of learning English. In Amsterdam, 40 percent of the school population was born outside the Netherlands. More than 50 percent of the school population in the Canadian cities of Toronto and Vancouver come from non–English-speaking backgrounds.

The new global economy is similarly characterized by a plethora of languages and cultures despite the current dominance of English in many cultural, scientific, and economic spheres. Thus, any pedagogical framework that aspires to promote literacy and prepare students for a globalized Information Age economy must address issues of linguistic and cultural diversity.

The increase of cultural and linguistic diversity in schools has created pedagogical challenges and opportunities. Specifically, is it feasible or reasonable to expect a one-size-fits-all homogenized curriculum to meet the needs of an increasingly diverse student body? What might a more differentiated curriculum look like and how should it be evaluated? To what extent should the education system acknowledge and promote the linguistic and cultural resources that students bring to school? If educators see it as educationally desirable to promote students' multilingual and multicultural potential in schools, then what kinds of curricula and pedagogy are likely to achieve this goal?

Technological change

Recent educational reform initiatives in countries around the world have been inspired by the transformation of the global economy during the late twentieth century from an Industrial Age economy to an Information Age economy, or what is increasingly called the *Knowledge Society*. Schools are now expected to develop twenty-first-century literacy skills, which are what the economy supposedly requires to thrive in an increasingly competitive global marketplace. These twenty-first-century literacy skills are heavily dependent on mastery of new technologies. The European Commission (2004), for example, in a report on its e-learning initiative, notes:

> Information and communication technologies (ICT) are opening up access to education, training and learning resources, while also establishing avenues of self learning. This is why the European Union believes the

proper use of such technologies may contribute to Europe's shift to a knowledge-based society. (p. 6)

This report makes explicit the belief that technology is fundamental to economic competitiveness in a knowledge-based society, arguing that "Europe should become, by 2010, the most competitive and dynamic knowledge-based economy in the world, capable of sustainable economic growth, with more and better jobs." The new mandate for schools, in Europe and elsewhere, therefore, includes producing increasing numbers of graduates who are capable of working collaboratively with others to analyze and critically interpret information, thereby participating in the generation of knowledge that fuels the new economy.[1]

This rhetoric, which is replicated in many countries around the world, appears at first sight to represent a radical departure from the ways in which schools have traditionally defined their roles. Unlike education for societal elites, education for the masses has never aspired to develop deep understanding or promote knowledge generation and critical literacy. Instead, more modest goals have been pursued. Historically, schools have aspired to develop sufficient literacy among students to enable them (1) to read and analyze sacred texts such as the Qur'an or the Bible as a means of saving their eternal souls and (2) to participate productively in the economic life of the society. Not surprisingly, major expansions of and investments in schooling have occurred at times of significant economic change and upheaval (e.g., from agrarian to industrial means of production in the 1800s). As noted earlier, the current preoccupation with educational reform has been a response to the shift from an Industrial Age to an Information Age economy. As John Guthrie (2004) notes, "Literacy has evolved . . . from a tool for religious education, to a skill for economic productivity, to a symbolic indicator of information management" (p. 7).

Despite the fact that the societal commitment to knowledge-based educational reform may be superficial and selectively applied to upper-income rather than to lower-income students, the current discourse provides a unique opportunity for educators to explore forms of critical pedagogy that potentially can exert a transformative impact on students and society. At this historical juncture, the rhetoric of the knowledge-based society urges educators to apprentice *all* students to the cause of higher-order thinking and deep understanding. Educators whose role definitions include promoting critical literacy among their students can use this rhetoric to implement transformative approaches to pedagogy in their classrooms.

In responding to societal expectations that they simultaneously transmit standards-based information and skills *and* prepare students for participation in a knowledge-based economy, educators not only make pedagogical choices but they also make identity choices with respect to where they position themselves in relation to the power structure of the society. These intersecting pedagogical and identity choices can be discussed in the context of four frameworks that attempt to articulate the relationships between learning and pedagogy. The first of these frameworks derives from cognitive psychology and synthesizes the empirical research on *how people learn.* The second outlines three broad orientations to pedagogy labeled *transmission, social constructivist,* and *transformative.* The third framework focuses on the construct of *multiliteracies* as a means of highlighting how schools might respond to rapidly changing global social realities. Finally, John Guthrie's *literacy engagement* framework emphasizes that engagement is a crucial component of all learning and highlights its specific relevance for sustaining literacy development throughout schooling. Each of these four frameworks contributes important insights to understanding the nature of effective literacy instruction in a globalized Information Age society. We briefly sketch these frameworks and then analyze their relevance to the pedagogical and identity choices faced by educators who aspire to develop strong literacy skills among all their students.

How People Learn

The volume written by Bransford, Brown, and Cocking (2000) entitled *How People Learn* and published by the National Research Council synthesized the research evidence regarding how learning occurs and the optimal conditions to foster learning. A follow-up volume edited by Donovan and Bransford (2005) examined the application of these learning principles to the teaching of history, mathematics, and science. The relevance in the present context is that instructional interventions should reflect these basic principles of learning if they are to be scientifically credible. Bransford and colleagues emphasize three conditions for effective learning: *engaging prior understandings, integrating factual knowledge with conceptual frameworks,* and *taking active control over the learning process.*

Engaging Prior Understandings

Donovan and Bransford (2005) point out that *"new understandings are constructed on a foundation of existing understandings and experiences"* (p. 4, emphasis in original). Prior knowledge, skills, beliefs, and concepts significantly influence what learners notice about their environment and how they organize and interpret it. Prior knowledge refers not just to information or skills previously acquired in a transmission-oriented learning sequence but also to the totality of the experiences that have shaped the learner's identity and cognitive functioning. This principle implies that in classrooms with students from linguistically and culturally diverse backgrounds, instruction must explicitly activate students' prior knowledge and build relevant background knowledge as necessary.

Integrating Factual Knowledge with Conceptual Frameworks

Bransford and colleagues (2000) point out that to develop competence in an area of inquiry, "knowledge of a large set of disconnected facts is not sufficient." Students must be provided with opportunities to learn with understanding because "deep understanding of subject matter transforms factual information into usable knowledge" (p. 16). Thus, knowledge is more than just the ability to remember; deeper levels of understanding are required to transfer knowledge from one context to another. This implies that instruction for deep understanding involves the development of critical literacy rather than simply literal comprehension of text. Literal comprehension involves understanding the content of the text (broadly defined) with respect to what the author is trying to communicate. Critical literacy, on the other hand, involves a deeper inquiry into the text with respect to the perspectives represented, the purposes of the text, the means by which these purposes are pursued (e.g., language, images, intonation, etc.), and the evidence supporting the views expressed.

Taking Active Control over the Learning Process

Learners should be supported in taking control of and self-regulating their own learning. Donovan and Bransford (2005) point out that "a 'metacognitive' or self-monitoring approach can help students develop the ability to take control of their own learning, consciously define learning goals, and monitor their progress in achieving them" (p. 10). When students take ownership of the learning process and invest their identities in the outcomes of learning, the resulting understanding will be deeper than when learning is passive.

Bransford and colleagues (2000) also emphasize the importance of support within the community of learners. Learning takes place in a social context, and a supportive learning community encourages dialogue, apprenticeship, and mentoring. Learning is not simply a cognitive process that takes place inside the heads of individual students; it also involves socialization into particular communities of practice. Within these learning communities, or what Gee (2001) terms *affinity groups,* novices are enabled to participate in the practices of the community from the very beginning of their involvement. Lave and Wenger (1991) describe this process as *legitimate peripheral participation.* The learning community can include the classroom, the school, the family, the broader community, and virtual communities enabled through electronic communication.

This account specifies some minimal requirements for effective learning. It also brings into immediate focus the lack of scientific credibility of approaches that rely primarily on simple transmission of knowledge and skills from teachers to learners. Exclusive reliance on transmission pedagogy is likely to entail memorization rather than learning for deep understanding, minimal activation of students' prior knowledge, and passive rather than active self-regulated learning. A narrow transmission approach would also view active and creative use of language by students as "off task" and thus, within this approach, there is minimal opportunity to establish a genuine community of learners. It is important to reiterate that transmission of information and skills is an important component of effective pedagogy. Transmission of information and skills becomes problematic only when it constitutes the predominant instructional focus.

> Transmission of information and skills becomes problematic only when it constitutes the predominant instructional focus.

Pedagogical Orientations

As illustrated in Figure 2.1, *transmission, social constructivist,* and *transformative* orientations to pedagogy are nested within each other rather than being distinct and isolated from each other. Transmission-oriented pedagogy is represented in the inner circle with the narrowest focus. The goal is to transmit information and skills articulated in the curriculum directly to students. Social constructivist pedagogy, occupying the middle pedagogical space, incorporates the curriculum focus of transmitting information and skills but broadens it to include the development among students of higher-order thinking abilities based on teachers and students co-constructing knowledge and understanding. Finally, transformative

FIGURE 2.1

Nested Pedagogical Orientations

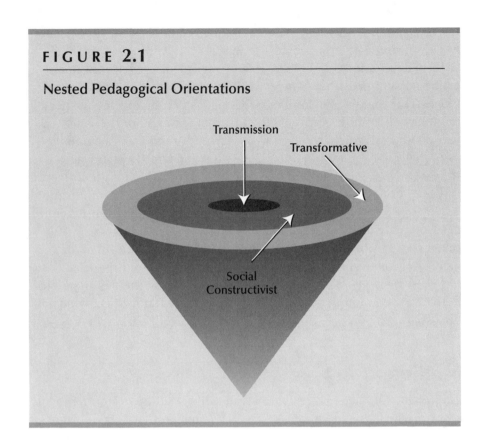

approaches to pedagogy broaden the focus still further by emphasizing the relevance not only of transmitting the curriculum and constructing knowledge but also of enabling students to gain insight into how knowledge intersects with power. The goal is to promote critical literacy among students.[2]

Obviously, these three broad orientations incorporate considerable variation in emphasis and implementation. For example, it is possible to acknowledge the importance of clearly and explicitly transmitting information and skills (as we do) without endorsing one-size-fits-all scripted instructional approaches that reduce students to passive roles within the teaching–learning process. Similarly, social constructivist approaches may vary in the emphasis they place on the *constructivist* aspects (Piaget, 1929) as compared to the *social* aspects (Vygotsky, 1978). Au (1998) points out that "the social is seen to encompass a wide range of phenomena, from historical, political and cultural trends to face-to-face interactions, reflecting group processes both explicit and implicit with intended and unintended consequences" (p. 299). The common thread, according to

Au, is that "social constructivists are interested in the collective generation of meaning among people" (p. 299).

The development of critical literacy is particularly relevant in an
era of global propaganda where skillfully crafted multimedia messages
broadcast by media conglomerates dramatically influence public perceptions and attitudes. Witness the fact that throughout the 2004 U.S.
presidential campaign, more than 40 percent of the U.S. population
continued to believe that Saddam Hussein was
instrumental in the 9/11 attacks despite the universal
acknowledgment (including the Bush administration)
that this was not the case. Thus, there is an urgent
necessity to teach for deep understanding and critical literacy, not so
much because the economy demands it, but because the survival of
democratic institutions in our societies may depend on it.

> Critical literacy is particularly relevant
> in an era of global propaganda.

These pedagogical orientations intersect with the themes articulated
in the New London Group's (1996) *multiliteracies* framework, which is
discussed next.

Multiliteracies

The concept of *multiliteracies* was advanced by a group of international
scholars who labeled themselves "The New London Group" as a means of
conceptualizing the implications of recent societal changes for how literacy
is taught in schools. Literacy is no longer simply reading and writing.
Outside the school, students are engaged in literacy practices that may
involve languages other than the school languages and technologies that
have moved far beyond paper and pencil. The essence of a multiliteracies
pedagogical approach is that schools in the twenty-first-century need
to focus on a broader range of literacies than simply traditional reading
and writing skills in the dominant language (Cope & Kalantzis, 2000;
Pahl & Rowsell, 2005).

The New London Group (1996) highlighted the relevance of new
forms of literacy associated with information, communication, multimedia technologies, and, equally important, the wide variety of culturally specific forms of literacy evident in complex pluralistic societies.
From the perspective of multiliteracies, the exclusive focus within
schools on linear text-based literacy in the dominant language of the
society represents a very limited conception that fails to address the
realities of a globalized, technologically sophisticated, knowledge-based
society. In urban contexts across North America and Europe, the stu-

dent population is multilingual and students are exposed to, and engage in, many different literacy practices outside the school. Within schools, however, the teaching of literacy remains narrowly focused on literacy in the dominant language and typically fails to acknowledge or build on the multilingual literacies or the technologically mediated literacies that form a significant part of students' cultural and linguistic capital.

The New London Group proposed a pedagogical framework that identified *situated practice, overt instruction, critical framing,* and *transformed practice* as central components. The essence of this framework is that students should be given opportunities to engage in meaningful experiences and practice within a learning community, and the development of concepts and understanding should be supported by explicit instruction as required. Students should also have opportunities to step back from what they have learned and examine concepts and ideas critically in relation to their social relevance. Finally, they should be given opportunities to take the knowledge they have gained—to put it into play in the world of ideas—and come to understand how their insights can exert an impact on people and issues in the real world.

Thus, as in the nested pedagogical orientations framework (Figure 2.1), a legitimate role is assigned to overt instruction (transmission pedagogy) but only as one component of a more inclusive and comprehensive framework for learning. In a similar way, the cognitive psychology research on learning synthesized by Bransford and colleagues highlights the limitations of an exclusive reliance on teacher–student transmission of information and skills. This research suggests that cognitive engagement and deep understanding are more likely to be generated in contexts where instruction builds on students' prior knowledge and learning is supported by active collaboration within a community of learners.

The fourth framework is focused specifically on literacy and highlights perhaps the major immediate goal of effective pedagogy: literacy engagement.

Literacy Engagement

Guthrie (2004) draws attention to the centrality of *literacy engagement* for reading achievement. Drawing on both the 1998 NAEP data from the United States and the results of the PISA study of reading achievement in international contexts, he notes that students whose family background was characterized by low income and low education, but who were highly engaged readers, substantially outscored students who came from backgrounds with higher education and higher income, but who themselves were less engaged readers. Based on a massive sample, this finding suggests the stunning conclusion that engaged reading can overcome traditional barriers to reading achievement, including gender, parental education, and income. (p. 5)

Guthrie notes that the term *engagement* incorporates notions of *time on task* (reading extensively), *affect* (enthusiasm and enjoyment of literacy), *depth of cognitive processing* (strategies to deepen comprehension), and *active pursuit of literacy activities* (amount and diversity of literacy practices in and out of school). He believes that engaged readers are active and energized in reading and use their minds with an emphasis on either cognitive strategies or conceptual knowledge. Furthermore, he asserts that engaged reading is often socially interactive insofar as engaged students are capable of discussion or sharing with friends despite the fact that much of their reading may be solitary.

Guthrie's (2004) classroom-based research has shown a direct relationship between increasing literacy engagement and higher achievement. He notes that the relationship is reciprocal:

Locked in a spiral, they grow together. . . . Young students who gain a modicum of skill in reading are enabled to read more stories and books, assuming they are available. With increased amounts of reading, students' fluency and knowledge expand, increasing basic word recognition. Contributing to this spiral is a sense of identity and selfhood; improving readers see themselves as capable, which is gratifying. Beyond self-confidence, however, students on the upward spiral see themselves as readers who are learners and thinkers; these students internalize literacy as a part of who they are. (p. 6)

Also, Guthrie notes that the relationships between engagement, identity, and achievement are equally potent in the opposite direction. Disengaged readers read less, experience fewer opportunities to learn from text, and gradually define themselves as disinterested readers.

Although numerous researchers have articulated the importance of cognitive strategy training, Guthrie (2004) expands and qualifies this focus in noting that "good strategy instruction cannot be provided with impoverished content" (p. 9). He also highlights the importance of texts that are well structured with respect to how knowledge is organized within the text (e.g., headings, bolding, italics, etc.). Students must also be given an opportunity to be self-directed in at least a portion of their learning from text, and discourse among students must be encouraged. He states that "if no social interchange is allowed, students' cognitive efforts to read and understand evaporate quickly" (p. 10). Finally, provision of ample time for engaged reading is crucial.

It is worth noting that the narrow research lens employed by the National Reading Panel (2000) did not enable the panel to address the relevance for reading achievement of self-direction, social interaction, or time for engaged reading. However, Guthrie's account of engaged reading is clearly congruent with Bransford and colleagues' synthesis of the research on how people learn. Unlike the National Reading Panel or the NCLB policy that it legitimated, Guthrie's analysis of the research includes the constructs of *affect, identity,* and *extensive reading* as significant components of engaged reading and reading achievement. The themes emphasized by Guthrie also converge with an earlier synthesis of research on reading comprehension carried out by Fielding and Pearson (1994). These authors highlighted four instructional components that research suggests are strongly related to reading comprehension outcomes:

Competent readers internalize literacy as a part of who they are.

1. Large amounts of time for actual text reading;

2. Teacher-directed instruction in comprehension strategies;

3. Opportunities for peer and collaborative learning; and

4. Occasions for students to talk to a teacher and one another about their responses to reading.

At this point, it is appropriate to revisit the construct of *reading* to understand better the nature of reading comprehension and the relevance of the four frameworks to the promotion of sustained reading development beyond the initial grades. We focus this analysis on low-income and English language learning (ELL) students, since these are groups that tend to experience the most disproportionate levels of academic failure.

Literacy and Academic Language Development among Low-Income ELL Students

In order to understand patterns of academic development among low-income and ELL students, one must distinguish between three very different aspects of proficiency in a language: (1) conversational fluency, (2) discrete language skills, and (3) academic language proficiency. The rationale for making these distinctions is that each dimension of proficiency follows very different developmental paths among both ELL and non-ELL students and each responds differently to particular kinds of instructional practices in school.

Conversational Fluency

Conversational fluency is the ability to carry on a conversation in familiar face-to-face situations. The vast majority of native speakers of English have developed conversational fluency by the time they enter school at age 5. This fluency involves use of high-frequency words and simple grammatical constructions. Certainly, conversational fluency evolves in complexity according to sociolinguistic context and the language registers required in particular situations (e.g., a job interview). However, for present purposes, it is sufficient to note that ELL students generally develop peer-appropriate fluency in conversational aspects of English within a year or two of intensive exposure to the language either in school or in the environment.

Discrete Language Skills

Discrete language skills involve the learning of rule-governed aspects of language (including phonology, grammar, and spelling) where acquisition of the general case permits generalization to other instances governed by that particular rule. Becker (1977) describes this process with respect to decoding as follows: "One can teach a set of sounds, blending skills, and rapid pronunciation skills, so that the student can read any regular-sound word composed from the sounds taught" (p. 533). Discrete language skills can be developed in two independent ways: (1) by direct instruction (e.g., systematic explicit phonics instruction) and (2) through immersion in a literacy-rich home or school environment where meanings are elaborated through language and attention is drawn to literate forms of language (e.g., letters on the pages of books). A combination of these two conditions appears to yield the most positive outcomes (e.g., Cunningham, 1990; Hatcher, Hulme, & Ellis, 1994). Students exposed to a literacy-rich environment in the home generally acquire initial literacy-related skills, such as phonological awareness and letter–sound correspondences, with minimal difficulty in the early grades of schooling (e.g., Neuman, 1999).

Some of these discrete language skills are acquired early in schooling and some continue to be acquired throughout schooling (e.g., spelling).

The discrete language skills acquired early include knowledge of the letters of the alphabet, the sounds represented by individual letters and combinations of letters, and the ability to decode written words into appropriate sounds. Some of these skills, such as phonological awareness and knowledge of the letters of the alphabet, show consistently moderate relationships with the acquisition of word decoding skills (National Reading Panel, 2000; Snow, Burns, & Griffin, 1998).

English language learners can learn these specific language skills concurrently with their development of basic vocabulary and conversational fluency. However, little direct transference is observed to other aspects of oral language proficiency, such as linguistic concepts, vocabulary, sentence memory, and word memory (Geva, 2000; Kwan & Willows, 1998). Similar findings are reported by Verhoeven (2000) for minority language students in the Dutch context and by Lambert and Tucker (1972) in Canada for English-speaking students in French immersion programs.

Academic Language Proficiency

Academic language proficiency includes knowledge of the less frequent vocabulary of English as well as the ability to interpret and produce increasingly complex written language. As students progress through the grades, they encounter far more low-frequency words (primarily from Greek and Latin sources), complex syntax (e.g., passives), and abstract expressions that are virtually never heard in everyday conversation. Students are required to understand linguistically and conceptually demanding texts in the content areas (e.g., literature, social studies, science, mathematics) and to use this language in an accurate and coherent way in their own writing. Figure 2.2 illustrates the complexity of the language that students are expected to acquire in content areas such as social studies.

Acquiring academic language is challenging for all students. For example, schools spend at least 12 years trying to extend the conversational language that native-speaking children bring to school into these more complex academic language spheres. It is hardly surprising, therefore, that research has repeatedly shown that ELL students, on average, require *at least* 5 years of exposure to academic English to catch up to native-speaker norms (Cummins, 1981; Hakuta, Butler, & Witt, 2000; Klesmer, 1994; Thomas & Collier, 2002; Worswick, 2001). In Israel, research has shown that Russian and Ethiopian immigrant students require at least 9 years to catch up to

> ELL students typically require at least five years to bridge the gap with native speakers, partly because they are catching up to a moving target.

FIGURE 2.2

Selected Vocabulary from a Grade 5 Social Studies Unit on the American Revolution

amend	consultation	perpetual petition	siege
annexation	convention	preamble	skirmish
bombarded	convince	ratify	statement
boundary	declaration	rebellion	surveyor
cavalry	dissolved	representatives	sustain
colonist	dynasty	resolution	traditions
commerce	independence	revolt	treaty
compromise	induced	revolution	tyrants
constitution	inference	sentiments	

their peers in academic Hebrew (Shohamy, Levine, Spolsky, Kere-Levy, Inbar, & Shemesh, 2002).

In addition to the complexity of the academic language they are attempting to acquire, ELL students must catch up to a moving target. Every year, native speakers are making large gains in their reading and writing abilities and in their knowledge of vocabulary. In order to catch up to grade norms within six years, ELL students must make 15 months gain in every 10-month school year. By contrast, the typical native-speaking student is expected to make 10 months gain in a 10-month school year (Collier & Thomas, 1999).

All three aspects of language proficiency—conversational fluency, discrete language skills, and academic language proficiency—are important. However, policymakers and the media frequently confuse them. Many ELL students who have acquired conversational fluency and decoding skills in English are still a long way from grade-level performance in academic language proficiency. Students who can "read" English fluently may have only a very limited understanding of the words they can decode. This is illustrated in the phenomenon of the fourth-grade slump.

The fourth-grade slump

Low-income and ELL students seem to be particularly susceptible to what has been called "the fourth-grade slump" (see Chall, Jacobs, & Baldwin, 1990; Chall & Snow, 1988; Rand Reading Study Group, 2002). Chall and

Snow (1988) report that "experienced teachers of low-income children have long reported a fourth-grade 'slump,' when their students' reading achievement slows down and reading problems increase" (p. 1). These students demonstrate grade-level reading performance in the primary grades (1 through 3) but begin to fall significantly behind grade norms starting at grade 4, with the discrepancy growing larger with each succeeding grade. Chall and colleagues (1990) report that low-income students in grades 2 and 3 are on grade level on tests of word recognition, oral reading, spelling, and word meaning. However, between grades 4 and 11, the extent of deceleration in reading performance is "overwhelming" (p. 43). These authors attribute these trends to low-income students' weakness in academic vocabularies. They point out that at grade 4 and beyond, "the reading materials become more complex, technical and abstract and are beyond the everyday experiences of most children" (p. 45). In the primary grades, where students were on grade level in word meaning, most of the words students were asked to define were common, familiar, and concrete words. Chall and colleagues note, "Whereas the major hurdles prior to grade 4 are learning to recognize in print the thousands of words whose meanings are already known and reading these fluently in connected texts with comprehension, the hurdle of grade 4 and beyond is coping with increasingly complex language and thought" (p. 45).

Numerous other studies have documented either significant gaps between decoding and comprehension performance or actual declines in reading comprehension among low-income students in the later grades of elementary school (Becker, 1977; Becker & Gersten, 1982; Venezsky, 1998). For example, Becker and Gersten (1982), in discussing students' performance on the DISTAR direct instruction program used between kindergarten and grade 3 in three school districts, document significant declines between grade 3 and grade 6 in Total Reading percentiles of the Metropolitan Achievement Test. In these districts, students' performance fell from the 31st to the 16th percentile, the 52nd to the 26th percentile, and the 28th to the 17th percentile, respectively. In a fourth district, there was a decline between grade 3 and grade 5 from the 40th to the 20th percentile.

A similar gap between word-level decoding and reading comprehension skills has been noted by Venezsky (1998) in reviewing data from the Success for All (SFA) program, which follows a highly controlled scripted approach in grade 1. A major gap was observed in students' performance on measures of word-level skills (word recognition, letter–sound decoding), which were close to grade expectations, in comparison to their performance on reading comprehension measures. Although there was a significant difference in reading comprehension at the grade 5 level between the SFA schools and controls, this difference was minimal (four months) and students were still about two years below grade expectations.

In short, the fourth-grade slump reflects the fact that neither language proficiency nor reading ability are unitary constructs. Reading comprehension does not develop automatically on the basis of decoding skills; similarly, academic language proficiency is distinct from students' conversational fluency in English or their knowledge of discrete language skills. A core component of academic language proficiency is vocabulary knowledge, and the vocabulary load in the curriculum increases dramatically after the primary grades. The development of academic language proficiency, for both ELL and non-ELL students, requires that students *gain access to academic language* by means of extensive reading and also that they are supported in *harvesting the language* they encounter in literature and content area texts.

The importance of vocabulary knowledge for reading has been frequently articulated (e.g., Corson, 1997). Nation and Coady (1988), for example, in reviewing research on the relationship between vocabulary and reading, point out that "vocabulary difficulty has consistently been found to be the most significant predictor of overall readability." Once the effect of vocabulary difficulty (usually estimated by word frequency and/or familiarity and word length) is taken into account, other linguistic variables, such as sentence structure, account for little incremental variance in the readability of a text. They summarize their review as follows: "In general the research leaves us in little doubt about the importance of vocabulary knowledge for reading, and the value of reading as a means of increasing vocabulary" (p. 108).

Although direct instruction of vocabulary has a place in supporting its development, this instruction is likely to be most effective when integrated with extensive reading and writing activities in which students are engaged. If low-frequency (nonconversational) vocabulary is found predominantly in written text, then extensive reading of text must be promoted as a crucial component of both vocabulary acquisition and reading comprehension development. There is overwhelming evidence for the importance of extensive reading in building up academic language proficiency in both first and second languages (L1 and L2) (e.g., Elley, 1991; Guthrie, 2004; Krashen, 2004b; Postlethwaite & Ross, 1992).

At this point, we have a basis for addressing the specific pedagogical issues that are in dispute regarding what constitutes effective literacy instruction.

Pedagogical Conflicts and Choices

Current disputes about literacy pedagogy revolve around one seemingly straightforward question: What forms of pedagogy will most effectively promote reading comprehension? There is actually a considerable degree of consensus around this issue. We suggest that the intensity of the current debate about literacy instruction derives primarily from underlying ideological orientations regarding the nature of learning and teaching—specifically, the extent to which proponents of alternative positions endorse behaviorist or social constructivist approaches to pedagogy. The misinterpretation and misleading communication of the NRP findings that we and many other commentators have noted (see Chapter 1) can be understood as an attempt to legitimate a programmed learning (behaviorist) approach to reading instruction.

Although its roots lie in the 1940s and 1950s behaviorist psychology of B. F. Skinner, recent incarnations of programmed learning derive from the work of Siegfried Englemann (1969), the developer of the DISTAR program. The instructional focus of programmed learning is on the design of appropriate skill hierarchies for efficient transmission of knowledge and content and is seen most clearly in scripted programs. The instructional science is in the script rather than in the actions of the teacher. Because the script is sacrosanct, there is minimal opportunity or encouragement to deviate from the script to address the learning needs of individual students (e.g., ELL students who may not understand the tasks dictated by the script).

By contrast, a social constructivist approach focuses on the collaborative construction of knowledge by teachers and learners. Pedagogical interactions build on learners' prior experience, helping them integrate new understandings or knowledge into their cognitive schemata. Since students come to school with very different cultural, linguistic, and personal experiences, teachers must orchestrate interactions in a flexible way that takes into account the diversity of experiences, needs, and talents within their classroom. In other words, by definition, within a social constructivist approach teacher–student interactions cannot be preprogrammed.

The Pedagogical Divide: Programmed Learning versus Social Constructivist Learning

Behaviorism for the masses?

As noted in Chapter 1, the architects of the Reading First component of No Child Left Behind continue to insist that "systematic phonics instruction produced significant benefits for K–6 students" (Lyon & Chhabra, 2004), omitting to note that systematic phonics instruction produced no benefits beyond grade 1 in reading comprehension among normally achieving and low-achieving students (i.e., a large majority of the elementary school population). This questionable interpretation of the NRP findings entails major consequences for schools. For example, in 2003, Reading First grants were withheld from the New York City school system until it agreed to adopt an additional intensive phonics-oriented program for the primary grades (K through grade 3).[3]

In addition, some school systems have implemented scripted phonics-oriented programs in highly prescriptive ways, perhaps even going beyond the intent of the authors of these programs. In many school districts, this has led to intense teacher frustration and anger (see, for example, Meyer, 2002). In discussions with teachers, we have heard on numerous occasions views such as those expressed by California elementary school teachers André Gensburger (2005) and Elizabeth Jaeger (2006). Gensburger highlights the widespread demoralization of teachers caused by scripted reading programs that leave no room for creativity and professional judgment in the classroom. He points out that all reading materials that were not included in the reading adoption were removed from his classroom despite the fact that these books were totally appropriate for "reading-starved children" and had been paid for by parents, the parent–teacher association, the school, and teachers themselves over the years.

Jaeger (2006), a teacher in the West Contra Costa Unified School District northeast of San Francisco, recounts the dramatic changes that occurred in her school reading program with the introduction of the Open Court reading series, "a scripted reading program that tells teachers what to say and do at every moment" (p. 39). Open Court instruction occupied between two and three hours each day and replaced the literacy curriculum that teachers had previously developed which, according to Jaeger, "more fully addressed the range of levels and the varied strengths and weaknesses of our students" (pp. 39–40). Noting that "teachers got laryngitis while children remained silent" (p. 40), Jaeger describes how the interaction between teacher and student was reduced to "a mechanical and impersonal back-and-forth" (p. 40):

> In kindergarten and 1st grade, teachers now taught the least meaningful aspects of literacy—letters and sounds—and postponed emphasis on meaning for nearly two years. These children faced a steady diet of so-called decodable texts ("The cat sat on the mat. The cat is fat. Where is

the cat?"). Teachers presented the lessons to all students at the same time, limiting the opportunity to differentiate instruction. (p. 40)

Jaeger goes on to discuss how trainers and consultants could enter classrooms at will, interrupting lessons, chastising teachers in front of their students, and going through personal files without permission. Furthermore, any teacher who veered from the mandated script by altering or expanding less effective lessons was threatened with disciplinary action by the principal. This "heavy-handed implementation" of the scripted reading program did not extend to the same degree to other schools that were located in middle-class neighborhoods with a greater percentage of white students:

> The district shackled teachers of poor children with generally lower achievement to a curriculum that did not let them modify their teaching. Teachers in more affluent schools could enrich the curriculum to emphasize higher-level thinking and aesthetics. These children had the opportunity to obtain an education that prepared them to assume demanding leadership roles. Poor kids received an education that prepared them for McDonald's, McMilitary, and McPrison. (p. 40)

Jaeger's active opposition to this type of program resulted in her being transferred to another school, giving a clear message to other teachers who might contemplate resisting top-down mandates: "Speak up and you will be punished; advocate for your students and you will be silenced" (p. 41).[4]

These accounts articulate some of the most problematic aspects of the literacy instructional approach being implemented in many low-income districts. Instruction is scripted and uniformly paced; all teachers are expected to cover the same material at the same rate regardless of whether students understand it or not. Many ELL students have no way of connecting cognitively with the one-size-fits-all instructional content but teachers are routinely told, "Trust me, this program is good for every child in your class" (Meyer, 2002, p. 53). Typically, ELL and special needs students are not permitted to be withdrawn for remediation during the phonics component of the program, clearly communicating that all other aspects of literacy instruction are secondary to systematic phonics instruction.

The instructional approach described by commentators such as Gensburger (2005) and Meyer (2002) goes far beyond simply the transmission of skills and information as one component of a broader instructional philosophy. It represents a programmed learning approach that is explicitly based on behaviorist psychology and ideology. Becker (1977) outlines the essential elements of Englemann's direct instruction approach:

> In common with other theories of programmed instruction, Englemann specifies teaching one thing at a time, providing adequate practice, and designing lessons for a low error rate. (p. 531)

Becker (1977) also articulates the role of instructional scripts within a programmed learning approach:

> The use of explicitly detailed lessons—scripts—has been criticized as restricting teachers' initiative. This may be a valid criticism, but one should consider the potential advantages of scripts in providing quality control in a delivery system. The scripts permit the selection and testing of sequences of examples that produce efficient learning if followed. Most teachers simply do not have time to find appropriate words and examples or to sequence skill hierarchies in the most efficient possible manner. When teachers phrase their own questions, they may choose terms unknown to lower-performing children or may include unnecessary verbiage. In choosing examples, moreover, they may teach incorrect rules because the positive examples have some irrelevant feature in common. (p. 523)

With respect to reading comprehension, Carnine, Silbert, and Kameenui (1997) note that in "each aspect of the comprehension model . . . instruction begins with the least complex form and moves to the most complex in hierarchical fashion" (p. 28). The focus is on the skills hierarchies built into the script rather than on what students may be bringing to the learning environment. This approach relies on what Iran-Nejad, McKeachie, and Berliner (1990) call *simplification by isolation,* where complex skills are broken down into their components and taught in isolation from other skills with which they are normally integrated.

The focus of programmed instruction is on the skills hierarchies built into the script rather than on what students bring to the learning environment.

Social constructivist alternatives

By contrast, social constructivist approaches draw their inspiration from the work of cognitive theorists such as Vygotsky (1978) and Piaget (1929) and emphasize both the importance of students' prior knowledge as a foundation for constructing new understandings and the role of the social context in facilitating this process. Particularly influential has been Vygotsky's (1978) notion of the *zone of proximal development (ZPD),* which he defined as the distance between children's developmental levels as determined by individual problem solving without adult guidance and the level of potential development as determined by children's problem solving under the influence of, or in collaboration with, more capable adults and peers. Expressed simply, the ZPD is the interpersonal space where minds meet and new understandings can arise through collaborative interaction and inquiry. Newman, Griffin, and Cole (1989) label this interpersonal space the *construction zone.*

We have argued that not only is *knowledge* collaboratively generated within this interpersonal space or construction zone but, equally significant for learning, *identities* are negotiated between teachers and students (Cummins, 2001). The reciprocal negotiation of identities and the collaborative generation of knowledge are intimately related to each other. Teacher–student collaboration in the construction of knowledge will operate effectively only in contexts where students' identities are being affirmed. Essentially, this conception extends the ZPD beyond the cognitive sphere into the realms of affective development and power relationships. It also makes clear that the *construction zone* can also be a *constriction zone,* where student identities and learning are constricted rather than extended.

> The construction zone, can also be a constriction zone where student identities and learning are constricted rather than extended.

Common ground and areas of dispute

Behaviorist and social constructivist pedagogical orientations entail very different implications for reading instruction and define the major issues of contention in current debates. This can be appreciated by considering the common ground that a large majority of researchers, educators, and policymakers are likely to endorse (see review in Cummins, 2001). There is considerable consensus, supported by the research, on the following:

- Immersion in a literate environment either in home or school (and preferably both) is a strong predictor of success in both decoding and reading comprehension.

- Development of phonological awareness, letter knowledge, and concepts about print is an important component in acquiring initial decoding skills.

- An explicit instructional focus on developing phonological awareness, letter knowledge, and concepts about print, *together with a significant instructional focus on actual reading and writing,* contributes to the development of decoding skills and early reading comprehension skills.

■ The extent to which students have access to print and the amount of actual reading that they carry out are major determinants of reading comprehension development.

The most significant points of contention appear to be (1) the extent to which reading instruction should be rigidly scripted and (2) the extent to which tight control should be exercised over students' access to authentic text (i.e., text that would not be classified as "decodable"). Advocates of scripted instruction see scripts as essential to ensure quality control in the delivery of reading instruction. They also tend to emphasize that decodable text should predominate in initial reading materials with only limited access to "nondecodable" text (e.g., children's literature). Mathes and Torgesen (2000), for example, express this perspective as follows:

> Likewise, to ask children to read text that they cannot decode using the alphabetic elements and skills that they have been taught is to communicate to them that the alphabetic knowledge and skill they have spent effort learning is not really relevant to reading, and that they must rely heavily on guessing the identity of words from context. (p. 12)

In other words, it is seen as problematic for children to encounter words in reading materials for which the letter–sound correspondences have not been previously taught in an explicit and systematic way. Becker (1977) makes essentially the same argument with respect to the teaching of vocabulary, arguing for a graded progression of reading materials in which "words in a proposed text that are not suitable for a given grade level would be replaced, emphasized in the text, or listed so that the teacher could teach them before beginning a lesson" (p. 539). Thus, a behaviorist approach assumes that students can reliably learn only what has been explicitly taught. Therefore, both letter–sound correspondences and also vocabulary-concept knowledge should be pretaught prior to students encountering new vocabulary in texts. One implication of this approach is that students will not be encouraged to engage in extensive independent reading because errors cannot be minimized when students encounter the uncontrolled vocabulary of trade books or other reading materials that have not been specifically programmed to fit into the skill hierarchy. This assumption underlies the removal of nonprescribed books from classrooms in contexts such as that described by Gensburger (2005).

Illustrative research studies

What does research say about the underlying theoretical assumptions of behaviorist and social constructivist orientations to pedagogy? Two illustrative studies point to the limitations of one-size-fits-all scripted programs. For example, in a study involving detailed observations in four classrooms, Juel and Minden-Cupp (2000) found that "children who entered first grade with some reading ability did exceptionally well in a classroom that included a less structured phonics curriculum and more reading of trade books and writing of text, . . . whereas children who entered with fewer literacy skills benefited from a curriculum with an early word-level focus" (pp. 484–485). They further point out that after a "strong dose of effective phonics and a rapid rise in word-level skill, these low-group children then benefited from the same type of increased vocabulary and text discussions, and reading from a variety of types of materials, as did their peers" (p. 485). The authors interpret the finding that phonics is critical for some children but may not be helpful for others (p. 484) as support for the self-teaching hypothesis (Share & Stanovich, 1995), which proposes that when children have developed phonological awareness and letter–sound knowledge, and are provided with rich exposure to print, they can ultimately teach themselves to read. The interaction between students' entering ability and the initial focus of teaching shows clearly the limitations of direct instruction approaches that ignore student diversity of language, culture, and prior experience in favor of a uniform script that attempts to transmit hierarchical skills to all children in the same sequence.

The second illustrative study also supports the basic principles of a social constructivist approach by showing that when students' identities are invested in the learning task, and learning is supported by a culturally responsive instructional context, students can acquire extensive literacy skills that have not been explicitly taught. This research consisted of a longitudinal case study carried out by María de la Luz Reyes (2001) of the "spontaneous biliteracy" of four low-income working-class Mexicano/Latino children in a bilingual program, two of whom were taught to read initially only in Spanish and two only in English, according to their language dominance on entry to the program. The children received structured phonics instruction (in English or Spanish) in kindergarten, but in first and second grades only minimal phonics were taught. All four children spontaneously transferred their literacy skills from the initial language of instruction to their second language

> In bilingual programs around the world, children spontaneously transfer literacy skills across languages without systematic and explicit instruction in the dominant language.

without formal instruction. Their "natural, spontaneous, and uncomplicated approach to bilingualism and biliteracy" was supported by their interest in writing in both languages and also by their social play where they challenged each other to read in the language in which they had received no formal reading instruction.[5]

In interpreting the spontaneous biliteracy development of the four children, Reyes (2001) emphasized the centrality of affective dimensions related to students' identity. She notes that the learning environment legitimated children's bicultural identity:

> There is no doubt that these students felt their languages and their culture affirmed. . . . Although each of the girls received [reading] instruction in only one language, all their learning from kindergarten to second grade took place in classrooms where the teachers supported and nurtured their cultural and linguistic resources. Each day they heard their teachers and peers use Spanish and English. Their teachers also made great efforts to treat English and Spanish as equally as possible, valuing both languages for personal, social, and academic purposes. (p. 116)

Reyes's (2001) documentation of the biliteracy development of these students clearly refutes predictions derived from the learning theory underlying scripted reading instruction. As a result of the supportive sociocultural environment, these four low-income students learned extensive literacy skills that had not been "systematically and explicitly" taught. This research is just as "scientific" as the quasi-experimental studies considered by the NRP and just as capable of contributing to scientific advancement and knowledge generation (Cummins, 1999). In most scientific disciplines, knowledge is generated by constantly testing and refining theory-based predictions and thus systematic observations such as those reported by Reyes contribute directly to the testing of hypotheses. In this case, they refute central hypotheses underlying programmed learning and scripted curricula.

In short, there is extensive research evidence from a variety of qualitative and quantitative research studies on reading development that is inconsistent with the pedagogical assumptions of scripted curricula and programmed learning. In addition, the principles of social constructivist approaches to reading instruction are not only consistent with the research evidence but also with the broader research-based principles of learning articulated by Bransford and colleagues (2000). Those who endorse a social constructivist approach to learning point to the extensive scientific

> Only transformative approaches to instruction focus on issues of student and teacher identities as they intersect with societal power structures.

research showing that children are capable of developing complex phonological and decoding skills that have not been explicitly taught when they are provided with a culturally responsive learning environment at home or at school and when their learning is guided or scaffolded by supportive adults. They argue that because children come to school with widely different degrees of preliteracy knowledge, such as phonological awareness and other concepts about print, as well as different degrees of knowledge of the English language, one-size-fits-all scripted instruction constricts the learning environment and limits students' potential for sustained growth in reading comprehension. The empirical research suggests that children's time would be much better spent applying their phonological awareness, knowledge of phonics, and knowledge of the world to reading engaging texts and exploring possibilities for expressing their identities through personal writing (Chow & Cummins, 2003).

However, although social constructivist approaches accurately capture important aspects of learning, they typically do not address broader social issues related to the nature of literacy and the goals of literacy instruction within a globalized Information Age society. There is general agreement among proponents of all pedagogical orientations that strong literacy skills are important for economic participation and national competitiveness. However, only transformative approaches raise issues of teacher and student identities as they intersect with societal power structures. The rationale for addressing these issues is that the *role definitions* or identities of teachers in relation to the overall goals of education will determine the kinds of pedagogy they orchestrate and the literacy abilities they aspire to promote among their students.

Pedagogical Images: Preparing Students for Civic Participation

As educators, our interactions with students are constantly sketching a triangular set of images:

- An image of our own identities as educators;
- An image of the identity options we highlight for our students; and
- An image of the society we hope our students will help form.

The intersection of these three "images" and the ways in which instruction opens up or shuts off identity options can be illustrated in the findings of large-scale studies of classroom interaction in the United States (e.g., Goodlad, 1984; Ramírez, 1992). In discussing the implications of Goodlad's finding that teacher-centered transmission instruction predominated in U.S. classrooms, Sirotnik (1983) pointed to the fact that the typical American classroom contained

> a lot of teacher talk and a lot of student listening . . . almost invariably closed and factual questions . . . and predominantly total class instructional configurations around traditional activities—all in a virtually affectless environment. It is but a short inferential leap to suggest that we are implicitly teaching dependence upon authority, linear thinking, social apathy, passive involvement, and hands-off learning. (p. 29)

In other words, an image of the society that students will graduate into and the kind of contributions they are being prepared to make within that society is embedded implicitly in the interactions between educators and students.

The ways in which these images are transacted in classroom interactions reflect the ways in which educators locate themselves in relation to the power structure of the society. When one chooses to frame the universe of discourse about underachievement primarily in terms of children's deficits in some area of psychological or linguistic functioning (such as phonological awareness), one expels culture, language, identity, intellect, and imagination from one's image of the child. Similarly, these constructs are nowhere to be found in one's image of the effective teacher of these children, nor in policies that might guide instruction.

The erasure of *imagination* from the images of children and teachers is particularly unfortunate in view of the major environmental, social, and economic problems that today's global society faces. It is also clearly at variance with the emphasis on knowledge generation and collaborative inquiry that both the corporate sector and many government reports have emphasized in recent years. Imagination can be defined as "the act or power of creating mental images of what has never been actually experienced" (Egan, 1986, p. 7). Egan (1986, 1999) makes an extremely persuasive case that school curricula have excluded the "most powerful and energetic intellectual tools children bring to school" (1986, p. 18). He suggests that educators need to reconstruct their curricula and teaching methods in light of a richer image of the child as an imaginative as well as a logico-mathematical thinker. Children's imaginations are revealed in their capacity for highly abstract and sophisticated thinking in relation to engaging stories (e.g., *Star Wars, Harry Potter*), yet children's opportunities to exercise these imaginative intellectual powers are systematically restricted throughout their schooling. Society views children, and particularly children of poverty, as relative intellectual incompetents ignoring the everyday experience of their creative intellectual energy and imaginative powers (1986, p. 22). One might add that the new regime of truth also constructs teachers as relative intellectual incompetents who must be policed to ensure that they do not deviate from the official script.

At issue are radically different conceptions of learning and education and their roles in society. Should education automatically reinforce the societal status quo or should it challenge societal structures and discourses that are at variance with the articulated (although perhaps only sporadically pursued) core values of the society, such as equality, social justice, and freedom? Do we truly want historically subordinated groups to develop active intelligence and imagination whose outcomes, by definition, can't be predicted? Shouldn't we rather prescribe exactly what is to be taught as a means of controlling what can be thought? Are we comfortable promoting the multilingual talents of our students in light of the different perspectives on reality that this multilingual access might provide? Do we really believe that inner-city children should be encouraged to take pride in their linguistic creativity and further explore the range of English varieties they command (Delpit, 1995) despite the fact that such varieties are stigmatized in the wider society?

The answers to these questions will depend on the extent to which society sees constructs such as power and identity as in any way relevant to children's education. The conceptions of literacy and pedagogy that underlie the analyses and instructional practices described in this book explicitly incorporate an image of society as needing all the intelligence, imagination, and multilingual talent it can get. Effective citizenship requires active intelligence and a willingness to challenge power structures that constrict human possibility. If instruction doesn't promote active intelligence from children's first day in school, or promotes it only in middle-class suburban schools, then it is failing both students and society. The case studies that we document in Chapters 5 through 9 and in the appendix illustrate clearly how various forms of technology can be harnessed to mobilize students' imaginations and active intelligence in ways that powerfully challenge the anemic pedagogical vision that currently holds sway in far too many inner-city and rural schools.

1 Think about an instructional situation with which you are familiar (e.g., your own classroom if you are teaching). Approximately what proportion of instruction is spent in each of the three pedagogical orientations discussed in this chapter (transmission, social constructivist, transformative)? What are some of the reasons for the patterns you have identified? In your ideal teaching situation, how would you organize instruction with respect to the three orientations?

2 In their book *How People Learn,* Bransford and colleagues (2000) highlight the importance of activating and building on students' preexisting knowledge. What implications does this have within a culturally and linguistically diverse classroom? What strategies might you use to activate students'

preexisting knowledge when their English language skills are still quite limited?

3 In addition to the rapid increase in low-frequency vocabulary that students encounter after the early grades of elementary school, what other aspects of academic language might contribute to the fourth-grade slump phenomenon?

4 Why do you think that the bilingual students that María de la Luz Reyes (2001) documented were spontaneously able to develop reading and writing skills in their second language without any systematic and explicit literacy instruction in that language? What are the implications of this phenomenon for monolingual "mainstream" classrooms?

Endnotes

1. Some skepticism in relation to the Knowledge Society rhetoric is warranted in view of the fact that the vast majority of new jobs that are being created in Western societies are in the service sector. Thus, only a relatively small segment of students graduating from high schools will work in jobs that require critical interpretation of data and generation of new knowledge. Most service jobs will involve greater use of new technologies (e.g., scanners at supermarket checkouts) but few will require significantly greater use of higher-order thinking or critical literacy skills than is currently the case. However, *all* students will require critical literacy if they are to participate effectively in the democratic process.

2. The metaphor of "nesting" these three pedagogical orientations within each other was developed in discussions between Eleni Skourtou, Vasilia Kourtis Kazoullis, and Jim Cummins. The visual depiction of these nested relationships was initially created by Vasilia Kourtis Kazoullis (see Skourtou, Kourtis-Kazoullis, & Cummins, 2006).

3. Abby Goodnough (2003) in the *New York Times* described the change in New York City schools as follows:

In addition to Month by Month Phonics, the program that Deputy Chancellor Diana Lam chose in January as part of a new system wide reading and math curriculum, kindergarten through third grade classrooms will use the New York City Passport program, developed by Voyager Expanded Learning of Dallas. . . . Reid Lyon, Mr. Bush's top reading advisor, complained in January that Month by Month did not have enough research backing it; he and other reading experts have warned New York City that it could lose millions of dollars in federal funds. (p. D1)

Part of the concern in regard to Month by Month Phonics appears to have been that it did not focus almost exclusively on systematic intensive phonics instruction. According to Goodnough:

> The curriculum will also require students to read books from classroom libraries and practice writing for several hours every day. But while [New York City Schools Chancellor] Mr. Klein and Ms. Lam have expressed more excitement about the daily reading and writing, critics have warned that the city's many struggling students should spend more time drilling in phonics. (p. D3)

A footnote to the confrontation over New York City's Reading Program is that when Reid Lyon resigned from the National Institute of Child Health and Human Development in May 2005, he took a high-level position with Best Associates, the founder of Voyager Learning. *Education Week* described the switch from public to private sector as follows:

> Best Associates is a merchant-banking firm that underwrites start-up companies, including education ventures. Randy Best, a founding partner, was the creator of Voyager Learning, a company that publishes commercial reading programs that have been approved for use in schools receiving federal funds under Reading First. The Voyager program, for example, was adopted for use in New York City schools that receive Reading First money after the district's existing reading initiative was criticized by Mr. Lyon as not being explicit or systematic in its approach to teaching the subject. (Manzo, May 24, 2005, www.edweek.org)

4. The frustrations of experienced and talented teachers were also documented in a *New York Times* article in May 2003 that profiled the experience of a Florida kindergarten teacher who refused to partici-pate in the test-preparation stampede (Winerip 2003). Ms. MacLeish had been named Orange County Teacher of the Year in 1998 and is described in the article as possibly "the best kindergarten teacher in Florida." She decided to move to a resource teaching position, helping children who were experiencing academic difficulties, rather than compromise her vision of what education should be. The letter she wrote home to parents announcing that she would not be teaching kindergarten next year explained:

> A single high-stakes test score is now measuring Florida's children, leaving little time to devote to their character or potential or talents or depth of knowledge. . . . Kindergarten teachers throughout the state have replaced valued learning centers (home center, art center, blocks, dramatic play) with paper and pencil tasks, dittos, coloring sheets, scripted lessons, workbook pages.

Winerip (2003) notes that "the breaking point for Ms. MacLeish was an article in the paper praising a kindergarten teacher who had eliminated her play centers and was doing reading drills, all part of a push to help her school get a higher grade on the annual state report card." By contrast, Ms. MacLeish's classroom is described as "crammed with books" and her focus on linking reading and writing to students' lives was far removed from the pedagogy of reading drills and scripted lessons.

5. This process of spontaneous transfer of literacy across languages parallels what is typically observed in Canadian French immersion programs (e.g., Geva & Clifton, 1993; Lambert & Tucker, 1972) and in U.S. dual language programs (Cloud, Genesee, & Hamayan, 2000; Freeman, Freeman, & Mercuri, 2005; Genesee, Lindholm-Leary, Saunders, & Christian, 2006; Lindholm-Leary, 2001). English L1 students are typically introduced to reading through their second language (French in Canada and usually Spanish in U.S. dual language programs) but quickly transfer their reading skills to English and acquire fluent English reading skills with no systematic or explicit instruction in English phonics.

CHAPTER 3

Assessment

When educational testing programs are mandated by school, district, state, or other authorities, the ways in which the test results are intended to be used should be clearly described. It is the responsibility of those who mandate the use of tests to monitor their impact and to identify and minimize potential negative consequences.

American Educational Research Association (1999, p. 145)

Ill-conceived educational accountability laws, whether state or federal, invariably erode instructional quality. They do so by causing teachers to engage in statute-spurred classroom activities that turn out to be incompatible with high quality instruction, for instance, curricular reductionism and excessive test-preparation.

W. James Popham (2004, p. 1)

Standardized test scores are widely regarded as an index of the quality of instruction within a particular school or district. No Child Left Behind mandates that yearly testing between grades 3 and 8 be used to assess the extent to which schools have made adequate yearly progress (AYP). Schools whose test scores do not meet the prescribed criteria are designated as in need of improvement or failing. We argue in this chapter that these legal provisions are highly problematic on the grounds that:

- There is no scientific evidence that increased standardized testing results in higher achievement.

- Standardized tests typically assess only a limited range of content standards, specifically those that can be assessed easily and relatively inexpensively.

- High-stakes testing narrows the curriculum such that teachers will teach only content that will be tested.

- Test scores reflect both instructional and noninstructional factors (e.g., poverty, proportion of ELL students, etc.). When the contribution of noninstructional factors to test score variance is ignored, the test scores no longer provide any scientific basis for policy decisions.

- Teaching to the test disproportionately affects students in low-income schools with the result that the pedagogical divide between low- and middle-income schools is exacerbated.

■ Enrichment programs, such as dual language programs for ELL and native-English-speaking students, are compromised because of pressure to meet test-defined AYP criteria in the early grades.

Introduction

Let us state at the outset that standardized tests have a legitimate and important role to play in promoting both equity and accountability in education. Evidence of major disparities between dominant and socially marginalized groups in standardized test performance provided significant impetus to the movement for equality of educational opportunity during the 1960s and continues to do so (e.g., Beykont, 2002; Mercer, 1973). Similarly, the failure of states to demonstrate any significant closing of the achievement gap between White and minority students on NAEP scores over the past 30 years (see Chapter 1) belies any claim that real progress has been made toward civil rights in education. Without the documentation of persistent achievement gaps across social groups provided by "The Nation's Report Card," it would be much more difficult to challenge discriminatory educational practices.

Standardized tests, however, also carry a sorry legacy of reinforcing coercive power structures by excluding low-income and minority students from educational opportunity (e.g., Sacks, 1999; Valdés & Figueroa, 1994). One of pioneers of the standardized testing movement in the early 1900s expressed clearly the power of standardized tests to determine who belongs and who should be excluded:

> The number of aliens deported because of feeble-mindedness . . . increased approximately 350 per cent in 1913 and 570 per cent in 1914. . . . This was due to the untiring efforts of the physicians who were inspired by the belief that mental tests could be used for the detection of feeble-minded aliens. (Goddard, 1917, p. 271)

Almost a century later, similar standardized tests are being applied to identifying and uprooting feebly performing schools. Sadly, this "untiring effort" has about as much scientific credibility as that of Goddard and his colleagues. It is also contributing just as effectively to the deportation of marginalized students into educational dead-zones, despite its expressed intention to do the opposite.

Popham (2005) distinguishes two forms of standardized achievement tests commonly used for high-stakes assessment: norm-referenced tests and standards-based tests. He argues that both forms of tests are instructionally insensitive, for different reasons.

Norm-referenced tests (e.g., the Comprehensive Tests of Basic Skills) are used to assess students' performance in relation to a norm group. The norm group may be the total population of school-age students or it may be a subgroup (e.g., African American students). These tests are constructed in such a way as to maximize variability among individuals. The goal is to rank an individual's performance in relation to the performance of other people. The score spread will result in most of the test-takers scoring in the average range (66 percent will be within one standard deviation of the mean) but will also permit fine-grained distinctions to be made among those at the top and the bottom of the distribution. In general, items are retained in the test only if they correlate well with the total test (or subtest) and are neither too easy nor too difficult. A consequence of this test construction procedure is that norm-referenced tests reveal nothing about how much a student has learned in absolute terms, only how well she or he did in relation to a comparison group. In Kohn's (2000) words, norm-referenced tests "are not about assessing excellence; they are about sorting students (or schools) into winners and losers" (p. 15). Because of the way they are constructed, norm-referenced tests tend to measure "not what students have been taught in school but what they bring to school . . . they're unable to measure improved instruction in a school even when it has definitely taken place" (Popham, 2005, p. 40).

By contrast, *standards-based tests* (e.g., the Texas Assessment of Academic Skills) are designed to measure the extent to which students have learned a particular body of knowledge or skills that has been specified in a set of curricular standards. This type of test has also been referred to as a *criterion-referenced test*. The major problem with these tests, according to Popham (2005), is that the standards upon which the tests are based usually constitute an extremely detailed listing of skills and knowledge and "teachers soon become overwhelmed by too many targets" (p. 40).

> Educators must guess about which of this multitude of content standards will actually be assessed on a given year's test. . . . After working with standards-based tests aimed at so many targets, teachers understandably may devote less and less attention to those tests. As a consequence, students' performances on this type of instructionally insensitive test often become dependent upon the very same SES [socioeconomic status] factors that compromise the utility of nationally standardized achievement tests when used for school evaluation. (2005, p. 40)[1]

Our specific concerns with assessment and accountability provisions are focused on the fact that the powerful forms of literacy pedagogy for low-income students that we document throughout this book risk becoming relics of an earlier age if current trends continue. Thus, it is imperative that we identify more appropriate systems of accountability that will advance the kinds of education students require within a twenty-first-century Knowledge Society. First, we summarize briefly the problems and contradictions within the NCLB-mandated system of accountability.

High-Stakes Tests and Educational Quality

High-Stakes Tests Do Not Improve Education

Several detailed analyses of the relationship between high-stakes testing and educational outcomes seriously undermine the widespread assumption that both teachers and students will work harder and perform better when their performance is closely monitored by high-stakes tests. Walt Haney (2002), for example, examined the data underlying the apparent surge in test scores in Texas during the 1990s subsequent to the introduction of the Texas Assessment of Academic Skills (TAAS). Test scores

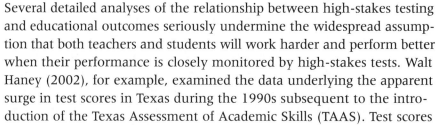

High-stakes tests are insensitive to the outcomes of powerful pedagogy.

climbed steadily upward during the 1990s and the gap between White and minority students decreased. In addition, high school dropout rates decreased and gains also appeared in NAEP scores. A Texas miracle? Unfortunately not, according to Haney. The illusion of educational improvement was due to a combination of measures taken by school systems to boost scores at the expense of truly educating students.

Among the patterns Haney (2002) documents is placement of low-performing students in special education classes where they are excluded from school accountability ratings. Between 1994 and 1998, the numbers of students taking the grade 10 TAAS, but classified as special education, increased from 3.9 percent to 6.3 percent. According to Haney, "This means that a portion of the increase in pass rates on the grade-ten TAAS is attributable simply to the increases in the rates at which students were diverted into special education and hence excluded from school accountability ratings" (pp. 32–33).[2]

Similarly, retention of Hispanic and African American students in grade 9 so that they do not take the grade 10 TAAS exit test represents a major contributor to the apparent reduction in the racial gap in TAAS scores. Haney (2002) points out that "compared with 9.6 percent of

White students who were retained in ninth grade, 24.2 percent of Black and 25.9 percent of Hispanic students were retained in ninth grade" (p. 33). Furthermore, Haney demonstrates that only one in five students who repeated grade 9 persisted in high school until graduation and that there was an *increase* in the number of students dropping out of school since the implementation of the standards-based education reform in Texas.

Haney's analysis has been presented here as illustrative of a range of similar reports, drawing on data from many states, documenting the absence of empirical support for the claim that high-stakes testing improves school performance (e.g., Amrein & Berliner, 2002; Klein, Hamilton, McCaffrey, & Stecher, 2000; Neill, Guisbond, & Schaeffer, 2004; Uriarte, 2002). The fragility of the Texas miracle also hit the news media in 2003. According to the *New York Times* (Editorial, July 21, 2003), accountability in the Houston school district owed more to "Enron-style" accounting than to any real improvement in student performance. Schemo's July 11, 2003, account in the same newspaper reported observations that many schools had assistant principals who act as "bouncers," pushing students who show up late to school or are frequently absent to quit. In addition, schools may hold back ninth-graders who do poorly on a pretest for the tenth-grade math exam, producing an artificial "ninth-grade bulge" in student enrollment.

Test critic Alfie Kohn (2000) also points out that "claims of miraculous improvement often turn out to offer more hype than hope" (p. 24), citing the fact that test score improvement during the 1990s in the San Francisco public schools owed more to the exclusion of thousands of ELL students from the testing process than to any improvement in educational outcomes.

High-Stakes Tests Do Not Assess Instructional Quality

It has frequently been observed that most of the information received from large-scale standardized testing could be obtained much faster and at considerably less expense simply by ranking schools and students according to the mean income of their zip code areas. Kohn (2000), for example, points out that the main thing standardized tests reveal is how big students' houses are:

> The main thing standardized tests reveal is how big students' houses are.

> Research has repeatedly found that the amount of poverty in the communities where schools are located, along with other variables having

nothing to do with what happens in classrooms, accounts for the great majority of the difference in scores from one area to the next. To that extent, tests are simply not a valid measure of school effectiveness. (p. 7)

Any standardized test score reflects variance that derives from both instructional and noninstructional sources. Significant sources of non-instructional variance are factors such as poverty or socioeconomic status (SES) and the extent to which ELL students in a school have had the time and/or opportunity to learn the test content. The impact of poverty on test score performance was apparent in the linear relationship between poverty and U.S. students' scores on the Progress in International Reading Literacy Study (PIRLS) study (National Center for Education Statistics, 2003) (see Figure 1.1, Chapter 1). Similarly, a study of 593 Ohio school districts (Hoover, 2000) reported a correlation of 0.80 (representing 64 percent of the variance in test scores) between poverty level and scores on the Ohio Proficiency Test (OPT). Hoover comments on the implications of this finding for using standardized tests as indicators of school and instructional quality:

> The primary finding is that OPT performance is affected most significantly by non-school variables representing the lived experiences of the children attending the school district. . . .
> Because of the discovery that OPT performance is overwhelmingly determined by the social-economic living conditions that the students of the district experience growing up, the inescapable conclusion is that OPT is not a valid measure of either school or teacher effectiveness and should not be used for accountability assessment. The OPT is invalid because the results of this study show that it does not measure what it claims to measure: Student performance on the OPT is, at best, academically meaningless. (Hoover, 2000; www.cc.ysu.edu/~rlhoover/OPTISM/3_primaryfindings.html)

Popular interpretation of standardized tests tends to ignore the impact of noninstructional sources of variance (SES, ELL status, etc.) and views the scores of a school, school system, or state as reflecting the quality of instruction. This point has been made clearly by Rothstein (2002):

> Researchers and policymakers have determinedly blinded themselves to the reality that learning outcomes of students are the product of the efficacy of schools, but also of families, communities, and peers, and that broader social, economic, and cultural forces also affect student achievement. . . . Nothing could be more dangerous to education reform than schemes to reward the first and penalize the second, measuring schools

by the level of student achievement produced jointly by schools and families, rather than by the "value added" schools contribute to socio-economically predictable results. By labeling all schools in poor communities with below-norm achievement failing (and all suburban schools successful), we paralyze our ability to distinguish good schools from bad. (pp. 11–12)

Linn (2004) has similarly pointed to the fact that the adequate yearly progress provisions of NCLB do not adequately specify how the impact of instructional and noninstructional contributors to test scores should be disaggregated. As a consequence, major anomalies are apparent in the assessment of whether a school has improved or not.

Although the NCLB accountability system might appear to focus on change, in many ways, it actually focuses on status. . . . Consequently, schools that have a high achieving level to begin with have a relatively easy time meeting AYP without any gains in achievement, at least in the first few years. On the other hand, schools with initially low achieving students would have to have extraordinary improvement in achievement to meet AYP. Consequently, many schools that are actually showing considerable progress, and deserve recognition for the gains they are making, fail to meet AYP because of their initial low performance. (Linn, 2004, pp. 7–8).

In other words, schools in low-income areas are expected to reverse the enormous impact of noninstructional variables, such as generations of poverty and racism, through their instruction, whereas schools in higher-income areas simply need to maintain the status quo. This mammoth task is to be carried out with considerably fewer funds than are allocated to higher-income districts, fewer well-trained and experienced teachers, and parents who frequently do not have the resources (e.g., money for tutoring, books, computers, etc.) or time (because of heavy work demands on both parents) to devote to supporting the school's mission.

> To meet AYP, schools in low-income areas need to reverse the impact of generations of poverty and racism, whereas those in high-income areas simply need to maintain the status quo.

It is little wonder that by 2005, the bipartisan support that NCLB had garnered at its inception had turned to bipartisan opposition from states required to implement its poorly conceived and punitive mandates. Across the United States, states have taken legal action to exempt their schools from compliance with a federal mandate that will cost far more to implement than the federal government has provided. Popham (2004) is blunt in his assessment of the unrealistic expectations of the AYP provisions that derive from both the inadequacy of the assessment measures used and the failure to acknowledge that social variables play a role in school achievement:

> At some point in the future, NCLB's AYP provisions will unquestionably cause the law itself to implode. American citizens will simply not accept the counter-intuitive notion that nearly all of their public schools are ineffective. However, until the moment of implosion arrives, many U.S. students will be getting a lower-quality education as a consequence of AYP's unrealism. (p. 12)

This lower-quality education is reflected in higher dropout and retention rates for marginalized students. It is also evident in the pedagogical divide that increasingly consigns low-income students to classrooms characterized by drill-and-practice test preparation, whereas more affluent students who are not considered "at risk" benefit from cognitively challenging instruction.

High-Stakes Tests Narrow the Curriculum and Promote Teaching-to-the-Test

Although NCLB does call for multiple measures that assess higher-order thinking, this has not happened in practice. As Neill and colleagues (2004) point out, "The call for measures beyond standardized test scores [is] essentially ignored" (pp. 146–147). Tests that might assess higher-order thinking are difficult to construct and expensive to score and thus are rarely used for large-scale accountability purposes. Amrein and Berliner (2002) express the widespread concern of many educators that in contexts of high-stakes testing, the test becomes the curriculum. They note that the "many anecdotes and research reports we read . . . document the narrowing of the curriculum and the inordinate amount of time spent in drill as a form of test preparation, wherever high-stakes tests are used." This pattern is particularly problematic for low-income students who receive the brunt of teaching to the test:

> Any narrowing of the curriculum, along with the confusion of training to pass a test with broader notions of learning and education are especially problematic side effects of high-stakes testing for low-income students. The poor, more than their advantaged peers, need not only the skills that training provides but [they also] need the more important benefits of learning and education that allow for full economic and social integration in our society. (Amrein & Berliner, 2002)

Neill and colleagues (2004) review a variety of recent studies that document the narrowing of the curriculum that is occurring under the influence of NCLB. For example, the Council for Basic Education (von Zastrow, 2004) found that "subjects like social studies, civics, geography, languages and the arts are being given short shrift because of increasing time devoted to reading, math and science" (pp. 47–48). In some states and school systems, even science is being squeezed out of elementary school to make room for a two-and-a-half-hour block devoted to scripted reading instruction. The rest of the school day is given to math (also tested) and the few other school subjects that can secure a foothold. Neill and colleagues (2004) also note considerable data showing that teachers are aware of the effects of high-stakes testing on their instruction and consider that "testing caused them to teach in ways that contradicted their views of sound instruction" (p. 46).

Linda McNeill (2000) documents the quandary of committed teachers with the example of a highly qualified Texas teacher who had spent considerable time and money assembling a rich collection of historical and literary works related to Latino culture. According to McNeill,

> Her students responded to her initiative with a real enthusiasm to study and learn. She was dismayed to see, upon returning one day from lunch, that the books for her week's lessons had been set aside. In the center of her desk was a stack of test-prep booklets with a teacher's guide and a note saying "Use these instead of your regular curriculum until after the TAAS." The TAAS test date was three months away. (p. 236)

The school had spent almost $20,000 on these materials, which constituted almost the entire instructional budget for the year, and for the next three months more than half of every class period was spent working through the TAAS preparation booklet rather than analyzing and discussing culturally relevant literature and issues.

High-Stakes Tests Conducted Only in English Undermine Culturally Responsive Programs for Culturally and Linguistically Diverse Students

Because NCLB assessments are conducted only in English, bilingual and dual language programs that spend instructional time in the early grades through another language (e.g., Spanish) are being assessed on the basis of what they have *not* taught rather than on what they have taught. There is extensive research data supporting the effectiveness of bilingual and dual language programs that may spend anywhere from

50 to 90 percent of instructional time in the primary grades (K–2) through the medium of a language other than English (August & Shanahan, 2006; Cummins, 2001; Freeman, 1998; Genesee et al., 2006; Lindholm-Leary, 2001; Thomas & Collier, 2002). Typically, both minority first language (L1) and majority L1 students in these programs have caught up to grade norms in English by about grade 6 or 7, despite considerably less instructional time through English. They have also developed literacy and oral skills in the minority language. Currently, however, these schools are under pressure to switch into all-English instruction faster because of the mandate to demonstrate AYP (in English) by grade 3. Thus, a model that has demonstrated considerable success across a wide range of contexts for bilingual and ELL students is being undermined as a result of arbitrary top-down mandates.

The negative impact of NCLB is outlined in a report on Native American bilingual programs in northern Arizona. We quote McCarty and Romero (2005) as an illustration of what is happening in bilingual and dual language programs across the United States:

> Prior to the passage of NCLB, Beautiful Mountain Elementary School [a pseudonym] had implemented a pre-K–6 Navajo bilingual, bicultural, biliteracy program, for which the school has good longitudinal data. The program used a process-oriented, literature-based approach to English and Navajo reading and writing, with subject matter instruction organized around culturally relevant themes. Program evaluations show that between 1988 and 1998, Beautiful Mountain elementary students consistently improved their oral English and English reading scores, as measured by a locally developed reading assessment, student portfolios, and standardized tests. At the same time, students were becoming bilingual and literate in Navajo. Overall, program evaluations show that students who had the benefit of initial, cumulative literacy development in Navajo significantly outperformed a comparison group on locally developed and standardized tests of English reading comprehension and vocabulary. . . .
>
> By 2002–03, funding for the bilingual program had ended and the full brunt of the No Child Left Behind Act was beginning to be felt. Beautiful Mountain School was labeled as "underperforming" on the basis of students' performance on English standardized tests, and faced the possibility of losing its funding or being placed in receivership by the Bureau of Indian Affairs. (p. 4)

The school changed course and implemented a direct instruction remedial teaching program that kept students "on task" but which teachers did not regard as *real* teaching. McCarty and Romero (2005) note that the new approach shows no evidence of improvement in student test performance despite the fact that students are now being drilled on test-related content.

The troubling fact in the present case is that there is no evidence that student achievement, as measured by the tests to which Beautiful Mountain is being held accountable, is improving as a result of the direct reading instruction prescribed by NCLB. Stanford 9 reading comprehension scores of LEP [limited English proficient] students at Beautiful Mountain Elementary School were higher in 1999 than they were in 2003; non-LEP elementary students' scores actually dropped by as much as 50 percent over this four-year period. . . . Sixth and eighth graders' total reading scores dropped from 53 to 29 NCEs [National Curve Equivalent, with a mean of 50 and range of 1–99] during this period; eighth, tenth, and twelfth graders' scores showed virtually no improvement, remaining at about 28 NCEs.

NCLB has undermined programs that have demonstrated the most promise in reversing academic failure among low-income students.

In short, NCLB has usurped local control and undermined exactly the kinds of programs that have demonstrated the most promise in promoting the academic achievement of bilingual and ELL students (Thomas & Collier, 2002). Contrary to the Guidelines of the American Educational Research Association, there has been virtually no attempt on the part of those who mandate the use of tests to monitor their impact and to identify and minimize potential negative consequences.

Assessment for School Improvement

Any accountability scheme that aims to assess what students have learned and to encourage high-quality instruction must meet at least two criteria:

1. It must assess what students have learned at school rather than what they have brought to school; in other words, the value that high-quality instruction adds to students' knowledge and skills should be the focus of the assessment process.

2. It should be sensitive to, and encourage, forms of instruction that promote the knowledge and skills that students need in a twenty-first-century Knowledge Society; in other words, assessment should be capable of identifying and rewarding evidence of higher-order thinking, critical literacy, and knowledge generation. Since these outcomes are not promoted by transmission orientations to

79

Chapter Three
Assessment

pedagogy, this form of assessment would strongly encourage schools to implement social constructivist and transformative orientations to pedagogy.[3]

A number of U.S. states have moved in these directions, and accountability blueprints consistent with these principles have been articulated by a number of commentators (e.g., Neill et al., 2004; Popham, 2004, 2005). We briefly review some of the directions that have been articulated and then illustrate the impact of these directions on student engagement and success with reference to the experience of the International High School at LaGuardia Community College in New York City.

Disaggregation of Instructional and Noninstructional Influences on Achievement

If current assessment procedures are measuring noninstructional background influences to a considerably greater extent than any instructional effects, then it should be a fairly simple procedure to disentangle the different influences so that the "value-added" effect of schools can be ascertained. Linn (2004) suggests the use of longitudinal student records to track the growth in achievement for individual students. Using students' initial performance as a baseline, growth that is attributable to instructional effects can be isolated from background factors.

Even if longitudinal monitoring of student records is not used, there are alternatives to the current model that permit instructional impact to be ascertained. One very simple way of isolating the value-added impact of schooling is to correct scores for the effect of background factors through statistical adjustments. Thus, one calculates the relationship between test performance and a set of noninstructional factors that influence performance (e.g., poverty, proportion of ELL students, single parents, etc.) and then statistically "removes" the influence of these variables from the score, thereby calculating an alternative score that better reflects the impact of instruction. To illustrate, some years ago the *Times Education Supplement* in Britain reported this kind of analysis for the General Certificate of Secondary Education (GCSE) national school examination results. Scores were corrected for the impact of poverty. According to the report, there were "huge variations in education authorities with apparently similar levels of deprivation" (Dean, 1999). Furthermore, some school systems with high poverty levels emerged as "winners" rather than "losers" when the data were disaggregated:

Arguably, the best-performing authority is the London borough of Tower Hamlets, where more than two-thirds of pupils are on free school meals, making it the most deprived area in the country on this measure. Though its GCSE score of 32.8 puts it well below the national average of 38.1, on the TES [Times Educational Supplement] analysis its pupils scored 7.3 GCSE points above what might be expected.

If this model were adopted (and there would be virtually no cost involved), schools, policymakers, and the general public could be provided with two sets of scores: (1) the uncorrected "raw" score obtained by the school that blends the impact of instructional and noninstructional factors and (2) the corrected score that provides a more accurate indication of school quality than the uncorrected blended score. Despite the simplicity and transparency of these measures, there appears to be very little interest among federal or state policymakers in identifying schools that are truly making a difference for low-income students.

Instructionally Sensitive Assessment

Instructionally sensitive assessment incorporates two closely related elements, both centered on pedagogy. First, assessment should be capable of capturing and evaluating student work that is evoked by the kinds of pedagogy that should be fostered in the nation's schools. Thus, if curricular goals include promoting students' ability to carry out research on a range of topics, synthesize this research coherently, and communicate it clearly by using appropriate multimedia tools, then the assessment system should be sensitive to the outcomes of this pedagogy. Second, the assessment system should actively encourage and support teachers in implementing pedagogy that responds to the realities of a globalized knowledge society.

In a similar vein, Neill and colleagues (2004) describe a number of approaches to what they term *authentic assessment* that are being pursued by several states and school districts around the country. They also present a number of principles for an accountability system that would improve rather than undermine the educational system. Among these are the following:

■ All students should be given a fair opportunity to learn a rich curriculum in a supportive yet challenging environment. Equitable funding is a prerequisite for this to happen.

■ Assessments should draw on multiple forms of qualitative and quantitative evidence of student learning, including a range of real student work such as portfolios, final projects presented to a panel of community members, and teacher evaluations of student achievement.

■ The assessment should provide feedback to both students and teachers aimed at improving student outcomes and the efficacy of instruction. Standardized tests or examinations "should supplement, not supplant or overpower, classroom assessment" (2004, p. 152).

Among the accountability systems that Neill and colleagues describe in detail is the School-based Teacher-led Assessment and Reporting System (STARS) implemented in Nebraska. This system involves multiple forms of assessment, including portfolios that are designed to promote powerful forms of pedagogy. Among the lessons that Gallagher (2004) argues can be learned from the Nebraska experience are the following:

■ Accountability systems must keep pedagogy at the center of concern rather than at the periphery.

■ Accountability systems must promote high-impact rather than high-stakes assessment.

■ Accountability systems must develop capacity within schools rather than try to control what schools can do.

The Nebraska experience has also been highlighted in the report of the National Conference of State Legislatures' Task Force on No Child Left Behind (2005). In discussing the limitations of standardized tests and the overly rigid implementation of the federal government's AYP provisions, the report notes:

> Multiple measures, such as portfolios, can provide a more accurate assessment of performance, but not as applied under the current AYP structure. NCLB allows states to use measures other than test results, but only to identify more schools as being "in need of improvement." In other words, additional indicators cannot be used to refine the model if it results in a decrease in the number of schools that miss AYP. The exception, however, is in Nebraska. The U.S. Department of Education is allowing Nebraska to use portfolios as an alternative to relying primarily on test results. The state received approval because its constitution guarantees local control over school accountability and because the state was able to demonstrate that the assessments were valid and reliable. (pp. 17–18)

Thus, it is likely that portfolio assessment will become more widespread as states and school districts explore alternatives to the exclusive use of standardized tests. The positive impact that portfolio assessment can exert in applying the principles articulated by Gallagher (2004) is apparent in the experience of the International High School at LaGuardia Community College in New York City. The pedagogy at this school aligns closely with the scientifically supported principles articulated by Bransford and colleagues (2000) (see Chapter 2). However, in a context of high-stakes standardized assessment where teachers are forced to teach to the test, the powerful forms of pedagogy implemented in this school might quickly be snuffed out.

The International High School at LaGuardia Community College, New York City

The International High School was founded in 1985 and offers learners of English a four-year comprehensive program where they can satisfy state-mandated subject matter requirements while they are learning English (DeFazio, 1997; DevTech Systems, 1996). The students come from more than 50 countries and speak a wide variety of languages. According to DeFazio, entering students score in the lowest quartile on tests of English proficiency, yet more than 90 percent of them graduate within four years and move on to postsecondary education. As a result of the success of the original program, the philosophy and vision have been extended to other international high schools in different boroughs of New York City.

The philosophy underlying instruction and school organization at the International High School includes the following principles:

- Language is key to learning, and increasing proficiency in academic language emerges most naturally in experiential, language-rich, interdisciplinary study.

- Fluency in two languages represents a resource for the student, the school, and the society.

- Students learn best from each other in heterogeneous, collaborative groupings and learning is facilitated when collaboration exists between the school and the larger community.

- Assessment must support individual growth and offer a variety of opportunities for students and faculty to demonstrate what they know and what they can do.

The latter point is particularly significant because ELL students entering high schools across the country with limited knowledge of English are severely handicapped by the inflexibility of the curricular and assessment requirements. They do not know enough English to gain access to and learn a challenging curriculum at the same pace as native-English-speaking students. Despite this, they are typically assessed with the same tests as native-English-speakers. Consequently, many are failing courses or receiving grades that would preclude them from going on to university or college.

Among the innovations of the International High School is an emphasis on career education throughout the curriculum to encourage students to explore their future life options and motivate them to continue to expand their language sophistication. In addition, cohesion of the school's educational vision is reinforced by the fact that new teachers are selected and hired by the teachers already working in the school. The teachers themselves have developed procedures for collaboration with each other to provide support and evaluative feedback.

Rather than being organized according to traditional subject matter, the curriculum is structured in an interdisciplinary way. The teaching staff has organized itself into six interdisciplinary teams with each team responsible for developing at least two interdisciplinary programs. Each of these programs runs for 13 weeks, with the team of teachers in the program responsible for overseeing a group of approximately 75 students. An example of the kind of interdisciplinary focus is one labeled "Origins, Growth, and Structure" that involves chemistry, mathematics, linguistics, and art.

Rethinking the assessment of students has been a fundamental component of the restructuring process. Portfolios and exhibitions incorporating self, peer, and instructor evaluations play a major role. DeFazio (1997) notes:

> Students at the International High School undergo portfolio assessment where they demonstrate their academic, linguistic and social proficiencies. Traditional testing is eschewed because it is often unfair and counterproductive to linguistically diverse populations who often know much more than they may be able to articulate in English. Portfolio assessment encourages retention, higher-level cognitive skills, development of internal standards, creativity and variety in solving problems.... Students undergo these assessments informally during the course of a semester and more formally at the end. Students also present a master portfolio as they prepare to graduate. (p. 102)

Although English is the usual language of instruction, the school is very much a multilingual learning environment. Students' first languages are integrated into all phases of learning and assessment. In developing their portfolios in the various interdisciplinary programs, students write in both their first language and English, according to their choice. Teachers will often ask other students or members of the wider community for assistance in translating material that has been written in a language they themselves do not know. For example, in the "American Reality" program, students formally explore their native language, human development, and career education, spending at least half their school day doing academic reading and writing in their native language. The first language resources to enable students to do this "include abundant native language materials that teachers, students, and parents purchased for the school" (DeFazio, 1997, p. 104).

Parents have also become significantly involved in the school. Teachers have asked students to write letters home in their native languages to describe the interdisciplinary program the students are involved with, to explain what they are learning, and to explain the portfolio/grading process. Parents are encouraged to respond to the letters in either the native language or English. When parents' letters come back in the native language, the student is requested to translate the letters for the teacher into English. According to DeFazio (1997):

> The letter writing campaign helped instantiate several aspects of the school's language philosophy: the importance of the native language; the need for the parent/guardian and school to work together regardless of language; the development and importance of bi- and multilingualism; language respect. (p. 103)

In other projects, students produce both native language and English language magazines and articles; their writing is read by teachers and students proficient in the native language, and if no one on the school staff is proficient in the students' language, "teachers go into the community to find volunteers willing to spend time reading and commenting on the students' work" (DeFazio, 1997, p. 104). DeFazio notes that students often comment on how much of their native language they had forgotten.

Other projects that students carry out in the "Origins/Growth/ Structures" program include writing an autobiography or a biography of another student (again in English, their L1, or both) and investigations into comparative linguistics. For example, students work with the International Phonetic Alphabet to practice the sounds in each others' languages, to write cartoon strips in phonetics, and to attempt tongue twisters and riddles in the various languages represented in the class.

Their linguistics projects culminate with a community research project that focuses on some issue or question related to language in the wider community. For example, students have interviewed members of their communities about bilingual education, dialect, and language prejudice and presented their findings as the last chapter of their linguistics book. Another project involves students writing multilingual children's books on some aspect of language or linguistics (e.g., *How the Chinese Got Language; The Monster that Ate Polish Words,* etc.).

The kind of rigorous research and critical literacy engagement that can never be captured by traditional standardized tests is well illustrated by a project carried out by International High School students in 2004 on the rights of immigrant workers. This project was published by the students in a booklet entitled *Fight for Your Rights! An Information Booklet on Immigrant Workers' Rights by Students at International High School.* Excerpts were also published in the web-based magazine *What Kids Can Do* (www.whatkidscando.org/index.asp). The International High School project was introduced as follows in this magazine:

> Grateful to have a job, many immigrant workers are afraid to speak up when wronged by an employer and don't know where to turn for help. Students at this New York City school for newcomers—from 51 countries—know this firsthand as they watch their parents scrape together a living, taking almost any job they can get. What problems do their parents face, they wonder, in finding jobs and on the job? What rights do all workers in New York City have regardless of their immigrant status? What local resources are available to educate immigrant workers about their rights and to help them with their problems? Through reading, research, surveys, and interviews, a team of juniors and seniors from several English and history classes at International High School/ LaGuardia Community College set out to answer these questions. (www.whatkidscando.org/studentresearch/InternationalHS.html)

The students also wrote a letter to New York Governor George Pataki (dated March 10, 2004) highlighting the plight of immigrant workers (86 percent of whom are heads of households) who receive minimum wage ($5.15 per hour).

How can any standardized test capture the intellectual richness and social commitment of collaborative projects such as this? There is simply no way. However, multiple facets of these students' research and other academic work *can* be captured and assessed when it forms part of a student portfolio. Although there is much work to be done in refining portfolio assessment so that it constitutes a valid and reliable component of an overall assessment plan (Neill et al., 2000), it represents a commonly used form of assessment in numerous societal institutions (e.g., application to Art College) and there are multiple promising directions that states and school districts are pursuing in this regard.[4]

Conclusion

Current assessment procedures implemented under the aegis of NCLB have resulted in multiple negative consequences for schools. The curriculum has been constricted, with the result that teachers are mandated directly or indirectly to teach only those curricular subjects that will be tested (usually language arts and mathematics). The constrictive effect has been much greater in those schools that are at risk of low performance on the tests—namely, schools serving low-income students. Instructional practices have mirrored the constriction of the curriculum. Drill-and-practice transmission approaches predominate in low-income schools, while schools serving more affluent students can focus more on "real teaching" (McCarty & Romero, 2005). Innovative programs that have demonstrated considerable success in enabling low-income and minority students to catch up academically have come under intense pressure to revert to mindless drill-and-practice test preparation. Bilingual and dual language programs, in particular, have been undermined by the fact that no provision is made within NCLB for testing in languages other than English.

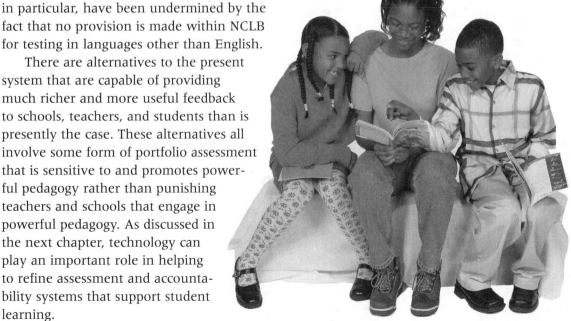

There are alternatives to the present system that are capable of providing much richer and more useful feedback to schools, teachers, and students than is presently the case. These alternatives all involve some form of portfolio assessment that is sensitive to and promotes powerful pedagogy rather than punishing teachers and schools that engage in powerful pedagogy. As discussed in the next chapter, technology can play an important role in helping to refine assessment and accountability systems that support student learning.

Discussion Questions for Study Groups

1 Why do you think the general public, the media, and most policymakers support standardized testing? What are some of the typical misinterpretations that are frequently made when standardized test results are published?

2 Discuss with a partner what some of the purposes are for administering standardized tests within schools. Could some of these purposes be better achieved through other forms of assessment or evaluation? Explain your answer.

3 When is it meaningful and potentially useful to administer standardized tests to ELL students? How should such tests be interpreted?

4 Write a brief explanation to parents about the purposes of the standardized tests administered in your school, focusing on what the test scores mean, what is actually being measured by the tests, and what cautions are necessary in interpreting the patterns of test scores.

Endnotes

1. In a discussion of curriculum expectations in Ontario, Canada, Leithwood, McAdie, Bascia, Rodriguez, and Moore (2004) point out that by the end of eighth grade, students are expected

> to encounter, learn, or otherwise come to grips with, a total of 3,993 specific expectations! (We counted them.) On average, there are about 500 specific expectations for each grade without much variation until grades 7 and 8 where specific expectations jump significantly. (p. 2)

Leithwood and colleagues calculated that this works out at roughly three minutes per expectation per student and suggest that this "mile wide and inch deep" curricular organization is highly counterproductive if deep understanding is a goal of instruction.

2. Both Haney (2002) and Amrein and Berliner (2002) note that Texas and other states with high-stakes tests are more likely to exclude limited English proficiency students and students with disabilities from participation in the NAEP. This results in artificially high scores and spurious "gains" on NAEP for these states. Ironically, this issue has led to conflict between Texas and the Bush administration as

outlined in the following report from the *New York Times*:

> In the dispute, which has nettled the Bush administration, Texas has refused to apply a provision that limits the number of students with learning disabilities who can be exempted from regular standardized tests. Last year, Washington said that only 1 percent of disabled students could be given easier alternative tests, but Texas officials allowed schools to administer the alternative examination to about 9 percent of its students. As a result, hundreds of Texas schools' standardized test scores were higher last year than they would have otherwise been, allowing the schools to meet the federal achievement benchmark known as adequate yearly progress. (Dillon, 2005)

The bad news on No Child Left Behind continued to mount in 2006. Twenty-seven percent of U.S. public schools (almost 25,000 schools) failed to meet adequate yearly progress (AYP) criteria in 2004–2005. The fact that in Oklahoma only 3 percent of schools failed to meet AYP (down from 25 percent the previous year), whereas in Florida 72 percent of schools failed to show sufficient improvement, raises the question of whether these figures are in any way meaningful. Shortly after these figures appeared in March 2005, it was revealed that schools were not counting the scores of almost two million students when they reported scores by racial groups. Minority groups made up the vast majority of students whose scores were being excluded (by a 7 to 1 ratio in comparison to whites). The exclusion of these scores enabled schools to meet AYP criteria despite the fact that minority groups within their schools might not have been making adequate progress (see www.msnbc.msn.com/id/12357165/).

3. Leu, Castek, Coiro, Gort, Henry, and Lima (2005) point out that state assessments that focus only on linear text-based literacy are totally out of touch with the reality of twenty-first-century literacies. They note that states have viewed the assessment of new literacies such as comprehending text on the Internet, composing e-mail messages, or writing with a word processor as technology assessment issues rather than as literacy assessment issues. State assessments do not include new literacy skills such as searching for information, reading and comprehending search engine results, critically evaluating information resources and communicating with various tools such as instant messaging, e-mail, blogs, and so on.

The fact that state assessments remain focused on Industrial Age literacy rather than expanding to include Information Age literacies has immediate consequences for the validity of state assessments. For example, Leu and colleagues (2005) point to the fact that no state permits students to use a word processor rather than paper and pencil on state writing assessments despite evidence that almost 20 percent more students are able to pass the Massachusetts state writing assessment when permitted to use word processors (Russell & Plati, 2000, 2001). Russell and Haney (2000) also report a variety of research studies that lead them to conclude:

> Recalling that nearly ten million students took some type of state-sponsored written test last year and that nearly half of the students nationwide use word processors in school, these results suggest that state paper-and-pencil tests may be underestimating the abilities of some five million students annually. (p. 5)

4. Unfortunately, the exemption that enabled the International High School to avoid administering state-mandated standardized tests was rescinded in 2005. The extent to which this will compromise their system of portfolio assessment remains to be seen.

CHAPTER 4

Technology

The billions of dollars already spent on wiring, hardware, and software have established the material conditions for frequent and imaginative uses of technology to occur. Many students and teachers have acquired skills and have engaged in serious use of these technologies. Nonetheless, overall, the quantities of money and time have yet to yield even modest returns or to approach what has been promised in academic achievement, creative integration of technologies, and transformations in teaching and learning.

Larry Cuban, *Oversold and Underused: Computers in the Schools* (2001, p. 189)

W e believe that technology *can* play a highly significant role in promoting literacy among all students and particularly among low-income and minority students. Technological tools such as the Internet and World Wide Web can also contribute in important ways to the development of a socially committed and intellectually critical citizenry.

We are also very much aware, however, that thus far technology has exerted minimal impact in helping schools attain either of these goals. Massive investments in educational technology during the past decade have been undertaken on faith rather than evidence. Despite increasing access to technology by teachers and students, no large-scale improvement in literacy or numeracy has been demonstrated.

The failure to realize the educational potential of technology has much more to do with *pedagogy* than with technology itself. The accountability mandates of adequate yearly progress (AYP) and high-stakes testing have resulted in a pedagogical focus on teaching to the test in many schools serving low-income and minority students. Because drill-and-practice transmission pedagogy predominates in these schools, computer use tends to conform to the same orientation. In this context, imaginative inquiry-focused teaching, with or without technology, is frequently considered "off task." Consequently, the potential power of technology is only rarely and minimally harnessed in these school contexts.

However, numerous case studies (such as those in Part 2 and the appendix) document how various forms of technology can amplify student learning in the context of social constructivist and transformative orientations to pedagogy. These case studies show that low-income students are very much capable of using technological resources for collaborative critical inquiry when they are given opportunities in school or out of school to do so. Thus, the ways in which technology is likely to be used in any school context are intimately connected to the pedagogical orientations operating in the school and the associated image of the student that is constructed in these pedagogical interactions.

Introduction

Throughout human history technological tools have been crucial to survival and the evolution of human intelligence. This is particularly evident in the case of literacy where a succession of tools (sticks, pencils, typewriters, computers) have enabled ever more sophisticated forms of communication. The focus of this chapter is on the potential educational impact of recently developed *digital* technologies that have transformed modes of oral and literate communication during the past 30 years. We examine initially the goals of technology investment in schools and then summarize data regarding differential access to technology across income groups. Research on the educational effects of technology access and use is then examined and analyzed in the context of the forms of pedagogy that are most likely to harness technology in powerful ways.

During the past decade there has been massive worldwide investment in educational technology by governments and the private sector. Affluent countries continue to fund the development of a technological infrastructure intended to increase students' access to computers and other forms of technology and to link all schools to the Internet. The United States, for example, invested more than $90 billion in computer technology for schools during the 1990s (Oppenheimer, 1997, 2003), and the Schools and Libraries Universal Service Support Mechanism, more commonly known as the e-rate, has provided $2.25 billion a year to assist schools and libraries to obtain affordable telecommunications and Internet access.

Two major rationales for this ongoing investment are particularly relevant in the present context:

1. To promote the development of the kinds of literacy (and numeracy) skills required to function effectively in the global economy and society of the twenty-first century (henceforth, *twenty-first-century literacy skills*);

2. To improve traditional learning outcomes for all students, but particularly for low-income and minority students who experience disproportionate underachievement.

Government and private sector policymakers are increasingly discussing the educational challenges of realigning school curricula and assessment systems to take into account the relationships between traditional literacy (reading and writing skills) and twenty-first-century literacies (e.g., International Information and Communication Technologies [ICT] Literacy Panel, 2002; 21st Century Literacy Summit, 2002). Wilhelm, Carmen, and Reynolds (2002) succinctly express the educational relevance of these emerging literacies: "There are enormous possibilities and opportunities ahead for young workers who possess '21st-century literacy'—that is, the knowledge and skills to take advantage of the new Internet-related technologies" (p. 1).

Although academic investigation of twenty-first-century literacies is in its infancy (see, for example, Leu & Kinzer, 2000), there is, in principle, little dispute at the policy level about the need to realign school curricula to promote and take advantage of these emerging literacies. We have moved from an era where print dominated the literacy landscape to one where multiple forms of electronic communication are inseparable from literacy development (Leu et al., 2005). However, for schools, the process of moving in this direction has not been smooth or unproblematic. Cuban (2001), for example, has documented numerous barriers to effective use of computer technology in schools ranging from adequacy of teacher preparation to reliability of the equipment.

We argue that the major problem in promoting an expanded range of literacy competencies for all students resides in the tension between inquiry-based and transmission-based orientations to pedagogy. As discussed in Chapter 2, inquiry-based orientations (both social constructivist and transformative) aim to support students in constructing curriculum-related knowledge, whereas transmission-based orientations focus on enabling students to internalize the content of the curriculum. Transmission orientations to pedagogy predominate in low-income schools as a result of the pressure on teachers to ensure that their students pass the high-stakes tests that dominate the curriculum. Thus, the pedagogical focus in these schools is considerably more narrow than in more affluent schools, and this pedagogical divide extends to the ways in which technology is used in these two school contexts.

> We have moved from an era where print dominated the literacy landscape to one where multiple forms of electronic communication are inseparable from literacy development.

Access to and Use of Technology

Access

Wilhelm and colleagues (2002) highlight the persistent "digital divide" that separates lower-income from higher-income families and the social and educational consequences of these disparities:

> Despite the rapid increase in computer use and Internet access during the late 1990s, there is still a formidable gap that separates the haves from the have-nots. Generally, children who are already disadvantaged are the least likely to have access to the new technology. Minority children, children living in poor families, and particularly those living in high-poverty neighborhoods are the least likely to have a computer at home or access to the Internet. Schools close some of the gap, but significant disparities remain even after access at school is taken into account. . . . (p. 1)

> In 2001, 83 percent of non-Hispanic white children lived in households with computers, compared to only 46 percent of black children and 47 percent of Hispanic children. . . . There are similar gaps in access to the Internet at home. Based on data collected in 2001, 50 percent of non-Hispanic white children were able to connect to the Internet at home, compared to only 25 percent of black children and 20 percent of Hispanic children. (p. 4)

Similarly, DeBell and Chapman (2003) report that in 2001, 5- to 17-year-olds whose families lived in poverty were less likely to use the Internet at home than 5- to 17-year-olds whose families were not in poverty (47 percent compared with 82 percent).

Within schools, access to computers has increased rapidly. Parsad and Jones (2005) report the following data on school-based Internet access:

- Between 1994 and 2003, the percentage of public schools with access to the Internet increased from 35 to almost 100 percent.

- Internet access was available in 93 percent of instructional rooms in 2003 compared to just 3 percent in 1994.

- In 2003, the ratio of students to instructional computers with Internet access in public schools was 4.4 to 1, a decrease from the 12.1 to 1 ratio in 1998.

- Schools with the highest poverty concentration in 2003 had 5.1 students for each instructional computer with Internet access, whereas schools with the lowest poverty concentration had 4.2 students to each instructional computer with Internet access.

- Schools with high minority enrolment (50 percent or more) had more students per instructional computer with Internet access than schools with low minority enrolment (less than 6 percent) (5.1 vs. 4.1).

- High-poverty schools and those with high minority enrolment were less likely to have a school website than more affluent schools and those with low minority enrolment (72 percent vs. 96 percent for highest vs. lowest poverty categories, and 80 percent vs. 94 percent for highest vs. lowest minority enrolment categories).

In summary, although the gap in technology access in relation to poverty and minority group status still persists, it has narrowed in recent years. There remains, however, a very significant gap in access at home to computers and to the Internet between these groups (DeBell & Chapman, 2003; Kleiner & Farris, 2002). The gap in home access is exacerbated by the fact that even when they do have access, low-income students benefit less academically from home computer access than do high-income students (Attewell & Battle, 1999). Warschauer, Knobel, and Stone (2004) suggest that this phenomenon may reflect teachers' assumptions that most low-income students do not have access to computers at home and so do not assign homework or projects that require technology access.

Use

Probably more significant for overall academic development is the way computers and other forms of technology are used in schools. Warschauer and colleagues (2004) reviewed a number of studies showing an emphasis on remedial or vocational uses of new technology by low-income or Black and Hispanic students and more academic uses of technology by high-income or White and Asian students.

One example is an analysis of NAEP Mathematics performance of grade 4 and 8 students (Wenglinsky, 1998), which reported that low-income students were significantly more likely to be taught lower-level skills on the computer than more affluent students. Furthermore, at the grade 8 level, the use of computers to teach lower-level cognitive skills (drill-and-practice activities) was negatively related to academic achievement, whereas the use of computers to teach higher-level cognitive skills through simulations and applications was positively related to achievement.

Warschauer and colleagues' survey of eight low- and high-income California high schools compared the availability of, access to, and use of information and communication technologies (ICT) within these schools. Although student-to-computer ratios in the schools were similar, significant differences emerged in the effectiveness with which computers were used in these schools. Low-income schools were affected by uneven human support networks, irregular home access to computers by students, and pressure to raise school test scores while addressing the needs of large numbers of English learners. Warschauer and colleagues (2004) elaborate on the differential impact of high-stakes testing in low- and high-income schools as follows:

> One important element in the successful or unsuccessful use of ICT in classrooms concerned the pressure of high-stakes testing. Teachers in all the participating schools, and especially in the low-income schools, where student test scores are lower, told us that they feel a great deal of pressure to focus instruction on covering standard curriculum material and raising test scores. Teachers repeatedly reported feeling torn between needing to prepare students for testing and wanting to engage in innovative instruction that made good use of new technologies. Less experienced teachers, in particular, appeared to feel these pressures more so than experienced teachers. (p. 582)

Warschauer and colleagues also identified a predominant pattern of computer use in the schools they studied as performativity. This construct "refers to situations in which teachers are going through the motions or ticking off checklists of skills without paying due attention to larger issues of knowledge construction and purposeful learning" (pp. 574–576). Performativity is illustrated in activities such as learning basic computer skills or how to use a particular program such as PowerPoint as an end in itself. Performativity was evident in both high- and low-income schools, but it seemed to have a special impact on students in low-income schools insofar as teachers often focused on basic computer skills because they assumed (often incorrectly) that students didn't have home access to computers. The authors suggest that the instructional focus on enabling students to acquire fluent skills in particular software applications acts as a distraction from more powerful applications of technology for knowledge generation and inquiry, a distraction that low-income students can ill afford.

Rather than reducing educational inequities, the introduction of information and communication technologies in the eight schools Warschauer and colleagues investigated served to amplify existing forms

> **Low-income schools were affected by uneven human support networks, irregular home access to computers by students, and pressure to raise school test scores.**

of inequality. They suggest that what emerges from recent research is not a single construct of a digital divide, but rather a variety of ways that technology amplifies existing inequalities in school and society.

In another study of computer use in two elementary schools serving diverse populations, Warschauer, Grant, Del Real, and Rousseau (2004) point to the kinds of technology-supported pedagogical applications that *can* promote powerful forms of learning.

> Both schools make highly effective use of technology to promote academic literacy among their students, resulting in sophisticated student products, highly engaged learners, and high standardized test scores in relationship to school demographics. The keys in both cases are a schoolwide commitment to excellence, equity, and development of classroom communities of inquiry. Technology is used to apprentice students into academic literacy through promotion of independent reading, support for language scaffolding, involvement in cognitively engaging projects, and student analysis and creation of purposeful texts in a variety of media and genres. (p. 535)

Unfortunately, this focus on knowledge building and critical analysis is still the exception rather than the rule in the ways computers are employed in low-income schools.

Warschauer (2006) reported on a multisite case study that examined literacy practices in ten culturally and linguistically diverse K–12 schools in California and Maine in which all the students in one or more classrooms were provided with laptop computers. The introduction of laptops appeared to increase students' engagement with literacy in a variety of ways. Teachers, students, and parents all reported that students spent more time on task, worked more independently, enjoyed learning more, and took part in greater variety of learning activities at school and at home than they had prior to receiving laptops. They incorporated multimedia into their assignments and in many cases demonstrated highly creative work (e.g., they probed literature more deeply by composing music to it). However, these enhancements of students' literacy experience and engagement did not show up in reading, writing, or language arts test scores, which remained flat. Warschauer attributes the discrepency between literacy processes and measured outcomes to several factors, including the newness of the laptop program at the schools and the fact that standardized tests are not sensitive to the kinds of literacy processes that laptops enhanced (e.g., ease of searching for information, revision of writing, incorporation of multimedia, etc.).

In summary, the initial quantitative disparity between schools in high-income and low-income areas with respect to technology access has been largely replaced by a *pedagogical divide* in the way new technologies are used to support instruction and a corresponding *cognitive divide* in the way students use the new technologies to support different forms of learning.

The next section examines the empirical evidence on the extent to which information and communication technologies are effective in supporting language and literacy learning.

Effectiveness of ICT in Supporting Student Learning

The Apparent Lack of Overall Impact

Despite the obvious promise of technology-supported instruction for both language learning and more general academic development, there is minimal evidence of any overall enhancement of academic learning among school-age learners. This finding holds true despite massive ICT expenditure in both North American and European schools during the past decade (Bennett, 2002; Fuchs & Woessmann, 2004; Goolsbee & Guryan, 2002). The apparent lack of impact is not surprising when digital technologies are viewed as simply one component in a complex ecology of learning and teaching. However, it is worth reviewing the evidence in order to debunk the naïve assumption that investment in technology, by itself, will result in educational gains. As Cuban (2001) reminds us, "The most serious problems afflicting urban and rural poor schools—inequitable funding, extraordinary health and social needs growing out of poverty, crumbling facilities, unqualified teachers—have little to do with a lack of technology" (pp. 188–189).

In the United States, critics of technological investment in education have pointed to the fact that there has been no overall increase in national reading achievement levels despite the fact that such an increase might have been expected if access to ICT were effective in strengthening teaching and learning. Bennett (2002), for example, notes that between 1994 and 1999, there was minimal overall improvement in educational achievement as measured by the National Assessment of Educational Progress:

> Results for 1999 showed no significant change in reading, mathematics, or science for the three age groups tested—9-year-olds, 13-year-olds,

and 17-year-olds—from 1994 through 1999. During this five-year period, schools acquired huge numbers of computers and hoped earnestly that this influx of technology would improve education. (p. 622)

Similarly, a recent Rand Corporation report (Carroll, Krop, Arkes, Morrison, & Flanagan, 2005) showed no gains in literacy achievement in California between 1990 and 2003 despite major curricular reforms and significant technology investment. Clearly, the causes of stagnant academic progress are complex, and technology access and use represents only a small component of an evolving ecology of educational provision. However, the data do serve to debunk the naïve belief that technology infusion by itself will transform students' educational progress.

Access to the Internet has also failed to show measurable benefits for student achievement. Goolsbee and Guryan (2002), in a study that examined the impact of the federal e-rate program, concluded that although the program had certainly increased access, there was no evidence that Internet investment had any measurable effect on student achievement.

A recent analysis of large-scale data from Organisation for Economic Co-operation and Development countries by researchers at the University of Munich suggest that access to computers might even exert a negative impact on achievement (Fuchs & Woessmann, 2004). The study involved a sample of more than 100,000 15-year-old students in 31 countries. The authors summarize their findings as follows:

> This paper has found that despite bivariate correlations that show a positive relationship, once family background and school characteristics are extensively controlled for, the mere availability of computers at home is negatively related to student performance in math and reading, and the availability of computers at school is unrelated to student performance. By contrast, student performance is positively related to the use of computers at home for accessing emails and webpages and to the availability of educational software at home. (p. 17)

Critics have pointed to the failure of virtually every technological innovation introduced to schools during the past century to improve learning in any significant way.

In a similar vein, Angrist and Lavy (2002) report data from a survey of Israeli school teachers who received an influx of new computers funded by money from the national lottery. The new computers appeared to increase teachers' use of computer-aided instruction but there was no evidence that this translated into higher test scores. In fact, the trends were in the opposite direction.

In summary, it is clear that simply providing access to ICT in schools or homes does little to improve achievement or reduce the gap between White and minority students. This lack of obvious overall impact has increased the credibility of critics who challenge the general assumption that investment in ICT will improve educational outcomes. Critics have highlighted the diversion of scarce resources from other areas of the curriculum and pointed to the failure of virtually every technological innovation introduced to schools during the past century to improve learning in any significant way (Armstrong & Casement, 1998; Cuban, 2001; Healy, 1998; Oppenheimer, 1997, 2003).

Experimental and Quasi-Experimental Studies

Despite the lack of demonstrable overall impact of technology investment on student achievement thus far, there is considerable evidence from numerous small-scale experiments that, under certain conditions, ICT can promote academic learning among both school-age and adult samples. Fletcher (2003), for example, reviewed a variety of studies on technology-assisted instruction that showed effect sizes ranging from .39 to 1.05, depending on the extent of individualization or "intelligent tutoring" incorporated into the program. These effect sizes are the equivalent of raising percentiles ranks from the 50th percentile to the 65th percentile (effect size of .39) and from the 50th percentile to the 85th percentile (effect size of 1.05). He concludes, "This review of technology-based instruction suggests that it will most probably lower costs and increase effectiveness for many applications" (p. 97).

Willis (2003) summarizes a range of meta-analyses of computers in schools that conclude that computers can positively impact learning: "The 15 or so meta-analyses of computers in schools are cited over and over in the literature to support increased use of technology in education" (p. 18). He argues cogently, however, that it doesn't make sense even to try to answer a general question about effectiveness of computers in education because there are so many specific contextual variables and so many ways that computers can be used in education that the general question is meaningless: "No single example is sufficiently typical enough to allow us to generalize from the research study to other examples of that type" (p. 22).

Burns and Ungerleiter (2002/2003) could make only four unambiguous claims on the basis of their review of the research literature on the impact of ICT in elementary and secondary education:

1. Student attitudes toward computers and computer-related technologies improve as a consequence of exposure to them.

2. The use of ICTs for group work can be beneficial if teachers are able to take into account the complex interplay among the age of the students, the kind of task, and the amount of independence allowed.

3. The use of ICTs for mathematics instruction has a significantly positive effect on teaching high-level concepts to students in grade 8 or above.

4. The majority of the research reviewed is contradictory and/or seriously flawed. (p. 45)

As suggested by these reviews, sweeping generalizations about the impact of information and communication technologies on achievement may not be possible (or even meaningful). However, individual research studies (both experimental and qualitative case studies) *can* contribute to understanding how ICT might influence learning under specific conditions and in particular subject areas, such as reading development.

The Impact of ICT on Reading Development: Meta-Analyses

In the area of reading, the National Reading Panel (NRP) (2000) focused on 21 experimental studies published between 1986 and 1996. They concluded, "All the studies in the analysis report positive results" (p. 6-2). These results spanned a range of decoding and comprehension skills. With respect to instructional applications, the NRP suggests that the ability of the computer to transform speech to print and the use of hypertext hold promise:

> Although the Panel is encouraged at the reported successes in using computer technology for reading instruction, there are relatively few specific instructional applications to be gleaned from the research. It is clear that some students can benefit from the use of computer technology in reading instruction. In particular, studies on the addition of speech to print suggest that this may be a promising alternative, especially given the powerful multimedia computers now available and those being developed. In addition, the use of hypertext and word processing appear to hold promise for application to reading instruction. (2000, p. 6-2)

However, the NRP authors go on to lament the fact that so little research has been carried out on the impact of computers on reading (a point also addressed by Kamil, Intrator, & Kim, 2000). Furthermore, they claim to have uncovered "few examples of truly new uses for computer technology to date. . . . For now, the computer seems to be used as technology to either present or augment traditional instructional practices" (2000, p. 6-2).

In the area of second language reading, there are also some studies that suggest a positive impact of the use of online glosses to render vocabulary meaningful. LeLoup and Ponterio (2003) report that "students using computer technologies to assist in comprehending reading passages and identifying vocabulary outperformed control groups of students who did not have this assistance available or chose not to use it" (p. 2).

A more recent meta-analysis that focused on the impact of computer support for beginning reading instruction was just as cautious as the NRP review in its conclusions (Blok, Oostdam, Otter, & Overmaat, 2002). These authors reviewed 42 studies of beginning reading published between 1982 and 2000, only 6 of which overlapped with the NRP review. The selection of studies in the two reviews differed partly because the authors focused on reading subskills related to decoding and fluency, excluding studies whose primary focus was vocabulary and reading comprehension. The NRP included such studies in its database and also did not restrict the focus to the beginning reading phase.

Blok and colleagues found an overall effect size of $d = 0.2$, indicating a positive but minimal effect. They note that the effect size rises to $d = 0.5$ when only studies involving beginning reading in English are considered. They consider the possibility that this difference is due to the less regular sound–symbol relationship in English as compared to many other languages. However, they warn against concluding that students do profit from computer-assisted instruction programs when English is the language of instruction. They point out that the effect size estimate is based on comparison with untrained control groups. In other words, the data may reflect the fact that any intervention might exert an effect regardless of whether it is technology based. Furthermore, they note that research on phonological awareness training reviewed by Foster and colleagues (1994) suggests that teacher-based training is more effective than computer-based training. Blok and colleagues conclude that if this pattern "withstood further scrutiny and if it could be generalized to other CAI program types, there is little reason for teachers of beginning reading to convert to computer-assisted reading instruction" (2002, p. 123).

Clearly, this conclusion may change as new products become available that make use of more powerful computing functionalities. The next section examines research into specific commercial computer products designed to promote aspects of literacy.

Research Involving Commercial Programs

Studies of commercial computer-supported programs that were not considered in either the NRP or the Blok and colleagues' reviews suggest that some of these systems can be highly effective components of an early reading program. For example, Scholastic's WiggleWorks beginning literacy system showed highly significant effects among grade 1 students despite the fact that participating classrooms at the time generally had only one computer per class (Schultz, no date). WiggleWorks is described as follows on the Scholastic website:

> This media-rich program integrates leveled books with technology and instruction to help children become successful readers and writers. WiggleWorks provides leveled reading practice, built-in instruction, and motivation to engage students in reading and writing. WiggleWorks helps teachers scaffold instruction and move students toward reading independence. (http://teacher.scholastic.com/products/wiggleworks/index.htm)

Another Scholastic product, Read 180, intended for struggling readers, entails a similar blend of video, leveled books (re-written to make them appropriate for students reading at different grade levels), and individualized computer-supported instruction. This product has also been very positively evaluated (see http://teacher.scholastic.com/products/read180/research/index.htm). Scholastic has also conducted an impact study for ELL students that reports strong gains in reading performance (http://teacher.scholastic.com/products/read180/research/pdf/ELLReport.pdf). These studies, however, have been reported by Scholastic's Research Department rather than being conducted by independent evaluators.

Another computer-integrated system, Accelerated Reader, is used beyond the beginning reading stages in about half the school systems in the United States, and its developers, Renaissance Learning Inc., claim considerable research support. However, little of this research has been published in refereed journals and the academic jury is still out as to whether Accelerated Reader improves reading performance and/or leads to more independent reading. (For a very useful overview of this debate see Jim Trelease's webpage: http://www.trelease-on-reading.com/whatsnu_ar.html.)

The few studies of commercial products conducted by independent researchers tend to be much less positive in their assessment. One example is a study of the Fast ForWord reading program published by Scientific Learning that is designed to improve students' language and reading skills (www.scilearn.com/). According to the product website, this software is used by 450,000 students and is aligned with the "scientifically based" requirements of Reading First and NCLB. Rouse, Kreuger, and Markman (2004) carried out a randomized experimental study to assess the effects of this program using four different measures of language and reading ability. The authors conclude that although the use of the Fast ForWord program may improve some aspects of students' language skills, these gains do not appear to translate into increased achievement on broader measures of language acquisition or reading abilities.

Motivation

One issue that arises in the research is the question of whether student gains in computer-supported environments are due to intrinsic features of the hardware and software or whether technology is simply motivating to students, thereby resulting in greater task engagement. There is no general answer to this question but certainly many students do appear to be motivated by the engagement with technology. As one example, McMillan and Honey (1993) conducted a one-year study with a class of grade 8 students who were given the use of laptop computers to keep journals, write stories, and complete assignments. The study reported a marked improvement in students' ability to communicate persuasively in writing, organize their ideas effectively, and use a broad vocabulary effectively. The researchers attributed this improvement to increased motivation to engage in writing as a result of access to laptop computers. The positive educational results associated with using computers for e-mail reported in the large-scale Fuchs and Woessman (2004) study may also reflect the impact of computers on students' motivation to engage in writing.

Meskill and Mossop (2000) also report evidence of increased motivation and excitement for learning as a result of technology use. The authors carried out a survey of technology use by over 800 ESL teachers and observed extensively in two classrooms over a two-year period:

For questions regarding use, survey and interview responses consistently cited the motivational feature of technology. Teachers observed that children were especially responsive when they were able to create products of their learning to share with others. Tremendous enthusiasm for learning with e-texts pervaded the class sessions observed and interviews with students. (p. 588)

Meskill and Mossop go on to describe patterns of classroom interaction that illustrate the potential of technology-supported instruction to increase both cognitive engagement and identity investment in learning. English language learners in the classrooms they observed were enabled to participate in classroom instruction to the full extent of their intelligence and imagination. This contrasts with many traditional classroom contexts where ELL students are unable to follow grade-level curriculum and participate in learning for several years after starting to learn English. As a consequence, they frequently receive instruction focused on lower-level skills, such as phonics and pronunciation (Fitzgerald, 1995). The ways in which technology-supported instruction can promote both cognitive engagement and identity investment are evident in the following excerpt:

Their [children's] finished work, whether a word processed, desktop-published document, an animated story, a multimedia presentation, or a fully functioning city of their own design, was consistently a source of great pride and, among peers and family members, admiration. . . . Learners' achievements extended from moment-to-moment successes in editing their own work or making decisions to demonstrating to the larger school and community what they could do with technology. . . . The ESOL children became [technology] experts in their classes and school. (Meskill & Mossop, 2000, p. 589)

More general reviews of the impact of technology on second language acquisition also report a positive effect on students' attitudes toward learning. LeLoup and Ponterio (2003), for example, state that "language learners report a positive attitude toward computer use overall when engaged in language learning tasks" (p. 1).

The Issue of Cost Effectiveness

Clearly, many of the commercial computer programs that are on the market are well-designed and motivating to students. But do they represent a cost-effective purchase for cash-strapped school districts? For example, consider any computer program designed to teach phonological awareness and phonics skills. Although some of these programs may be effective (despite the minimal support for overall effectiveness reported by Blok et al., 2002), the more relevant question is, Are they sufficiently more effective than a program such as Jolly Phonics in teaching phonological awareness and basic decoding skills to justify the considerable additional cost? Jolly Phonics, developed in the United Kingdom (Lloyd, 1993), is a daily 15-minute program for kindergarten students involving "playful, creative, flexible teaching" (Ehri et al., 2001, p. 422) with research supporting its effectiveness for ELL students (Kwan & Willows, 1998; Ehri et al., 2001). Is the considerable additional cost for a computer program justified by differential outcomes? Probably not, although there may be cost-effective benefits for students who have specific reading or learning disabilities.

The reality is that a large majority of students (ELL and native–English speakers) acquire relatively fluent decoding skills in English when they receive appropriate instruction (e.g., Geva, 2000; Kwan & Willows, 1998). Expensive technological supports are neither necessary nor cost effective to teach basic literacy skills to the general student population.

However, many low-income students do experience difficulties in sustaining growth in literacy development beyond the primary years. Some programs have been developed specifically to support struggling readers and ELL students in the later grades of elementary school and beyond (e.g., Accelerated Reader, e-Lective Language Learning Program [Chascas & Cummins, 2005], Read 180, The Thinking Reader [Rose & Dalton, 2002], etc.). It is possible that programs designed to develop vocabulary and reading comprehension may help sustain literacy development for ELL and underachieving students because vocabulary knowledge is a crucial component of overall literacy development beyond the primary grades, and the academic vocabulary knowledge of many underachieving students is far below that of their more successful peers (Wood, 2001).

Skeptics, however, are unlikely to be convinced until definitive research demonstrates not only the effectiveness of computer-based interventions but also their cost effectiveness. Among the most articulate skeptics with respect to computer technology and literacy is Stephen Krashen, Professor Emeritus at the University of Southern California. Krashen has critiqued the success reports of several of these programs in a variety of articles and letters to the editor (see www.sdkrashen.com/

main.php3). His major point is that the positive impact of computer-supported reading programs derives from the fact that they provide opportunities and encouragement for students to read extensively. However, this effect can be achieved much more simply and at much less cost through sustained silent reading programs and by investing in books rather than machinery. The two quotes summarize Krashen's perspective:

> There is consistent evidence that those who have more access to books read more [Krashen, 2004b], and that those students who are provided with more time to do recreational reading (e.g., sustained silent reading programs) show better gains in reading achievement than comparison students. The effect is especially strong when such programs are allowed to last for one year or longer. . . . On the basis of this research it would be expected that reading management programs that provide reading time and access to books will indeed result in gains in reading comprehension. The issue is whether the addition of tests and rewards makes any difference. (www.trelease-on-reading.com/ whatsnu_ar.html)

> The research says that students who receive rewards for reading do not read better or read more than those who do not. There is, however, plenty of evidence that reading itself encourages more reading; for example, children who participate in sustained silent reading programs read more on their own than those who do not, even years after the program ends. This research suggests that when programs such as Accelerated Reader and Reading Counts! appear to work it is because of the increased access to interesting books, not the tests and rewards. The money spent on such programs might be better spent on books. (Letter sent to the editors, *The Washington Post,* March 19, 2002; www.azusausd.k12.ca.us/bilingual/Krashen.html)

For Krashen, the potential impact of additional supports that may be included in electronic texts, such as hearing the text read or using the glossary, are less significant than the impact of simply reading (or listening to audio recordings of) a wide variety of texts with comprehension.

In summary, the jury is still out on whether computer-supported instruction is either effective or cost effective for promoting literacy development. This broad question is not particularly helpful in understanding the conditions under which technology interventions might be effective. In the remainder of this chapter, we attempt to specify a set of design principles for effective technology-supported instruction. These design principles are aligned directly with the empirical research on learning and literacy development discussed in Chapter 2.

Design Principles for Technology-Supported Instruction

Bransford and colleagues (2000) highlighted the fact that optimal learning environments should promote deep rather than superficial understanding, invoke and build on learners' prior knowledge, and promote active and self-regulated learning rather than passive learning. The impact of these learning environments will be enhanced when they are supported by a meaningful learning community. Any effective technology-supported activity or intervention should incorporate these principles if it is to align with what is known about how people learn.

With respect to the development of literacy, the research suggests that ELL and many low-income students experience greater difficulty in reading to learn than in learning to read. A Research Brief published by the RAND Corporation expressed this point clearly: "Despite recent progress in reading achievement among children in primary grades, many children are not moving beyond basic decoding skills as they advance to the fourth grade and classes in history, mathematics, and science" (RAND Education, 2004, p. 1). The complexity of academic language (vocabulary, grammar, discourse features, etc.) that is characteristic of content areas in the later grades of elementary school represents a major barrier for many students. As noted in Chapter 2, sustained engagement with written language is crucial for expanding vocabulary knowledge because low-frequency vocabulary is found almost exclusively in written text. In addition to extensive reading, the research suggests that instruction focused on helping students develop effective comprehension strategies is also an important component of reading comprehension development (Postlethwaite & Ross, 1992; Pressley, Duke, & Boling, 2004).

So the issue becomes: What software programs or technology-supported learning activities will (1) promote deep understanding, build on learners' prior knowledge, and permit learners to control the learning process, and (2) engage learners in extensive reading, support them in accessing curricular content, and enable them to harvest the language they are reading?

The case studies that we document throughout this book and many others that have been discussed in the research literature (e.g., Durán, 2005; Leu et al., 2005; Parker, 2005) provide ample evidence that technology *can* play a central role in supporting this kind of learning among low-income and culturally diverse students. Before examining a variety of case studies in the appendix, we articulate six design principles that derive directly from the scientific research on learning and literacy development. The specification of these design criteria draws on Wood's (2001) analysis of computer programs that could potentially support children's vocabulary development. Based on the research literature, Wood identified five criteria for evaluating the nature of the vocabulary instruction in software products:

Criterion 1: Does it relate the new to the known?

Criterion 2: Does it promote active, in-depth processing of new words?

Criterion 3: Does it provide multiple exposures to new words?

Criterion 4: Does it teach students to be strategic readers?

Criterion 5: Does it promote additional reading?

Wood's analysis of 16 software products revealed that many products that made no explicit claims about fostering vocabulary learning reflected the five criteria better than many that made explicit claims. Programs designed explicitly to teach vocabulary often simply presented drill-and-practice routines rather than helping students develop a deeper understanding of a word.

We express the design criteria in the form of questions that address the major principles of learning and literacy development outlined in Chapter 2.

1. Does the technology-supported instruction provide cognitive challenge and opportunities for deep processing of meaning?

2. Does the technology-supported instruction relate instruction to prior knowledge and experiences derived from students' homes and communities?

3. Does the technology-supported instruction promote active self-regulated collaborative inquiry?

4. Does the technology-supported instruction promote extensive engaged reading and writing across the curriculum?

5. Does the technology-supported instruction help students develop strategies for effective reading, writing, and learning?

6. Does the technology-supported instruction promote affective involvement and identity investment on the part of students?

It is clear that these conditions are seldom present in instructional environments that are predominantly transmission oriented. They align much more easily with social constructivist and transformative pedagogical orientations. Leu and colleagues (2005) discuss of a variety of successful technology-supported new literacies projects involving linguistically diverse students. They make explicit the linkage between a social constructivist and/or transformative orientation and the learning possibilities embodied in these projects:

> We see that technology projects seem to work best when they present students of diverse backgrounds with challenging, generative tasks that require them to read, write, and think in new and demanding ways. The time, energy and thought students devote to participate effectively in these projects suggest that they are readily able to take advantage of constructivist forms of instruction that give them the knowledge and strategies needed to engage with new forms of literacy and electronic media. (p. 18)

A characteristic of most of the projects reviewed by Leu and colleagues (2005) is that the projects generally required no special computer programs but rather used the common functionalities available on most modern computers (e.g., presentation software, web-creation tools, photo and video editing software, etc.). Jonassen coined the term *mindtools* to highlight the power of these technological tools to support knowledge construction and critical thinking (Jonassen, 1996, 1999; Jonasson, Carr, & Yueh, 1998). Jonassen and colleagues argue that

> technologies should not support learning by attempting to instruct the learners, but rather should be used as knowledge construction tools that students learn *with*, not *from*. In this way, learners function as designers, and the computers function as Mindtools for interpreting and organizing their personal knowledge. Mindtools are computer applications that, when used by learners to represent what they know, necessarily engage them in critical thinking about the content they are studying. (1998, p. 24)

Jonassen (1999) elaborated a framework designed to help analyze the extent to which computer applications are being used as mindtools to generate knowledge and promote critical thinking. He specifies *engagement* (active to passive), *generativity* (focus on creation rather than presentation), and *control* (residing in the student as compared to the teacher or machine) as key dimensions. Knowledge generation and critical thinking require that the instructional emphasis be on student control, active engagement, and creation. This emphasis is clearly consistent with the six design principles and with the learning principles articulated by Bransford and colleagues (2000).

The logic underlying the articulation of these principles is that if an educator can answer all or most of these questions affirmatively in relation to any particular project or activity, then it is highly likely that this activity is promoting both engaged learning and literacy development. Therefore, these design principles can be used both to evaluate particular programs or activities (in a similar way to Wood's [2001] study) and to plan the implementation of new technology-supported initiatives. We will apply these design principles to the interpretation of the various case studies in Part II, and in Part III we integrate them into a broader conceptual framework designed to support school-based planning for change.

Discussion Questions for Study Groups

1 If you were given $3,000 to spend on classroom materials or resources, would you buy a computer with the money or spend it in other ways? Justify your response in relation to how you might use the computer as compared to other kinds of materials or resources.

2 Think about digital technologies other than computers (e.g., cell phones, digital cameras, video cameras, iPods, etc.). How might you use these new technologies to enrich your students' learning?

3 The chapter discusses the *pedagogical divide* that separates instruction for low-income and for more affluent students. Identify three technology-supported strategies for overcoming this pedagogical divide.

4 Examine three computer programs or tools that are used in your school to support students' literacy development. To what extent do they reflect transmission, social constructivist, or transformative orientations to pedagogy? Are they compatible with the design criteria discussed in this chapter for the promotion of technology-supported literacy development? Support your answer.

Part 2

From Literacy to Multiliteracies
Narratives from the Frontier

Part II moves from pedagogical theory to classroom practice, documenting in rich detail the kinds of technologically mediated instruction that can address and potentially resolve the pedagogical inequities that we have identified. These projects depart from the rote memorization of content unconnected to students' experiences and life aspirations so prevalent in low-income and inner-city schools. Is it possible to ignite curiosity, imagination, and social commitment while also promoting academic achievement and meeting curricular standards in students from low-income backgrounds? The answer is a resounding yes. The educators in these classrooms argue forcefully that far from detracting from academic achievement, inquiry-based, identity-affirming instruction, with technology as a powerful amplifier, opens the door to amazing forms of learning for a much wider range of students. These conditions also make teaching and learning an intellectually challenging, engaging, and affirming process for teachers.

The chapters that follow are a series of portraits. They represent more than a static snapshot at a particular point in time. Each tells a story that traces the experiences of a teacher and students, and often their families and communities, engaged in educational projects in which technology served as a powerful amplifier. In many cases, the process of gathering the data to write these portraits involved numerous conversations with the teachers about what they felt were the turning points in their classrooms and projects as they moved toward their goals and visions for their students. The teachers, and often the students and parents as well, had a chance to tell us what they thought made a difference, and what the real outcomes were, including but going beyond the kinds of skills that show up on paper-and-pencil tests.

In the six chapters that follow, we present portraits of educators who have involved their students in learning projects with a range of challenging activities that promote academic growth, foster identity development, and encourage the critical awareness necessary for effective social action. Technology-mediated learning plays an important role in each of these projects, ranging from photography and tape-recording to more contemporary technologies including digitized media and the Internet. Yet what links each portrait is the vision of educators and students using the learning tools at hand to engage in what we have termed *collaborative critical inquiry.*

Chapter 5 is a portrait that spans nearly three-quarters of a century, describing the learning partnerships possible between classes separated by distance, sometimes called *sister classes, partner classes,* or *twinned classes,* but more broadly termed *global learning networks.* First, we visit students participating in the networking project *De Orilla a Orilla* as they discover the myriad of instructional and learning possibilities opened up by sister-class exchanges and group projects. Then we travel 30 years back in time to the plains and valleys of northern Italy, where Mario Lodi was similarly discovering how minds can meet over geographic and cultural distances. Finally 40 years earlier, we visit a tiny village in the French Alps and Célestin Freinet, whose vision transformed the educational experience of students and teachers in the 10,000 schools in 33 countries that participated in the learning network of the *Mouvement de l'École Moderne* (Modern School Movement).

Chapter 6 presents Proyecto FRESA (Project Strawberry), in which third- and fifth-graders studied the strawberry field work of their migrant and agricultural families. They tracked the movements of strawberries from seeds to export markets. Students interviewed parents, used the Internet for additional research, and then invited community experts to speak to their class. They created a website that contained poetry, artwork, graphs, and the results from their community investigations. Students engaged in dialogue on local economics and profit analysis as part of their math curriculum. They then carried their investigation beyond their community by connecting through e-mail with students in a coffee-growing area of Puerto Rico and in a strawberry-growing area of India. Through this project, students used language and technology to facilitate dialogues regarding global issues of commerce, agriculture, and equity.

Chapter 7 details an oral history project in which junior high school students from various cultural backgrounds linked classroom assignments in world history with their families' histories as well as with the history of the larger community. As students conducted interviews with parents and relatives to gain insight and information regarding their family histories, they also uncovered connections with the history of their community. Technology-mediated learning was integrated at every stage of the process, from using the Internet for researching their ancestors to recording and producing an edited video documentary. As they opened a dialogue with their extended families about the people, places, and events of the past, students became confident in their ability to respond to challenges facing their community.

Chapter 8 narrates the unfolding of a partner school project on biographies that took place between primary grade classes in Livermore, California, and students on the other side of the bay in San Francisco. Both schools participated in a global learning network project called Connecting Math to Our Lives/Conectando las Matemáticas a la Vida. Students categorized the biographical holdings in their school libraries by race, class, gender, and disability, and shared their findings with their partner school using percentages, fractions, graphs, and written narratives. Their joint statistical analysis of the many gaps in the biography holdings of their school libraries led them to engage in a series of literacy activities as well, including the writing of their own autobiographies made available for lending in the library. A culminating activity was a joint visit to the largest public library in San Francisco, where they analyzed the biography section of its children's collection. Their formal recommendations for future acquisitions to staff librarians there and in their schools have helped make three libraries' holdings more representative.

In Chapter 9, elementary school students in a Spanish–English dual immersion program used dictionary-building software designed for university-level linguistics courses to create their own bilingual dictionary. These student lexicographers worked as partners, an English-speaking student paired with a Spanish speaker, to produce original definitions for essential vocabulary items from the thematic units they were studying. They consulted with peers, parents, and teachers and conducted extensive research using reference works and the Internet. Finally, they audio-recorded their definitions for each entry, illustrated them with digitized images, and included links to multiple websites, using the Internet to transform their bilingual dictionary into an encyclopedia.

Access to sophisticated technology is not essential for academic learning and engaging in intercultural learning networks, as illustrated by the extensive MSM network established by Célestin Freinet in France in the early twentieth century (see Chapter 5), but equity of access is a central issue for any serious attempt at educational reform in today's schools. Chapter 10 places our discussion in a global context, highlighting innovative and large-scale efforts in other parts of the world to close the technology divide for students, their families, and their communities.

In these portraits, technology and pedagogy can be viewed together, revealing the power of technology as a pedagogical amplifier. Too often there has been a tendency to focus on technological tools in isolation from any analysis of what pedagogical options are available to promote different forms of literacy. Part II offers an alternative to the narrow emphasis on technical skills in isolation based on a consideration of what content is worth presenting by means of these tools, for what purposes, and to which audiences, and what level of cognition or problem solving we want our students to exercise.

CHAPTER 5

Vignettes of Classes in Global Learning Networks

We use the term *global learning networks* to describe confederations of teachers and students employing technology as an integral part of collaborative learning exchanges over long distances. Student projects in three such networks are briefly described here.

Vignettes

De Orilla a Orilla (From Shore to Shore)

For more than a decade students from dozens of countries around the world participated in an annual project of the *Orillas* global learning network. They collected proverbs from parents, family, and friends, and organized, analyzed, and eventually shared and compared their collections with those of distant students in other *Orillas* classrooms, using technology at every phase of the project.

Participation in the Proverbs Project took many forms and involved students from every grade level. In primary classes, students produced charming drawings to illustrate sayings such as "People who live in glass houses shouldn't throw stones," offering perhaps the most literal interpretations of proverbs. Some older students took a page from fabulists such as seventeenth-century poet LaFontaine and produced their own fables, concluding with a proverb as a succinct punch line. Intermediate grade students in Puerto Rico exercised their analogical thinking skills in their analysis of the Spanish proverb *El mismo perro con diferente collar* (The same dog with a different collar); one student wrote that a mathematical principle they were studying in class at the time—namely, that 2 plus 2 plus 2 yields the same result as 2 times 3—reminded him of this proverb that he first learned from his grandmother. High school students wrote editorials disputing the veracity of proverbs such as "A woman's place is in the home." "This is how my parents thought," concluded one New York city student in the editorial she wrote in Spanish, "but not me, because I am a rebel" (Cummins & Sayers, 1995, pp. 55–56).

Year after year, collecting and sharing proverbs allowed students in Orillas classrooms

Moments of discovery occur in partner class exchanges as students compare and contrast their worlds.

from different nationalities, languages, and cultural backgrounds to compare, critique, and comprehend traditional folk wisdom embodied in proverbial sayings. It also proved to be a popular project among the parents and extended families of students in every country—not surprising, perhaps, since the Proverbs Project brought the younger generation to them asking eagerly for the kind of folk knowledge that had been handed down since time immemorial from their ancestors. Yet here intergenerational contact was being facilitated and disseminated through the most modern technology.

The Cooperative Education Movement

Bruno Ciardi's class in mountainous Certaldo formed a learning partnership with Mario Lodi's students in the distant plains of Vho; these Italian educators, part of the Cooperative Education Movement, also employed a number of technologies as "cultural amplifiers" to heighten students' classes' collaboration on joint projects, especially those that centered on producing and sharing journalism through co-edited newsletters.

The linguistic realities of Italian education helped thrust one technology in particular to the forefront. Although standard Italian is the *lingua franca* of schools in Italy, the country is in fact a patchwork quilt of regions with unique and at times mutually unintelligible dialects of Italian as their primary languages. How better to explore and comprehend these realities than to share slide shows and audio samples of comparable language and cultural phenomena such as folktales, proverbs, traditional games, and lullabies, analyzing differences and similarities between standard Italian and two regional dialects? Yet their decision to do so ignited a firestorm of controversy reminiscent of the one that followed the decision of Oakland, California, educators to employ Ebonics, the version of English spoken by their students and millions of African Americans in North America (Perry & Delpit, 2001). Mario Lodi articulated the rationale for educators in the Cooperative Education Movement to bring the language of the home into the classroom through technology:

> To start out where the children are simply means to accept them with everything they bring with them from their homes, but also to value what they bring and to help them understand that what they possess is important, and that while they are in school we will be working with and building upon what they bring. (cited in Tonucci, 1981, pp. 46–47)

Educators in the Cooperative Education Movement took care to maintain the language of the home as a vital means of communication in their classrooms, both out of an appreciation for its intrinsic value and a realization of its immense potential for motivating academic learning. And they used technology to achieve this goal.

The Modern School Movement

Like the *Orillas* network, the Modern School Movement arranges pairings and wider partnerships on a worldwide basis between classes of teachers and their students in dozens of nations. The first such pairing was between two teachers in different parts of France: Célestin Freinet from rural Bar-sur-Loup in the Maritime Alps and René Daniel from the coastal village of Trégunc in Breton. The technologies employed by Freinet and Daniel in their first long-distance collaborations centered on classroom printing and journalism; the two classes produced books and newsletters of student writings to share both locally with students, family, and friends, and with their distant partner class as well. To make the exchanges more meaningful and less abstract, the two teachers also worked with their students putting together "cultural packages" that they exchanged weekly by mail. Freinet wrote in his diary about how he and his students felt on the day they received their first cultural package from Breton, filled with fruits, dried flowers, perfumes, fossils, seashells, photographs, figurines, lace, ribbons, and folk costumes: "*Maintenant, nous ne sommes plus seuls*" (Now we are no longer alone) (Freinet, 1969/1975, p. 45).

Back to the Future

In fact, these three vignettes have been a journey backwards in time. Célestin Freinet's diary entry was dated October 28, 1924, and marks the beginning of the history of global learning networks; his and René Daniel's classes employed the technology of printing presses, *typeset by students themselves,* to produce books and newsletters, and they exchanged their work not via computers or the Internet—technologies not yet dreamed of—but via the national postal service. Indeed, so many thousands of French schools in the Modern School Movement (MSM) eventually used the national post for educational exchanges that teachers organized a successful national drive, unique in the world, to secure franking privileges; to this day, French teachers pay no postage to exchange materials between schools. The Modern School Movement that

Freinet founded has endured eight decades, incorporating over the years newer technologies, including photography and photographic slides, tape recording, motion pictures, video, and most recently computer-based technology and the Internet, into their collaborative exchanges between schools.

Mario Lodi established the Cooperative Education Movement (CEM) in the early 1950s as a sister organization of the international MSM, but with a particular focus on Italian schools and on issues of language and dialect. Not surprisingly, then, Lodi and Ciardi found the newer technologies of voice recording, using early wire recorders in their first exchanges and, later, tape recorders to "sample" their local dialects for sharing and comparing between classes. Teachers in both the MSM and the CEM wrote and published prolifically. Their writings have guided the educators of the *Orillas* network, established in 1985 by Kristin Brown, Enid Figueroa, and Dennis Sayers, from the days of its original partnerships among classes in Puerto Rico, Connecticut, and California, to the present, with worldwide collaborations stressing multilingualism, collaborative and critical inquiry, and social action.

A fuller discussion of the Modern School Movement and of the Cooperative Education Movement, key precursors of contemporary global learning networks, will help us situate the sister class partnerships described in this book in a rich historical context—a key aspect too often ignored in discussions of classroom technology.

Blueprints from the Past

While considering the early history and later development of global learning networks, one is immediately struck by the wide-ranging inventiveness of the teachers in the MSM and CEM as they experimented with technology-mediated approaches to learning. A frequent theme in Freinet's writings is the distinction between "techniques and instruments" on the one hand, and "methods" on the other. Freinet and his MSM colleagues called their approaches "techniques," and the technology tools they used to implement these experimental techniques, were termed "instruments."

> Pedagogical technique—and this is its superiority over any method— comprises by definition every kind of investigation and every sort of activity which . . . coincide to make possible the work of the community educator. Someday, when pedagogical science has progressed

considerably, when the workings of children's minds are finally known and comprehended by educators and when, moreover, there exist optimum social conditions for education, only on that day will we be able to speak of definitive methods that are scientifically ordered; in fact, they will be the result of innumerable trial-and-error probings by pedagogical technicians such as we are now. (Freinet, 1969/1975, pp. 134–135)

Methods, in Freinet's view, impeded the general improvement of educators by encouraging uncritical imitation of preestablished curricula, whether authorized by centralized regional and national authorities or recommended by educational experts. Pedagogical techniques, on the other hand, employ innovative tools and instruments that help establish new relationships between students and teachers, providing invaluable feedback as educators reflect on and improve their practice. We will focus on two key techniques in our discussion of MSM and CEM schools: classroom printing and interschool exchanges.

Classroom Printing

Classroom printing, perhaps the technique for which the early Freinet schools are best known, grew out of two practices: the "learning walk" and "free texts." Every day, weather permitting, Freinet would lead the students of his one-room school on excursions through Bar-sur-Loup and the surrounding countryside. Later, back at school, students would jointly author compositions at the blackboard that summarized the ad hoc interviews they had just conducted with townspeople, or that described the local flora and fauna. They then copied the resulting communal text into their notebooks. As motivating as these practices proved with his students, Freinet was concerned that the ephemeral nature of their notebook jottings seemed an inadequate expression of the high-level thinking represented in the free texts. He began to explore the possibilities of more permanent renderings, ordering his first printing press in 1921. As his students became adept at the crafts of typesetting and printing, Freinet discovered more and more outlets for their folios of writings, as classroom texts, of course, but also as documents children were proud to share with family, relatives, and friends. Indeed, classroom printing led directly to the discovery of a second technique, as Freinet's students and those of other French teachers who soon introduced printing presses in their classrooms all sought wider and wider readerships.

Interschool Exchanges

Freinet and Daniel were the first teachers to exchange their students' printed publications; however, the number of MSM "interschool exchanges" grew rapidly during the years leading up to the Second World War. In large part, this growth was due to a simple but ingenious scheme of structuring several teacher partnerships into larger clusters of collaborating classes, illustrated in Figure 5.1. Within these

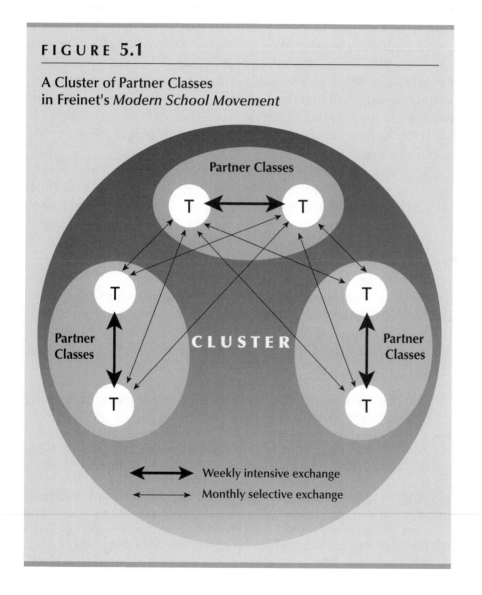

FIGURE 5.1

**A Cluster of Partner Classes
in Freinet's *Modern School Movement***

Partner Classes

CLUSTER

Partner Classes

Partner Classes

Weekly intensive exchange

Monthly selective exchange

clusters, pairs of teachers engaged in postal exchanges of their students' work on at least a weekly basis, often several times a week; additionally, each partnership was assigned to a cluster of three or more other partnerships, and each class sent to the other cluster classes monthly samples of their current publications and classroom investigations as well as students' comments on previously shared writings.

Thus, each MSM classroom was literally flooded with constant examples of student writings as well as responses to locally authored work that had been exchanged previously. "Having something to say, writing to be read, to be discussed, to be responded to critically, this is the grand motivation for literacy we should be seeking, and which is realized through classroom printing and the interschool exchanges" (Balesse & Freinet, 1961/1973, p. 89). But as valuable as audience can be for students' writing development, the technique of interschool exchanges provided much more than a wider readership to students and teachers in the MSM; for as their experience deepened, a new theory of literacy acquisition began to form.

Their emerging theory becomes easier to understand if one keeps in mind that typically MSM partner classes wrote about *shared topics*. Thus, both classes in a partnership would write about local geography and later compare their findings; or each class might conduct a survey of their community's attitudes on a social issue, then share and contrast the results. In this context, the language used in both classes would possess certain commonalities: a similar vocabulary of geographic terminology, for instance, or the words used to express opinions about a particular issue. As one class wrote and edited its texts for a project, students in that school became quite familiar with this core vocabulary, and with the words of their localized writings on that topic. But once the writings of the partner class arrived, new challenges were introduced:

> If on the one hand the child . . . creates new texts to satisfy his need for self-expression, utilizing words and expressions without worrying himself about the technicalities of syllables and letters, then on the other hand the practice of interschool exchanges places reading in an entirely different context. Now that the task is to decipher a written page, there is a totally different motivation, but equally personalized. . . . This is the moment at which the child really moves into decoding and becomes aware of it as a process. Familiar words are immediately discovered and ones that have never been seen are analyzed perspicaciously. . . . The teacher's intervention, even an exercise sheet, is wanted to aid in easily decoding those words that might clarify for us what we want to know.

The teacher's observations and help with syllabification are not an imposed system, but rather a necessity integrated with something lived, and are therefore received with the same enthusiasm as for everything that extends the child's life. (Balesse & Freinet, 1961/1973, pp. 64–65)

Thus, a "scaffolding" context, or zone of proximal development, was created within each interschool exchange, to use the terminology of Vygotsky, a contemporary of Freinet. While based in the familiar grounding of a shared topic, interschool exchanges helped create a felt need among students for assistance from teachers with decoding and mastery of the unfamiliar and slightly more challenging vocabulary in writings arriving constantly from their partner class. And so the technique of interschool exchanges led to a new definition of literacy attainment in the MSM: "Our students know how to read and write when they can easily read all the works they and their classmates have written, and when they can read passably well the texts sent from their correspondents" (Balesse & Freinet, 1961/1973, p. 68).

From the technique of interschool exchanges also arose what we have termed elsewhere a "pedagogy of distancing" that proved very influential in the development of the MSM and other sister global learning networks like the CEM, founded by Mario Lodi. Indeed, it is illuminating to discuss distancing in the context of Lodi's work with student dialects and the study of Italian, the official language of schooling in Italy. Students who speak a minority language everywhere—not only in Italy, of course—are largely unaware of their home dialects prior to schooling; too often, their encounter with schools is a negative one that involves suppression, even denial, of their mother tongue. Their mastery of the dominant language of schooling is hard won and usually occurs at the expense of the home language, the loss of which can handicap these students' viability as effective members of their community.

But in the context of an interschool exchange between two classes with differing dialects, a dynamic is created for positive language contact in school settings. In CEM partnerships, students recorded culturally salient examples—lullabies, proverbs, songs—in their respective dialects, and then employed standard Italian, the language shared by both classes, for extended discussion, first through voice recordings and later in writing. Thus, through a comparison of two dialects as powerful tools of communication conducted in standard Italian, students gained expressive power both in their home language and the official language of schooling. Modern School Movement teachers described the reflective distancing process fostered by interschool exchanges as follows:

> The child, because she needs to describe them, develops a consciousness of the conditions of her life, of the life of her town or her neighborhood, even of her province. She has been living too close to these conditions and through interschool exchanges she has distanced herself from life . . . We must take advantage of this impulse of curiosity, this new vision, these instances of discovery. (Gervilliers, Berteloot, & Lemery, 1968/1977, p. 31)

Cooperative Education Movement teachers took advantage of these "instances of discovery" by building literacy skills on the sure foundation of their students' oral language abilities. Teachers viewed the discipline required of students to produce and record "audio letters" destined for their partner class as a compelling introduction to the demands imposed by writing (Tonucci, 1981, p. 41):

- To communicate with someone who isn't present, to whom it is necessary to be explicit and explain everything;

- To plan the speech, anticipating its parts and assigning them to different speakers;

- The impossibility of using gestures, facial expressions, and other indicative movements that simplify the understanding of oral language so much; and

- Not receiving an immediate reply and having to wait for one.

The technique of exchanging voice recordings, a humble technology by contemporary standards, made the recorder an instrument that validated the language and culture of the home while promoting sophisticated literacy skills. As Mario Lodi insisted,

> Our school will not destroy so as to construct afterwards, but rather we will cause their heritage to grow. The difference is substantial. In the first case, a basis is created for a lack of confidence, both in oneself and in one's previous experiences away from school, while in the second the basis is created for self-confidence that serves as the foundation for all knowledge that will come later. (cited in Tonucci, 1981, pp. 46–47)

CHAPTER 6

Project FRESA

Cultivating Community-Connected Learning

Using an educational process based on dialogue and problem posing, and employing computers as a communication and research tool, third- and fifth-grade students from farm-working families investigated their parents' work in the fields and shared the results of their investigation. The students published their work online in a multimedia, cross-curricular anthology about the relationship between their lives and the strawberry crops that surround their school and sustain the local community and economy.

Strawberry fields surround Mar Vista Elementary School in Oxnard, California, a fertile farm community 60 miles north of Los Angeles. The strawberry business sustains the local economy and employs many of the parents of the children at the school. The berries' fragrance permeates the halls, and field workers sometimes delight the children in the playground by throwing strawberries over the fence. In 1999, third-grade teacher Amada Irma Pérez, fifth-grade teacher Michelle Singer, and their students created Project FRESA (*fresa* means "strawberry" in Spanish), a unit of study that has given legitimacy to the students' own lives as content worthy of study, while also providing a highly motivating context for advancing the students' literacy and academic skills.

The teachers come from vastly different backgrounds: Amada has taught for 30 years, Michelle for just 3. Amada, like the students she teaches, grew up in an immigrant farm-working family in an agricultural area of California and spoke Spanish at home. Michelle grew up in an urban area, speaking English and studying Spanish at school and later through travel and study in Mexico and Spain after she decided to become a bilingual teacher. In spite of these differences, Amada and Michelle share a deep interest in education for social justice and a belief that when children's lives, communities, and interests are part of the curriculum, learning begins to breathe. They were inspired in part by the work of Brazilian educator Paulo Freire, who in the 1950s, created effective literacy programs for Brazilian peasants, focusing on helping students not only to "read the word" but also to "read the world." Several decades after Freire's success, with the advent of new tech-

Note to new teachers from Amada and Michelle:

New teachers and veteran teachers are a perfect complement. Veteran teachers bring experience and expertise in classroom management, whereas new teachers have a lot of ideas and perspectives, and often more recent technology training. Keep your enthusiasm and knowledge with you.

nologies, Pérez and Singer used their classroom computers to make instruction more relevant to their students:

> We wanted to conduct a unit of study that would interest and intrigue our students, open up communication at home, bring the reality of our students' lives into the classroom, and elevate their respect for the tough and important work of their parents and grandparents. We hoped that the children would come to appreciate the strawberry workers more while becoming empowered to take action and have a better chance at transforming their own lives. Since strawberries not only surround our school, but also the lives of our students, it was a natural topic of study when deciding on the focus of our Telementor Project. (Michelle Singer & Amada Pérez, personal communication, October 14, 2001)

The CLMER-CABE Telementor Institute

During the 1999–2000 school year, Michelle Singer and Amada Irma Pérez were selected with 24 other exemplary bilingual educators from California to participate in the diversity-responsive CLMER-CABE Telementor project. This year-long institute, designed and organized by director Kevin Rocap and staff at the Center for Language Minority Education and Research (CLMER) at California State University, Long Beach, in collaboration with the California Association of Bilingual Education (CABE), builds its theoretical framework on six "lenses" related to twenty-first-century teaching and learning: community learning theory, critical pedagogy, antiracist education, language acquisition and development, standards and assessment, and technology fluency. During this year of extensive reading and dialogue with other bilingual educators, each team of participants was challenged to design, implement, and showcase a project that they could share with other educators. The Telementor Institute deepened Amada's and Michelle's knowledge of technology, and the dialogue with their peers inspired them to make their students' lives even more central to the teaching and learning at their school. It was from this professional development experience that Project FRESA emerged. In 2005–2006, a new cadre of diversity-responsive telementors was established with a focus on technology integration into dual language programs. This is a joint project with Long Island University Brooklyn, New York University, and San Diego State University.

Project FRESA:
Planting the Seeds of Learning

Michelle and Amada envisioned Project FRESA as a cross-age joint project for their two classes. Since the beginning of the year, their third- and fifth-grade students had met weekly on Fridays for half an hour for shared writing and art activities. Each fifth-grader served as a "big buddy" to a student in the third-grade class and there was already a feeling of trust among the students in the two classes. The Friday meetings were an ideal time to launch the project.

From the start, the teachers designed Project FRESA so that their students would feel a sense of ownership.

> We didn't write up what the project was going to be and then say, "Guess what, kids, this is what we're doing." That would have gone against our knowledge of critical pedagogy.... I remember saying to Michelle, "We'll need butcher paper and markers to grab their thoughts and put them up. Let's just put the word *strawberries* up. It's something they're so familiar with." (Amada Pérez, personal communication, January 15, 2003)

When the students first met for Project FRESA, the classroom walls were covered with butcher paper and chairs were in a circle. To help create a safe setting in which the students would feel free to express their opinions, the teachers each took a moment at the beginning of the period to tell the students about their own connections to the strawberry fields. Amada told how her father picked grapes in California's Central

Valley when she was a child. Michelle told of her drive to school each morning through the strawberry fields, observing the hard-working laborers, and the questions it raised for her about whether the people who buy the strawberries at the store know where they come from, who picks them, and how hard the work is. The teachers followed their stories with an invitation for the students to share their ideas through a Think-Pair-Share activity—a strategy they had found effective in ensuring that even the students who were shy or spoke

FRESA student displays a class-authored book on the parents' work in the strawberry fields, jointly written and illustrated by the fifth-grade students and their third-grade buddies.

another language at home could express their thoughts. They asked the children to think about their own connection to the strawberries and to share something they knew or wanted to know about strawberries with one other student in the class.

The room buzzed with conversation as the children put their heads together. While the children talked, the teachers wrote on one wall: *What We Know,* and on the other *What We Want to Know,* and on a third *What We've Learned* (a question they would come back to in future class meetings).

Asking New Questions

The teachers publicly recorded each of the students' comments about strawberries. "At first we were kind of disappointed," Amada and Michelle remember. "They could only come up with the most obvious things: 'They're red. They're sweet. They're juicy.'"

Michelle and Amada realized how often students are asked obvious questions and are expected to give obvious answers—and how infrequently students are taught to ask more probing questions. The teachers remember thinking, "How are we going to encourage the students to raise the deeper questions that might be on their minds?" They turned to the students and asked: "What do you wonder about strawberries? What have you always wondered?" "The questions became more perceptive and critical. They asked about the working conditions in the fields where their parents worked and wondered why only Mexicans worked in the fields" (Amada Pérez and Michelle Singer, personal communication, February 1, 2002). "I wonder why the seeds are on the outside?" said one student. Another asked, "I wonder why the people who pick the strawberries wear scarves across their noses and mouths." As the discussion turned to strawberry field work, one hand after the next was raised as the children shared the questions that had been on their minds: "I wonder why they have to work outside even when it's raining and cold." "I wonder why only brown people work in the fields."

Amada and Michelle filled the butcher paper with the students' questions. As the teachers explained that the questions would help guide the FRESA investigation, the students showed amazement at all the questions they had generated. Amada and Michelle recall, "There were so many questions and none of us had the answers."

The teachers reminded their students, "Your teachers don't have all the answers. We're learning with you." They asked the children to think about where they could go to find the answers to the questions they had listed. "Books, the encyclopedia, the Internet," responded the students right away. Michelle and Amada waited to see if there were other suggestions. "We could ask our parents," one girl offered. The children nodded with approval as Michelle and Amada added "parents" to the list of potential resources.

The teachers began the next session by asking students to form two lines—a line on one side of the room for those who had family members who worked in the fields, and a line on the other for those who did not. Everybody remembers what happened next. Nearly all of the students—45 out of 50 students—moved to the side of the room for those with family members who worked in the fields. The students looked around with wide eyes. With hushed but excited voices they marveled at the number of their classmates whose families worked in the fields, saying: "Your dad? My grandfather," "Mine too!" "My mom and my aunt both work in the fields," "Look, there are so many of us!"

Although many of the students had studied together at Mar Vista School for four to six years, having family members who labored in the fields wasn't necessarily something the children had mentioned. To do so risked revealing that your father came home with black hands or that you lived in the substandard housing with other migrant farm-working families. The teachers noticed how willingly, in this activity, the children shared that they were from farm-working families. "The students saw that it was a shared experience. In Project FRESA, it was more of a pride than an embarrassment" (Amada Pérez, personal communication, January 15, 2003).

At the following meeting, students quickly formed small groups to review the questions they had generated and to decide which questions would be appropriate to ask their parents. They formulated a questionnaire that allowed for both open and closed responses in order to get answers to their questions. "Just like researchers at a university," Michelle explained to the students. When all the teams had finished creating their lists, the teachers helped them compile the questions that had been raised most frequently into a two-page bilingual questionnaire for the students to take home over the weekend. Even so, the teachers realized that they hadn't yet talked about what to do with the information the students brought back. "Many times it felt as though the students were leading us rather than us leading them. It was like the students were on horses and we were trying to keep up with them" (Amada Pérez, personal communication, January 15, 2003).

The teachers' grounding in critical pedagogy led them to trust that the process of dialogue would take the students deeper in their analysis. They selected several key questions to open the discussion with the students the following Friday, pleased that the students were so engaged and that the parents would play a significant role in the project's next phase.

Analyzing the Data

At the next meeting, the teachers divided the group into two discussion circles. The students sat in circles outside on the grass with their completed questionnaires in hand. One student would read the question and say whom they had talked with and how the person had answered the question. But each child took responsibility for adding their data. "That's the same thing that my mom said," "My tía said the same thing." So the students were able to see the connections between the information they had all gathered. And that's also when they became aware of the injustices that characterized their families' working lives (Amada Pérez, personal communication, January 15, 2003).

Students began seeing patterns. They saw how long people had worked in the fields and how it had affected their health. "My dad used to work in the fields but he can't work now because of his back," one child said. "Really?" commented another, "That same thing happened to my grandfather." Many of the most disturbing answers mentioned *fertilizantes*, the Spanish word the parents used for "pesticides." "Why do you have so many headaches?" the children had asked their parents. "Por los fertilizantes" ("Because of the fertilizers," one father said). Another child responded, "No wonder my mom always has a headache. I didn't know that was why."

The children mentioned to their teachers that until Project FRESA, they had never asked their parents these questions or talked with them about their work, a comment that the parents would repeat later to the teachers during parent conferences. "When I heard the parents say that they didn't think their children would be interested," Michelle commented, "I realized that when we study occupations in elementary school, policemen, firemen, and lawyers are typically valued."

Questionnaire results reflected the complex realities of agricultural work. In particular, the question, "Do you like working in the fields?" elicited varied responses, some positive: "I like working outdoors. I can talk with my friends. I can make money. I help provide people with food." Other field workers mentioned the work's drawbacks: "It hurts my back. The days are long. I don't make much money."

As the children shared the responses they had gathered to the question, "Why do you work in the fields?" they began to see how people's lives are affected by the opportunities open to them. Some of the replies were: "It was the only job I could find," "I never went to school," "I don't speak English," "This is the first job I found when I came here."

The children were amazed at the number of years many people in their families had worked in the strawberry fields, and were concerned about the unclean bathrooms and the poor conditions under which farm workers labored. It quickly became obvious that bad backs, poor health, inadequate wages, and cramped or shared housing weren't just problems of one family. Students who earlier may have felt humiliation about their parents' occupation now understood that they weren't alone, and began to ask why so many parents had these similar experiences.

The students used their Friday sessions productively, dividing into several new teams to continue the investigation. Some of the students searched on the Internet for answers to questions such as, "Where do strawberries grow?" Others continued the dialogue about the questionnaire data, and still others formed a group that would reflect on what they were learning through art, poetry, and writing. In this collective investigation, it was important for team members to keep track of what they were learning and to share it with the rest of the group. The students took detailed notes. In their class technology journal, those who searched the Internet kept track of each website they researched and what new information they found. In addition, the students each began a FRESA journal for their personal reflections and writing and artwork—journals that the students would later choose to represent them at the school authors' fair for all in the

Poems, writing, maps, and detailed illustrations of the lives of strawberry workers fill the pages of the students' FRESA journals.

wider school community to read. Michelle and Amada remember that the children asked constantly, "'Are we having FRESA? Is it almost time?' They couldn't wait."

Students began arriving at school early and asked to stay in at recess to work on the project. Michelle worked regularly with a group of fifth-graders who volunteered to come to school 30 minutes early. She and Amada had only one computer each in their classrooms, so this time allowed her to teach the students new computer skills. She taught her fifth-graders to use the scanner, various drawing and graphing programs (including KidPix and ClarisWorks), and Microsoft PowerPoint presentation software, which they used to create graphs of their interview data. The children used a tiny digital camera to take pictures of everyone in the FRESA project and import these into other drawing and writing programs so that all students had both a hand-drawn self-portrait and a printed photograph to add to their journals. The fifth-graders, in turn, took their third-grade buddies, one at a time, to teach them the same programs.

Upholding Content Standards

Project FRESA expanded to other periods of the day, as the teachers found numerous connections to district and state curriculum and content standards. In geography classes, students created clearly labeled, detailed United States and world maps to illustrate where strawberries grow and to where they are exported. They were surprised to learn

Parents

Project FRESA helped students see that their parents' experiences are valued enough by the school to be part of their education, and that parents were sources of expertise. Parents served as consultants to the children and teachers throughout the project about the growing cycle of strawberries and the working conditions of the field workers. Parents and teachers communicated more frequently and parents reported feeling pleased that they could help their children with their schoolwork. Some visited the school on days when the weather didn't allow them to work in the fields, offering to assist in the classrooms. Parents and their children also reported that they talked more at home not only about the realities of work but also about the importance of educational opportunities and their hopes for the children's futures.

"It placed even more value and emphasis on the parents. Because whenever we had questions we would go back to the parents. The families were the primary source of information in this project" (Michelle Singer, personal communication, February 16, 2003).

that strawberries grew in every state of the U.S., and on every continent of the world, and were proud to discover that the largest were exported to Japan and Germany and England—even served at the Wimbledon tennis classic!

In language arts, teachers combined opportunities for the students to write poems reflecting on their FRESA investigation with a lesson on parts of speech. Here's an example:

> *Strawberries*
> *Juicy, delicious*
> *Eating, Picking, Packing*
> *Strawberries are part of our family*
> *Fruit*
>
> *Fertilizer*
> *Poisonous, dangerous*
> *Killing, helping, growing*
> *Medicine that's good and bad*
> *Fertilizer*

My language arts class that year had many recently transitioned students who were in just their first or second year of reading in English. I looked at the English language arts standards and asked, "How can I have these students meet this target?" I found that the grammar standards that they ask for in fifth grade could be taught through poetry about *fresas*. (Michelle Singer, personal communication, February 16, 2003)

Letter writing is another important standard, so teachers helped students with the format of their letters. Again using the Internet, the children created a partnership through the *Orillas* global learning network project with a class in a coffee-growing area of Puerto Rico. Teachers guided them in writing "friendly letters" to their new correspondents. Project FRESA students also gained extensive practice with the fifth-grade standard of persuasive writing. Michelle commented, "With FRESA, the students had a cause they felt deeply

Fifth-grade students, studying U.S. history and geography, discovered through Internet research that strawberries are cultivated in every state of the United States.

about, many ways to answer the arguments that somebody with a different opinion would have, and a strong interest in writing letters."

> Because the students had so much background knowledge in this area and strong desire to keep studying about FRESA, it was a natural lead into the standards. It gave them a reason to want to write and to analyze statistics. In that way standards became meaningful to them and to me, and not just like an arbitrary "to do" list, without any connections between them. There are some pretty abstract things that we have to teach. It made a world of difference having something the students could connect to and relate to. (Michelle Singer, personal communication, February 16, 2003)

> We wanted to make sure that everything we did related to the standards somehow because we have a responsibility to our students and to our school, but that didn't mean that we couldn't continue raising their consciousness, which was the greater goal. (Amada Pérez personal communication, January 15, 2003)

During math class, the students collated and analyzed the quantitative data they had gathered from the 50 questionnaires. To teach the fifth-graders statistics and analysis standards, Michelle used the FRESA questionnaire data to teach about bar graphs, line graphs, pie charts, and pictographs. "What was neat is that they gained extensive practice in thinking about what types of graphs are best for different kinds of data. The great thing about PowerPoint is that you just click and it shows you the data in different forms." The students created a presentation of their graphs using the classroom computer, and converted

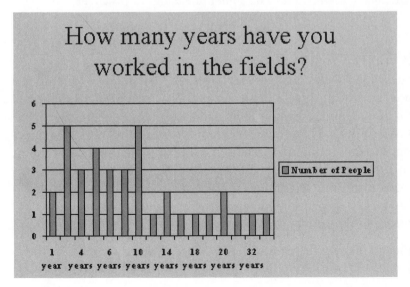

PowerPoint and other graphing software made it easy for students to experiment with different ways to display the data gathered during their parental interviews.

their PowerPoint slides to HTML web-browsing code to publish online. They also found rich material in Project FRESA for understanding math story problems. Transitioning from math facts to math story problems can be a challenge for students learning English, but they were eager to grapple with the real-world math story problems they found in the responses from the growers to their questions about wages and profits.

> In one growing season (six to seven months of producing), a field worker picking our company's berries earns an average of $13,000. If you were to annualize this number, a contract grower employee would earn approximately $19,800 per year! (excerpt from letter from an Oxnard strawberry grower)

The students, who knew that the growing season was not 12 months, analyzed the numbers and the logic and did not find that argument persuasive. The children's letters and journal entries were filled with the data and numbers they had gathered in their investigation of the inequities they were finding, and reflected a new interest in math.

> I think that the workers don't get paid well. They pay the workers $1.50 per box. They sell the boxes of strawberries for $10.00. They pay the workers $8.50 less. I don't think this is fair. That is not fair because they work very hard for the money. (Fifth-grade Mar Vista student)

> The students looked at the differences between what the workers were paid, and how much strawberries sell for, and asked what happens to all that money in between. I think that's when some of the inequities really hit home. The working conditions, the wages, the pesticides—all of that made them want to do something about it. (Michelle Singer, personal communication, February 16, 2003)

Community Action

The issues of pesticides, inadequate wages, and harsh labor conditions continued to concern the students. Community organizations helped them fill in some of the gaps in their understanding. Two guest speakers came to Mar Vista to share their wealth of knowledge with the students, one from the Environmental Defense League and the other from the California Rural Assistance League. Both speakers brought pictures, stories, and disturbing factual information about farm-working conditions and wages, environmental concerns, and the economic impact of strawberries in the county, state, and nation.

> Although the speakers provided a lot of very specific information, the students came back from the presentations with new questions. The

old questions might have been answered but they came back with new ones. It's just like as an adult learner, your questions never really get fully get answered because you always come up with new ones. Because once you find out something then you want to learn—you ask what about this and what about that—and so that kind of unique experience of wanting to know more and more and more was something that came from them. It wasn't something that was imposed on them. (Michelle Singer, personal communication, February 16, 2003)

The children were fascinated with the information provided by the classroom visitors and asked sophisticated questions using the new vocabulary they had learned from their reading. One speaker brought photos of the renowned labor activist César Chávez and had students volunteer to demonstrate how one must bend over to use a short-handled hoe. "We started to get this 'Aha, so that's why their backs hurt. No wonder.' All of our awareness shot up. The guest speakers really answered the students' questions" (Amada Pérez, personal communication, January 15, 2003).

The students decided to write letters to California's Governor Gray Davis to express their concerns about the use of pesticides and the working conditions in the fields. "It was really important to them to feel that they could do something to help," Michelle commented.

The governor's response was soon received, showing them that they were being listened to and that he would investigate their concerns. At first, they were excited to be communicating with a high-ranking political leader and to have the official seal from the office of the governor in their hands. (Amada Pérez and Michelle Singer, personal communication, February 1, 2002)

The teachers photocopied the governor's letter so that each child could keep a copy in his or her FRESA journal. The children admired the seal of the state of California and frequently reread the governor's words encouraging them to continue "to take an active role in public policy development." Nevertheless, the teachers note on the Project FRESA website, "In analyzing the letter, however, many students believed that his letter was not from the heart and felt that he would not follow through and truly investigate their concerns."

Students wrote in their FRESA journals:

I think the most interesting part of Project FRESA was the letter I wrote. It was the first time I wrote a letter to someone so important like the government of our state, California. (Mar Vista Elementary student)

When we sent the letter to the governor Gray Davis we asked him to tell people not to [use] pesticides.... They are still putting pesticides in some strawberry fields. I think he should take our advice. It would help a lot of workers and other people that work or live next to the field. People get sick because of the pesticides. (Mar Vista Elementary student)

My class wrote a letter to the governor to see what we could do about pesticides. When he responded he did not help. He only said how proud he was about us. All remained the same. (Mar Vista Elementary student)

In class, students discussed what directions the FRESA project should take next. The students reminded one another that César Chávez had struggled for decades to create real change for agricultural workers. They also realized that letters from children—even well-researched letters to the governor—wouldn't be enough. Michelle discussed with the students the ongoing nature of participating in the democratic process, "So even though we wrote once, and didn't get the response that you were expecting or hoping for, doesn't mean that we can't write again. And it doesn't mean that you can't keep on writing and expressing your opinions." "We can find adults who will listen to kids and then help them understand that they can take the message to the governor," proposed a fifth-grade girl.

Cognition

Community-connected learning and long-term research serve as a valuable context for sustained questioning, critical analysis, and academically rigorous teaching and learning that allow students to meet and exceed district and state standards.

First, the teachers felt that the kind of questioning encouraged by a long-term investigation was closer to the kind of learning that adults do—where one continually poses new questions as one learns, "where your questions never really get fully get answered because you always come up with new ones."

Second, the students' extensive background knowledge and passion about their subject led to deeper interest in and more extensive analysis of the topics studied.

Third, real-world situations give rise to more complex and challenging tasks than those assigned in more traditional classroom settings. Project FRESA students sought to convince legislators and businessmen to provide better working conditions for farm workers. Through their letter-writing exchanges with adults, who had differing opinions, and who were adept at employing statistics and skilled writing to argue their points, they sharpened their reading comprehension and persuasive writing skills.

The students continued writing letters to the strawberry companies, and continued talking in class about different ways to participate in the democratic process. After discovering which companies had fields located in Oxnard, the students investigated the companies' websites and decided to e-mail pressing questions such as: "How often do the workers receive breaks?" "Do they supply clean drinking water to the workers?" "Are there clean bathrooms on site?" "How much do you pay the workers per hour?" "How much do you pay the workers per box?" And many more important questions.

Many companies did not reply. One company replied with a four-page letter explaining and defending their working practices and citing the labor laws with which they complied. They also sent stickers, coupons, and pamphlets.

> These activities transformed the children into active, enlightened, empowered young citizens practicing civic responsibility, doing something about their concerns, practicing their freedom of speech, and participating in our democracy. (Amada Pérez, personal communication, January 15, 2003)

Project FRESA generated a tremendous amount of local cross-teaching. What the older students learned, they taught the younger students; what the research teams learned, they shared with the larger group. What one class worked on, they brought to the FRESA meetings to show the other class. And all the students discussed the findings with their parents. Teachers and students continued to consult with and learn from the parents about the growing cycle of strawberries and working conditions.

Project discussions extended beyond the local fields and into the global community. The children were able to use computers as one more way to communicate what they were learning. They created a partner class project with a class in Puerto Rico, and shared letters and cultural packages with their distant peers—the children and grandchildren of coffee-growers, many of whom had left agricultural work due to low wages. The children also became very interested in helping Ms. Singer create and promote the Project FRESA website.

Publishing on the Web and Community Sharing

When the students learned that their teachers were putting up a website, they chose their best work to display. "It made them work even harder because they wanted their artwork or poem or essay or quote to be selected. They put a lot more effort into it." Michelle commented. The first people to whom the children wanted to show the site were their families. Michelle showed them how to print webpages to share with people who didn't have computers at home. Jessica took her grandfather, who had worked in the fields for 35 years, to the public library to see the pages with the data from the questionnaires he had helped answer. Other families began going to the library in the evening, where the children taught them how to search online and showed their parents their writing, poetry, drawings, and research on the FRESA webpages.

> I think the parents were very surprised that this is something we were studying and that it was valuable enough to have a whole book about and a website for other people to see. (Michelle Singer, personal communication, February 16, 2003)

> The parents told us nobody had ever done a project like this before. They were amazed that the children were truly interested in their work—the work that they hoped their children never had to do. (Amada Pérez, personal communication, January 15, 2003)

Project FRESA forged new relationships between the parents and the school, and the children and their parents. "The children appreciated more the things the parents did for them. They would say, 'I appreciate

Tools

What is remarkable, given the extensive use of technology in the project, is that the teachers had only one computer in each of their classrooms. Although teachers and the students recognized that much more could have been done with better access to technology, some important lessons can be learned from the experience.

Teachers made maximum use of existing resources through careful classroom management and team work.

First, the teachers were able to maximize their use of technology through creative use of inexpensive hardware—a set of a half-dozen Alphasmart portable keyboards available for use at the school. The fifth-graders worked in teams with a single keyboard at each table, and with students taking turns in designated roles as composers, typists, and proofreaders.

Second, the teachers were highly skilled in organizing students to work in cross-age pairs or small grade-level teams. For example, to ensure that all students learned to use the different software programs, Michelle taught a small group of fifth-graders who volunteered to come to school early. This group taught their fifth-grade peers. The fifth-graders, in turn, took their third-grade buddies to the computer, one at a time, to tutor them in using the same programs.

how hard my parents have to work to buy me food'" (Amada Pérez, personal communication, January 15, 2003). Project FRESA also started new conversations between the parents and their children. During the November parent–teacher–student conferences, the parents of the fifth-graders spoke openly in expressing their wishes for their children, saying: "I want you to graduate from high school," "I want you to go to college," "I don't want you to have to work in the fields unless that is something you choose. I want you to have more options than I do." Michelle commented, "It really connected the kids to why it is so supremely important to the parents that they do well in school and that they behave and do their homework. Because their parents know that education is the way out." In class Michelle would hear the students say, "My parents believe in me." "This is what my parents want for me. And I'm smart enough I can do it." Michelle commented, "It gave them added resiliency to keep going."

As word of the FRESA website spread, the project grew. Children began corresponding via e-mail with students in Paraguay who had worked picking strawberries, and with strawberry growers in Chile who wanted to learn more about working conditions in the United States. Students continued their discussions about fertilizers and pesticides with children of strawberry growers in India. They were excited to learn from Ganesh, Swati, and other new Indian friends that the best strawberry seedlings are considered to be those imported from Oxnard. They also learned that small family farms gave the parents more control over how they grew strawberries. The Indian children were pleased to receive information from their new friends in California about growing strawberries organically. The children worked in teams to write their messages using portable Alphasmart keyboards and then upload their e-mails to the classroom computer at the end of the day.

The teachers, as part of their Telementor activities (see page 129 for a description of the CLMER-CABE Telementor Institute), also shared the Project FRESA webpages with other teachers and professors of education. Soon, Mar Vista Elementary students were corresponding with teachers at other California schools and with future teachers at the local university, stimulating the children's interest in college. The teachers passed e-mail questions about Project FRESA to the real experts—the students. The students responded to the future teachers' questions about life in a farm-working family, and to their requests for advice on organizing a classroom for community-connected learning. The students also recommended ways that teachers can raise difficult subjects such as racism with their students. They added new sections to the website in response to the teachers' and future teachers' questions, so that the site could become a teaching resource for professors and future teachers at the local university.

> They had never communicated with anybody before in Paraguay, or Chile, or India, or Puerto Rico, or even future teachers in Channel Islands not far from us. They were able to communicate about something that they were knowledgeable about and were willing to share, and here was a tool that could connect them to people who wanted to hear what they had to say. And that was a very unique experience. (Michelle Singer, personal communication, February 16, 2003)

> The project, the website, and correspondence online helped the students understand their parents, themselves, their communities, the people who represent them, their political system, their connection to the other places in the world. They communicated with children like them and children who are different from them, people who have things in common and people who don't. We discovered that the Internet is all about connecting people and connecting thoughts. (Amada Pérez, personal communication, January 15, 2003)

Project FRESA Continues to Grow

Since Project FRESA started, it has taken many new directions. Ms. Pérez's third-graders became Ms. Singer's fifth-graders. At the beginning of each school year, project "veterans" teach the students who are new to the school about FRESA. The questions about why only brown people work in the fields has led to an entire unit on racism. The children

have become a resource to other teachers not just on life in a field-working family but also on teaching and learning about racism.

Teachers sometimes wonder whether it's depressing for students to study real problems at school. Students' comments about Project FRESA make it clear that as they explore the problems in their communities, they also have a chance to talk about their dreams and ideals, and that participating in change is an exciting and affirming process.

A fifth-grader shares with pride the FRESA journals that she and a classmate entered in the schoolwide Young Authors' Fair as a portfolio of their writing during the year.

Pérez and Singer comment, "Students learned that even sweeter than strawberries' fragrance is the knowledge that they have power to take action and do something about injustices in their lives. And we teachers, with pressure from politicians and the public, know that curriculum content standards can still be met while engaging students in something much more meaningful and important." The students say it best:

> When I am working on Project FRESA I feel nice inside because I know that with all this work some day we will make César Chávez's dream come true. He wanted to have people that work at the fields to be paid more money. We are also helping them learn about how sometimes strawberry fields are dangerous. (Mar Vista Elementary student)

> I enjoy doing projects to help many people learn about strawberries and many chemicals they use at work like pesticides and other kinds of chemicals. I think Project FRESA will be a success in the future and the kids will make Project FRESA a famous Internet site. (Mar Vista Elementary student)

> I enjoyed this because it is exciting. It is exciting because I could express the feelings that I have in my head. (Mar Vista Elementary student)

Assessment and Identity Texts

Portfolios can help students demonstrate a wide range of academic, linguistic, and social proficiencies, not usually measured on traditional tests.

The students' FRESA Journals served as portfolios of their learning throughout the year. The teachers guided the students in saving samples of their work, including creative and expository writing in English and Spanish; reflections on the visits by the guest speakers and other key events; copies of letters they wrote and received; reports on pesticides and other issues they investigated; maps, drawings, and artwork; and other documentation of their roles in the project. They also encouraged the children to include the poetry, drawings, and reflective writing that expressed how they felt about their participation in the project.

As a result, each journal is a treasure, with original artwork or illustrated poems on nearly every other page. The front and back covers of each journal feature an original watercolor by the child depicting work in the strawberry fields.

The journals provided evidence of student learning. These hand-illustrated books were also important identity texts. Clearly, the children created their journals with great pride. The teachers report that these were the books that the children from both classes chose to represent them that year at the Mar Vista School Young Authors' Fair and asked to take home with them at the end of the year.

Project FRESA's Sweet Success

On November 13, 2000, California newspaper *The Desert Sun* reported on Project FRESA's many benefits, excerpted here:

■ *Increased academic performance and higher test scores.* Pérez attributes a portion of her students' 2000 standardized test scores gains to more effective, meaningful instruction. Teaching to the test is not the only way to make test scores go up.

■ *Parent participation.* Many parents began taking their children to the library to use computers. Some even saved up to buy computers for their homes.

■ *Higher aspirations.* Now that some Mar Vista students correspond with university students about how Project FRESA works in class, college is more tangible. (Lynn, 2000: www.thedesertsun.com/news/stories/local/974080923.shtml)

Clearly, through a thoughtful and critical approach to teaching and learning, these Oxnard, California, teachers helped their immigrant students feel more at home not only in their school but also in their new community and country as a whole.

Discussion Questions for Study Groups

1 Consider the following four areas cited by McCaleb (1997, pp. xii), who believes that community-connected learning and strong school–home–community collaborations can help promote a positive sense of personal identity in students and greatly enhance their possibilities of academic success. What did the Project FRESA teachers do to accomplish the following? What else can you do in each of these areas as you develop your own approaches to teaching?

a. Develop your classroom as a community of learners in which each student is valued.

b. Affirm each student's cultural and linguistic identity by using the knowledge he or she brings to school as the primary "text" for developing literacy.

c. Achieve collaborative relationships in a way that respects the students' family and community as valuable contributors to the educational process.

d. View one's role as a teacher not as an all-knowing authority, but as a human being in relationship with students and families and a co-investigator in a learning community.

2 The editors of *Rethinking Schools* assert that a social justice classroom is also an academically rigorous classroom, stating, "A social justice classroom offers more *to* students than do traditional classrooms and expects more *from* students" (in *Rethinking Our Classrooms: Teaching for Equity and Justice,* Vol. 1, 1994, p. 5). To what extent do you agree or disagree with this statement? For whom and under what conditions is it true? Support your answer with examples from your readings and your own experiences.

3 What are the lived realities of the students' families in the community where you live/teach? As a teacher, how can you use these in developing authentic writing where students not only develop literacy skills but also a sense of voice? How can these lived realities be central in the curriculum? What can you do, as a teacher, to learn more about the lives of your students?

4 The Internet provided Project FRESA students with connections to both human resources (people they came to know and corresponded with) and information resources (information they needed to have for their investigation). Consider an investigation you might do with your students that draws on their community and family knowledge. What role might each of these kinds of Internet resources play in your investigation? What role might each play in literacy development in your classroom?

CHAPTER 7

The Oral
History Project

*From a Shrug to "How Much
Time Do I Have, Mr. Green?"*

"Homework" took on a new meaning when students in a seventh-grade World History class used the methods of oral history to investigate their own family histories. Using audio, video, and computer technologies, the students became historians, recording their families' hopes, struggles, and accomplishments. In the process, they took control of their learning, made decisions about technology use, and learned their own roles as actors in and creators of history. History came alive, as students learned where they fit into large social structures. Through the project, they connected the dots of their own lives with the dots of history—encouraging them to see themselves as important young people with a future.

James Green, a social studies teacher at Slauson Middle School in Azusa, California, developed the oral history project for the 2001–2002 school year to help his students see history and themselves differently. The seventh-grade World History curriculum, required of all California students, is an in-depth survey that takes them from the fall of the Roman Empire in the fifth century to the heyday of the Industrial Revolution in the late 1800s. The course content is vast and requires students to absorb large amounts of material by reading. The subject matter is also far removed in time and place from the lives of 12-year-old students who come from immigrant and working-class families in an older community in the San Gabriel Valley (now subsumed by Los Angeles sprawl).[1]

James, in his fifth year of teaching, is the only African American teacher at the school. Having attended elementary, middle, and high school in East Los Angeles, he is no stranger to the challenges that face poor and ethnically diverse students in large urban districts. Three-quarters of the student population at Slauson are Latino, from families who have their roots in Mexico or other Central or South American countries. The other quarter is of African American, European, Asian, Pacific Island, Middle Eastern, and Native American descent.

> I'm looking at my kids and I'm seeing that some of these kids may not go to college. I want to defy the odds and make it so that instead of 2 percent going to college, it's 75 percent or more. I want to do my part. I want to give them everything I can give them. (James Green, personal communication, January 25, 2003)

To make the textbook facts more compelling, James involves his students in discussions, art projects, role-plays, readers' theater, and student presentations about the social, cultural, political, and economic contexts in which historical events take place—as well as their connections to modern-day events and life in Azusa. When students research the medieval period, James asks them to debate whether parallels exist between the Crusades and present-day terrorism. When students research the agricultural revolution, he asks, "Why do we have so much food in our local supermarkets? How did it get there? What does the agricultural revolution have to do with all that?" To help students do well in the world history course, and grasp unfamiliar concepts and vocabulary drawn from political science, history, anthropology, and economics, James supplements the text with films, visits to webpages, and books with photographs and drawings from the places they are studying. Still, for most of his students, many of whom don't read at grade level or for whom English is not a first language, the reading load can be overwhelming.[2]

A New School Year—A New Approach

James developed the oral history project after noting the disturbing way in which his students often simply shrugged when asked about their futures. He spent the entire summer of 2001 reflecting on his teaching of history. His reading included works by Paulo Freire, the Brazilian educator, who noted that members of marginalized communities often have a fatalistic attitude toward life, which can be changed through education. James thought about the impressionable, identity-forming age of his seventh-grade students and how important it is to recognize the lessons students take from school, consciously or unconsciously, and decided to design their instruction in identify-affirming ways. What can schools and teachers do, he wondered, to help students see that they can take action and have a positive impact on other people and the planet—not just stay on the sidelines of history?

That fall he launched an oral history project in which the students themselves become historians by interviewing their families about past events and ways of life. He encouraged the students to do plenty of questioning and reflection not only at home with their families but also in his world history class as they shared their findings, decisions, and experiences as historiographers. He was also intrigued by the idea of placing a range of educational technologies in the hands of the students to give them a more active role in the study of history.

James envisioned a several-week project that would run concurrently with the regular study of world history. Although much of the students' work could be done at home, he would also set aside class time for the students to report back and discuss what they were learning. Since the students would be actively involved in the documentation of history, the project would provide an ideal opening to deepen their understanding of the world history standards that focus on inquiry, perspective taking, and meaning making. The required "historical inquiry skills"—a set of skills that include constructing historical questions, comprehending and working with information from primary and secondary sources, reconciling conflicting accounts, and constructing explanations and accounts—are among the most interesting and important, yet challenging, skills for a history teacher to teach.

Students would record and write histories that may never have been recorded before, and take a more active role in class and in relationship to the subject they were studying. By learning more about the histories of their families, students would be documenting the lives of minority and working-class communities not usually reflected in textbooks. For at least several weeks, the project would place the students themselves and their families at the center of the curriculum.

Becoming Historians:
New Definitions and New Roles

To warm up the class, James talked about the concept of oral history from various angles. He asked students to write a reflective "Who Am I?" piece. He focused on the fact that ordinary people make history in big and small ways, even when they or others don't see their actions as significant at the time. James also described the important societal function played by those who record history. He intentionally chose an example of nontraditional historians, using the West African "griots" as an example of oral historians who were highly skilled and highly revered in their culture. Griots, selected carefully as children and trained by their elders to take on the role of historians, recite and remember genealogy and historical information for their villages. James spoke about the role students could play as historians and tradition-keepers, as "griots" in their own families and communities.

James outlined the broad requirements of the oral history assignment. The students would conduct individual investigations of their own histories and write reports with their findings and reflections. Additionally, students could present their investigations to the class as oral reports.

As a class, students decided on two broad research questions: (1) What kind of history can we find in our families? (2) Where do we come from? Within this broad framework, James encouraged the student historians to take an active role in making the decisions about what sources and research tools they would use, and more. They were given access to a wide range of technology tools, including audio cassette recorders that they could take home, a digital video camera that they could use at school to record the process, and time in the computer lab to view examples of other oral history projects on the Web and to write up their reports.

Early in the project, a student of European descent typed his ancestral names into a genealogy website and discovered that he

Oral History Internet Resources

History Matters

http://historymatters.gmu.edu/mse/oral/

This website offers a place for students and teachers to begin working with oral history interviews as historical evidence, including a guide to finding and using oral history online.

Step-by-step Guide to Oral History

www.dohistory.org/on_your_own/toolkit/oralHistory.html

Suggestions and strategies for collecting and preserving oral history are given. The website also addresses conceptual and ethical issues related to conducting and using oral histories.

Digital Historical Inquiry Project

http://dhip.org

The Digital Historical Inquiry Project is a consortium of schools and colleges of education interested in promoting historical inquiry in the preparation of preservice social studies teachers. Digital historical inquiry takes full advantage of current and emerging technologies to support approaches to learning history that stress developing inquiry, perspective taking, and meaning making over the current textbook-driven model.

came from a long line of German beer-makers. In less than a minute, he had identified nearly a dozen generations of relatives. To his class-mates, who looked on in awe, he explained that he had simply fol-lowed the prompts, typing in names and birthplaces. When other (non-European) students tried to follow suit, they didn't get the same results. This was a pivotal moment, with a fruitful class discussion about the reasons why.

To meet the challenge, non-European students had to refine their search strategies. They realized that to ask the right questions they needed background information, such as the full names of their relatives, the maiden names of female relatives, where their families had lived, birthplaces, and dates of birth.

James discussed the importance of critically evaluating Internet-based information, which can be incomplete or inaccurate. He showed the stu-dents various kinds of primary source material and historical documents on the Internet, but stressed that information found on the Internet is neither complete nor totally reliable. Although the students at first felt disappointed not to find out more about their families on the Internet, they realized later that they had an untapped wealth of knowledge available to them in their parents and family members. In their reports, almost every student revealed the value of talking with family mem-bers—as in the case of Anita, a student of Armenian descent who didn't find much information in either the library or the Internet. "The only place I got a lot of information," she said, "was from my family members: my mom, my grandmother, and my aunt."

In another key moment, the class found an online program for creating family trees. Students were initially fascinated by the tool but became frustrated when they tried to use it. The program allowed for only one kind of family structure—a traditional, symmetrical structure. Students found it discouraging that their family trees had so many empty boxes. "What if I don't live with my dad?" "My parents are divorced and I don't know as much information about one side of my family as the other." "Where can I put my step-sisters?" The Internet demon-stration software was "one size fits all," and not many of their families fit neatly.

When the students saw how much information some of their class-mates found about their families and how little others could find, they raised the question of which would be given more credit in class. Mr. Green was clear and insistent throughout the project that every student who went through the process they had talked about in class of becoming historians would get full credit. "The choice of how to define the question 'Who am I and what is my history' is for you to make," Mr. Green reassured them.

> I dealt spontaneously with many similar questions throughout the project. "Will I get less points if I don't have my father's side?" they asked. "No, you won't get fewer points," I always replied. "You can have two generations on your mom's side. Or you can have a single other family member. If you go through the process, you will get full credit and someone with details about the dates of birth and death of six generations won't get anything extra." I was very clear about that to everyone, and I think it freed the students up to talk in class. (James Green, personal communication, January 25, 2003)

At every point in the project, James sought to convey to the students that no one family was inherently more valuable than another. The students discussed the computer program's narrow assumptions about family structures and explored other ways to complete the task. The next day, James showed them a new tool—the AppleWorks Draw Program, which allowed them to create family trees of any size, dimension, or shape, for an infinite number of family configurations. The students worked in teams, creating individualized trees with sprawling branches, or criss-crossed vines, beginning wherever the students chose to begin— with their own generation, or as many generations back as they chose, on one side of the family, on two sides, or more. When the program doesn't fit, James told them, find some way to use a powerful tool to find a fit that works for you.

Seventh-graders meet in the computer lab to conduct historical research on the Internet and to use a drawing program to design individualized family trees.

Interviewing Family Members— Learning to Question

In the classroom, students prepared to interview their families. James reviewed strategies that oral historians use to gather information: how to design interview questions, take notes and organize information, and use tape-recorders to capture the voices and later transcribe the interviews.

When the students drafted interview questions, it was clear that they were operating with a narrow definition of history. With few exceptions, questions fell into three categories: Who in my family (1) fought in wars, (2) fought for liberation, or (3) healed others. In the six years they had taken social studies, students had learned what kinds of stories are worthy of being told and what counts as history. James encouraged students to question their assumptions and helped them brainstorm open-ended questions that began with phrases such as, "What do you remember about. . . ," "What was life like when. . . ," and "Tell me about. . . ."

Although the oral history assignment was given at school and the questions drafted in class, the real work took place at home, where students interacted in new ways with their families. As historiographers, students discovered the value in identifying and seeking out the "tradition-keepers" in their families. Henry explained, "I was excited to get the names of my mother's grandparents and some others, because my grandmother Tita keeps a little notebook with all the names and dates of her family." Once students got started, they interviewed even distant

Parents

The project helped forge new relationships between parents and school and encouraged greater communication at home between children and their parents. According to Mr. Green, "The students are talking with their parents. The parents are learning from the questions that their children asked the grandparents. I saw that when this becomes part of the history curriculum, the families talk."

The talk at home has also led to greater interaction between the parents and the school. James points out that this is important because "too often parents don't feel comfortable coming to the school of their middle school students."

"There's much more communication between myself and the parents. The kids have been talking at home about what's happening at school. And the parents know that the kids have been talking at school about what's happening at home. The parents are in much closer touch with me now. I even have parents volunteer to coach the basketball team" (James Green, personal communication, January 25, 2003).

relatives. With parental support, they made telephone calls or used the Internet to reach relatives in other countries. "On my father's side it was a little more difficult because most of his family members were born in different places in Peru," explained Henry.

The students' excitement mounted as they reported on their searches. "Should I stop now, Mr. Green?" they asked. More than once he told them, "Go as far as you want to go." The students learned the possibilities and limitations of each of the technology tools they were using, and had mixed reactions to the use of tape-recorders. Although some students thoroughly enjoyed capturing the voices of their family members and listening to them again and again as they transcribed the tapes, others found the transcription process tedious. A number of students noticed that their families spoke much more freely when they weren't speaking into a recorder. James suggested alternative approaches to foster flexibility in his students and to encourage their problem solving. Instead of capturing every word on tape or taking notes in front of the person, they might listen carefully and later return to their rooms to write down what they learned, or recount events into the tape-recorder with questions they still had.

This led to an unexpected and valuable outcome. As time went on, James observed that students were getting used to holding unanswered questions in their minds.

> We talked about how data gathering and filling in the gaps in one's knowledge is an ongoing process . . . a really interesting skill. I tell them, "You'll learn a bit of information, and this bit of information is a little gem. Put it on the shelf. Take it down when you need it." (personal communication, January 25, 2003)

Although some students had initially balked at doing oral histories, thinking it was not challenging, they admitted later that it was more difficult than expected.

Returning to School with New Questions and Information

Once the students began their home interviews, there were other changes. Students started coming to James's class before school at 7 A.M.—students who may not have been scheduled to come to his room until third, fourth or fifth period. Each day, students discovered new details that they couldn't wait to tell their teacher. "They told me, 'Mr. Green, my great uncle rode with Pancho Villa in the Spanish-American War.' And, 'Mr. Green, I never knew I had uncles in Peru'" (personal communication, January 25, 2003).

The students also asked new questions at school about the events and places they were learning about at home. "Mr. Green, what is the Battle of the Bulge? What is D-Day?" asked a student whose grandfather fought in World War II. James encouraged the students to share their stories and raise these questions during the world history class, when he helped them use the resource materials on classroom shelves and in school libraries to locate cities and look up the events. Often James was able to connect their stories to the history they were studying.

Telling Untold Stories

Students indeed discovered people in their families who had "fought in wars, fought for liberation, healed others," or were otherwise recognized publicly for their accomplishments. A number of students found relatives who had excelled in their fields or who had served as community leaders. Robert told the class, "I was excited when my mom told me that my uncle was a pro soccer player." Summer found that she was directly descended from a Cherokee tribal leader. Selene delighted the class with details of a relative whose clothes and artifacts are in a Mexican museum: "I have a great-great-grandpa who is really famous in Mexico. He was a priest who was killed because of jealousy. They say that in the museum over there you can see the blood stains on his clothes and they look like they're wet, really real."

Cognition

Too often students, particularly those who attend underperforming schools in urban areas, are expected to passively absorb history as a set of facts, dates, and names. Not surprisingly, these are quickly forgotten. This portrait illustrates a more active approach to teaching history in which students are enabled to engage in active inquiry and build on the funds of knowledge in their families and communities. In this way, the process of creating and interpreting history is demystified.

It was in the process of doing their own oral histories that Mr. Green felt that the students began to understand history. To get at history, one needs to go beyond yes/no, factual questions, and learn to probe—to think like a historian. "The project explained something to them. The students came to understand that all kinds of interesting things happen historically that never make it into the history texts. Once you know that, it becomes much more interesting to look for original source material or documents that might not have made it into the textbook, and to consider issues that might not be discussed in the text, or to speculate about how things got that way, or to look for other perspectives that may not be represented. Our investigation of our family 'case studies' taught the students firsthand about the nature of recorded history" (personal communication, January 25, 2003).

The students shared stories about family members confronting challenges and standing up for what they believed in. One student admired her grandmother, who insisted on marrying the man she loved even though he was from a lower social class. Adrian reported, "I learned that my grandfather was one of the instructors to help build the first roads in Mexico."

Other students described how families passed down knowledge, helping to preserve cultural traditions. Aleira reported on "the important role Mariachi music has had through my family's history." Her classmates viewed historical photos of the musicians in silver-studded *charro* outfits and learned how, during the Mexican revolution, Mariachis wandered from town to town, singing songs of revolutionary heroes and enemies, carrying news from one place to another.

The students uncovered stories of people in their families who had been divorced, had run into trouble with alcohol, or otherwise had taken paths that the parents hoped their children would not take. One girl confided to the class, "On my grandfather's side, they weren't very good with relationships, but they were very good at making money." Yet these accounts were balanced by those of relatives whom students felt exhibited more admirable qualities.

Resources—The Power of Oral History

A number of museums and organizations offer oral history collections where students can see and hear firsthand accounts of those who witnessed social and historical movements and contributed to social change.

The U.S. Holocaust Memorial Museum
http://www.ushmm.org/research/collections/
The museum's oral history collection is one of the largest for Holocaust testimonies in the world, with audio and video accounts of those who experienced, witnessed, or perpetrated the events of the Holocaust.

The Schomburg Center for Research in Black Culture
http://www.nypl.org/research/sc/sc.html
Information by and about people of African descent throughout the world, including a video oral history gallery and other audio and video resources.

Putting the Movement Back into Civil Rights Teaching
http://www.civilrightsteaching.org/links.htm
The Teaching for Change website provides links to oral histories and other web resources for teaching about the Civil Rights Movement.

Other resources can be found by searching for "oral history" on educational websites. GEMS, the Gateway for 21st Century Skills, at www.thegateway.org, has a vast array of educational resources linked to K-12 standards. MarcoPolo, at www.marcopolo-education.org, includes high-quality, standards-based content. Edutopia, at www.edutopia.org, features resources and powerful examples of teaching and learning in the Digital Age.

The students speculated about people who might have been leaders if they had be given the opportunity. They reviewed obstacles to success, including a lack of formal education (a critical discussion in a group with a high dropout rate), scarcity of economic resources, and the challenges often faced by immigrant, indigenous, or other minority groups. For example, Henry described a relative who ran for political office in Azusa, but who didn't have the money to continue his campaign. Just to place one's name on the ballot cost $800—far more at the time than a month's rent. This led to discussions about material that doesn't make it into history books: the reasons why minority-group individuals who were significant leaders have not been described in the history texts, and how opportunities may have been closed to people from poor or working-class backgrounds—people these students could grow up to become.

Changing Relationships at School and at Home

The students shared dimensions of their families that their classmates, and sometimes they themselves, had never known existed. As James commented, "What it did for all of us is that you find that you can't stereotype or generalize easily. It's a dangerous thing to make up scenarios about how a person is beyond what you see in them" (personal communication, January 25, 2003).

Students began to see one another not only as individuals but also as members of an extended family, and in the process the students became more willing to tell their stories. As James explains, "The students lost embarrassment about who they are. We learned how fragile we all are. We became much more interested in learning about one another, and much more respectful of one another" (personal communication, January 25, 2003).

James saw the importance of making the oral history project part of the official curriculum of the school. "The students tell me that they would not have asked those questions at home on their own, but now because they are part of a school assignment they feel freedom and a sense of space to do so."

The students valued their roles as historiographers in their families. Several students reported that they were proud to be the first to write down parts of their family's history. The parents were extremely supportive and told James that they were learning from the questions their children were asking grandparents and great-aunts and great-uncles.

Creating the iMovie for the Open House

Every student had class time for sharing stories. Some brought folded poster-board displays mounted with family photos, or family tree collages, or important letters, documents, anecdotes, or student artwork. With the students' permission, these remained on display in the classroom. When the day of the presentations came, the students referred to beautiful graphs, flowcharts, arrows that showed connections between people, and photos. Significantly, their definition of history was changing: One girl introduced her presentation saying, "I found a lot of history in my family."

James used the school's digital video recorder to capture the entire experience of researching and presenting the oral histories. He and the class transferred the video footage to iMovie, a technology available through Apple Computer that allowed them to edit the video and add an audio track, titles, subtitles and credits. The first part of the movie was set to music and showed every student in James's World History classes working in the classroom and computer lab, sharing with others in cooperative groups, engaged, talking, and teaching others. The second part of the movie showed the class presentations. This part required more complex preparation and recording of the sound track. Because not all of the parents spoke English, the students decided to include native-language voiceovers in the reports section of the movie, so the parents could understand.

Tools

James did not promote uncritical acceptance of technology. He encouraged his students to critique the effectiveness of each tool in achieving different tasks, and to reject them in favor of other alternatives when necessary, or to be creative in adapting them to suit the goals of the project.

On several occasions, the teacher and students decided against the use of certain technologies or tools in particular contexts because they interfered with rather than enhanced the task at hand (such as the use of tape-recorders when speaking with some family elders). Some tools had limitations or assumptions that made them inappropriate for the tasks that this group of under-served students from nontraditional families hoped to accomplish (such as reliance on the Internet for family research on immigrant Latino families or the use of genealogical draw tools that assumed traditional family structures). However, students also used technology in creative ways to accomplish their goals (such as adding Spanish-language soundtracks to an English-language iMovie so that it could be shared with their parents).

Through the project, the students became more critical and creative technology users, aware of the assumptions that may be part of the use of a particular technology.

Resources—Digital Storytelling

Both Macintosh and PC platform computers come with software that allows students to create movies using video footage or still photos with voice-over narrations. Presentation or slide show programs also offer possibilities for adding voice. With these new technologies students can become multimedia producers in schools or after-school programs, telling stories through digital media in a wide range of content areas.

Helpful resources and examples can be found on the Web, including: Center for Digital Storytelling, at www.storycenter.org. This nonprofit organization assists young people and adults to use digital media to tell meaningful stories from their lives. Digital Underground Storytelling for Youth (DUSTY) at http://oaklanddusty.org also provides valuable examples. DUSTY is an after-school technology and literacy program for urban students that combines popular culture, writing and digital media.

For a list of other digital storytelling sites, compiled by the Learning, Equity, Achievement and Reform Network (LEARN), see www.orillas.org/storytelling. This annotated list highlights examples of community digital storytelling, which integrates aspects of popular education, oral history, creative writing, and digital media in telling the stories of individuals and communities. Children and adults use materials from their lives (e.g., photographs, letters, drawings, newspaper clippings, voice recordings, etc.) to "tell their own truths in their own voices."

The parents came to the Open House in larger numbers than usual. James and the students had made multiple copies of the class iMovie, with a copy in each computer. When the parents arrived the video was playing in a loop at each of the six computer stations. A group of parents clustered around each of the computers, eager to see in action the project they had heard so much about from their children.

> The parents seemed amazed and overwhelmed that this is taking place in a school classroom. That a classroom is no longer just about learning out of the textbook and doing your school homework—it's about using technology at this level, creating films, having the students stand up and make presentations. They didn't know that that their kids were capable of this kind of work. They realized perhaps for the first time that their children were multidimensional and had many talents. It's not Johnny who comes home and watches TV and plays with his friends and asks what there is to eat. It's Johnny the student who is learning a lot. (James Green, personal communication, January 25, 2003)

Changes in the World History Class

After the oral history project, James noticed that his students' study skills had improved significantly. The students were more prepared to complete long-term course assignments, from beginning to end. "Now the students don't even question that each project during the year will have an investigation, followed by a written and oral report. They have completed each with confidence" (personal communication, January 25, 2003). James commented that the students used to make lots of excuses about why they didn't get their work done. Now the students are "a little more arrogant, in an appealing way, and more responsible," and rise to his expectations in turning in their work.

James also noticed improved academic skills, noting that his students are more able to offer informed opinions on the critical thinking questions that are included in each chapter of their history text. These questions begin with phrases such as "If you were . . . ," "What do you think . . . ," and "What do you believe the reasons were. . . ." The students used to be very reluctant to offer their own opinions. Now they are eager to speculate and give insightful responses. They also remember more about what they read and study. One set of students working in a small group on a historical time-line activity later that spring were able to share with their teacher and classmates detailed information about the Toltec and Olmec civilizations in Mexico. These Latino students added, "We may have some Aztec blood in our families."

Parents—Identity Texts

An important "identity text" that resulted from the project was the creation of the class iMovie with the bilingual soundtrack shown during Open House to the parents. This video provided important documentation of the project and was shown not only to the students and parents but also to teachers and administrators. The video was a source of pride for the students as well as the families who had participated in the oral history project. During the Open House a group of parents clustered around each of the computers, eager to see in action the project they had heard so much about from their children and to which they had contributed.

"The parents were glued to the video. The parents were so impressed and so proud that they were featured. You could see it in their eyes and hear it in their voices. It's pride on two levels. There's the family level. That 'Yes, here we are. We're the Gonzales clan.' That's one. But there's also a pride in their children that's even more important. The pride that their child pulled this off, something that no one in their family has done before, and they think that their child is already on the road to becoming a great human being—and they are" (James Green, personal communication, January 25, 2003).

After gathering oral histories in her extended family, a seventh-grade "historian" shares her findings and reflections on the research process in a written report.

The seventh-graders were also learning to question. James attributes their abilities to ask more probing historical questions to their experiences in interviewing their parents. In the family interviews, the students started out by asking straightforward questions to elicit geographical information or other facts, such as "Where did you grow up?" As the oral history project continued, they became skilled at asking follow-up and relational questions. For example, if their parents answered that they had grown up in Mexico City, the students would try to figure out what else was happening in Mexico at that time, or ask if their parents had climbed the pyramids, drawing on other historical and geographical knowledge.

Their new interest in asking questions led to dramatic changes in the kinds of class discussions James could have with the students. "Now the students are curious and ask all kinds of new questions," James noted. The students approached their course text differently, with a new appreciation of the personal experiences of those living in the periods they studied.

> This project opens the kids up to the fact that history is not just a lot of dates in a book. When we look again at the textbook, we try to personalize these people and figure out why they act that way. (James Green, personal communication, January 25, 2003)

Now, when the students tackle a new period in history, students themselves seek connections to their own lives. The students have become more aware of the divisions of labor and social organization in different societies, and they love to speculate about what life would have been like for them in another era. When the class studied Asian dynasties, with their societal hierarchies and military rankings, the students asked, "Where would you be, Mr. Green?" "Where would I be?"

Their questions served as a welcome point of departure for new discussions about the concepts they needed to master to meet the world history curriculum standards. "We need to consider the degree of social mobility; it's likely you'd be doing what your parents do," James suggested. "Your mom owns a store? A person who owns a store is a merchant."

"Hey everyone, my mom is a merchant," the student announced to his classmates. Other students relayed stories about family members who drove trucks and speculated with pride that they might have been in "commerce"; those who had stories to tell about relatives in the military felt proud to imagine that they might have been related to "warriors."

As students sought to leap from their own period of history to the periods studied in class, James posed questions such as "Compare the Ming Dynasty to twenty-first-century U.S. life." Students were more interested in and able to respond to questions comparing two or more historical periods—the kinds of questions that are prevalent on the World History Advanced Placement exam and other exams taken by college-bound students.

During these discussions, James found that students now had a mental framework for approaching the study of unfamiliar historical periods and for understanding key concepts needed to study each era in history. The oral history project had helped them understand basic sociological and historical concepts. Their own family and school connections had given them a structure in which to understand other clan, tribal, and community networks as well as social, political, and economic networks. The students were now more able to see the different eras as distinct and meaningful, and had begun to see the options open to people of different eras and the decisions that people had taken.

> As a teacher, you want to make it seem as though the people you are studying are distinct and individual and have contributed to the world. The oral history project gives students the notion that they're different too, that they are part of a global historical movement. (James Green, personal communication, January 25, 2003)

Going Forth

James concluded that the oral history project offered his students a chance to connect to history in a personal way. By helping students understand basic sociological and historical concepts, they were able to then go forth and absorb information about distant events in time and place quickly and proficiently.

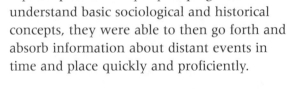

The students' written reports and family displays are featured on the walls of Mr. Green's classroom and are used throughout the year as a point of departure for discussions about world history.

What's more, the pride that students developed in their families and heritage fostered goals beyond the achievement of state standards. "The oral history project helped bring me closer to my family," Nathan commented. Pride echoed through the students' comments at the end of the project. Said one student:

> This project was totally worth my time, effort, and hard work. My favorite part of my oral history project was that I learned that my great-great-great-grandfather was the chief of the Cherokee tribe for 15 years. Knowing I was Indian I never thought my family would be a part of history, but now I know my grandfather will always be remembered. After I completed my history project I was proud of my family. I was proud of my ethnicity and religion, and most of all I was proud of myself. (Seventh-grade student)

James's greatest reward as a teacher came from this change in the way the students saw themselves. He says that before he started the oral history project, he would say to students, "Tell me about yourself," and students would reply, "I grew up in Azusa and that's it."

Now they answer, "How much time do I have, Mr. Green?"

Discussion Questions for Study Groups

1 The notion of youth engaging in oral history projects was made popular in the 1960s through the "Foxfire" concept where youth from a rural area of the Appalachian Mountains documented their community's history by tape-recording and transcribing interviews with community elders about past events and ways of life (www.foxfire.org). James adapted and broadened the concept for his urban and school-based realities, and encouraged the students to do plenty of questioning and reflection not only with their families but also in his world history class as they shared their findings, decisions, and experiences as historiographers. How might you incorporate oral history, community narratives, or family interviews into the subjects you teach?

2 Antiracist educator, Enid Lee, describes a classroom she visited where the teacher consciously used language to help to build positive identities in the students. The math teacher would say to his students, "We mathematicians have many ways of solving problems. How would you as a mathematician yourself solve this?" (See Lee, Menkart, & Okazawa-Rey [Eds.], *Beyond Heroes and Holidays,* "Anti-Racist Education: Pulling Together to Close the Gaps," p. 30.) Lee suggests that one of the ways that teachers can encourage success is by treating every student in the class like a scientist, a mathematician, an author, or a historian. What did James do to encourage his students to see themselves as historians? What might you do as a teacher to encourage your students to see themselves as scientists, historians, authors, or mathematicians?

Endnotes

1. James Green developed the oral history project through participation in the CLMER-CCCE Tele-mentor Project, a professional development project of the Center for Language Minority Education and Research at California State University, Long Beach, under the direction of David Ramirez and Kevin Rocap, in collaboration with the California Consortium of Critical Educators.

2. To further help the students, James (with school permission) created a new elective at the middle school—a semester-long course on reading. He encouraged all his world history students to enroll so that they would have an extra period for free reading. During this period the texts could include a wide range of enticing materials, including the morning newspaper, novels and historical fiction, biographies, and other high-interest books and magazines. Through offering more pleasurable reading about events beyond their everyday experience and an opportunity to talk about what they were reading, the course helped rekindle an interest in reading, while also immersing the students in increasingly complex language and thought.

CHAPTER 8

The Biographies Project

Opportunities for Math—and Change—in the School Library

Coauthored with Enid Figueroa

Thanks to expert and well-prepared teachers, a group of primary-level California students sharpened their math skills and learned the power of communication to change their world. They also delved deeply into issues of fairness and equity by analyzing biographical collections in an innovative learning project that took them from the classroom to the largest public library in San Francisco. During the 1997–98 school year, teachers at Almond Avenue School in Livermore, California, involved their bilingual first-, second-, and third-graders in a global networking exchange. Through the exchange, the students and their teachers conducted an investigation that integrated math with language arts and science curricula, and provided ample opportunities for questioning and learning.

The multilingual "Connecting Math to Our Lives/Conectando las Matemáticas a la Vida"[1] (CMTOL) global learning network project invited students to (1) explore how math is used in their families and communities, (2) use math and data analysis skills to investigate community or social concerns, and (3) take action to promote greater equity in the world around them.

The CMTOL project announcement, sent out to schools at the beginning of the 1997–98 school year, provided examples of how math can be used as a tool to help students not only understand and interact with their world, but also to take action to make the world a better place. The activities suggested in the "Promoting Equity at Our School Site" section of the project announcement highlight opportunities for students and teachers to take purposeful action at their own school campus. In one suggested activity, students categorize the biographies in the school library on the basis of race, class, disability, or gender using percentages, fractions, and bar graphs to analyze and describe the library's biography collection.

Project Planning and Design

In January, 1998, Patti Purcell McLain, resource teacher and Project LinC (Language in Community) coordinator at Almond Avenue School, met with the school's three primary-level (grades 1, 2, and 3) teachers, Mrs. Kerry Barger, Mr. Peter Hetherington, and Ms. Kerry Mattimore, to plan their students' participation in the Connecting Math to Our Lives Biographies Project. The teachers at Almond Avenue, a school that offers second-language classes to all students, welcomed the opportunity that this computer-networking project would provide to partner with another bilingual school and enable their students to use their Spanish. Classes at Fairmont Elementary, a two-way bilingual immersion school in San Francisco where all students study in both English and Spanish, also expressed interest in exploring issues of representation. The two schools, located on opposite sides of San Francisco Bay, decided to conduct parallel local investigations of the biographies in their school libraries and then compare and discuss their results online.

The investigation would challenge the students at Almond Avenue to think in new ways about a question of fundamental interest to young children: What is fair and what is not? It would also touch on an issue that the teachers dealt with each year in their culturally and linguistically diverse schools: how to involve everyone at the school in ensuring that their school is fair and welcoming to all. Almond Avenue, a science magnet school, draws students from widely dispersed neighborhoods, and a number of the students had not studied together in school the previous year.

Before the Almond Avenue teachers presented the project to the students, they communicated via e-mail and phone with the Fairmont teachers to plan the exchange. With a sense of excitement, Patti and the Almond Avenue teachers felt they were stepping out into new territory. In asking students to consider issues of representation in the school's biography collection, the teachers would be taking emerging readers in their primary-level classes into a new section of the library—one that contained nonfiction books and volumes far larger than most the children had ever read before. The teachers would also be asking the students to apply concepts to which they had been introduced in both their science classes (hypothesizing, observing, assessing the generalizability and validity of data, and drawing conclusions) and math classes (sorting, classifying, and graphing) to complex social problems. Clearly, the pedagogical assumptions of Patti and her colleagues diverged markedly from those embodied in scripted reading programs that tightly control children's access to "nondecodable texts" (see Chapter 2).

These experienced teachers planned the classroom management in great detail, designing cooperative learning activities and preparing easy-to-use data collection forms and charts for the students to use in the investigation. At the same time, they expected that the project design would evolve, and stayed in close touch each step of the way to modify the project as it progressed.

The teachers realized immediately that they would need to work more with their young students to explain the term *biography*. After rereading with their students the section on "stories about people" from their adopted reading series, the teachers at Almond Avenue developed a joint writing activity with the teachers at Fairmont to ensure that students at both schools understood the concept of a biography.

Writing Their Own Biographies

The teachers at Almond Avenue had their students work in pairs to interview one another and write biographies of their classmates. The students, through the stories they had read of famous African Americans in the reading text, now had a working definition of a biography and brainstormed possible interview questions. Soon, as the students interviewed their partners, the room was alive with conversation. "Where were you born?" "What things are you good at?" "What do you want to be when you grow up?" The students "researched" and "published" the biographies of their peers with great care, serving as both authors and illustrators. During their art class, for example, the students posed so that their partner could draw a portrait for the cover of the book. When finished, the students' biographies were included in the classroom's lending library. With delight at seeing their names and the names of their classmates in print, the students took down from the shelves the biographies they had written, and shared them among themselves, reading and rereading the stories of their lives.

Cognition

Usual curricular divisions in schools teach math with science, in isolation from the social studies and language arts curriculum. When mathematics is instead taught "across the curriculum," multiple opportunities arise to use mathematics to uncover stereotypes, understand history, and examine issues of inequality (Peterson, 2001).

Too often, the development of students' math skills is conducted only through paper-and-pencil exercises and is limited to performing discrete calculations. Students later have trouble applying what they have learned. In cross-curricular project-based learning, students have greater opportunities to apply the concepts and operations to which they have been introduced in their math and science classes to more complex social problems than those usually presented to children this age. These real-world activities are both demanding, in that students are challenged to justify and explain their conclusions, and highly motivating for students who experience firsthand the importance of data gathering and analysis skills in understanding the nature of social realities and ultimately in making a difference in their world.

The now experienced "biographers" started on their second set of biographies—about the life of a student they had been paired with from the partner school in San Francisco. The student authors again formulated interview questions, but instead of conducting face-to-face interviews, they sent their questions via e-mail. Then they composed short biographies, sharing their stories electronically with the students they had been paired with to make sure they got the details right.

> The students saw themselves not only as writers but also as "scientists." We were impressed with the questions they raised about the data-gathering process. When the e-mail questions came in from San Francisco, the kids were trying to figure out how to respond to the question "Do you play soccer?" "We could say yes," they said, "but that might give the idea that we're really good at it, and we're really not!" "Would they ever know?" another student asked. This led to a deeper discussion about the challenges involved in framing questions and interpreting data. The students wondered, "How do you know the data is correct if you don't actually see it for yourself or see something firsthand?" (Patti McLain, personal communication, October 29, 2002)

The students used the information gathered to introduce their distant partners to their local classmates. Even at this early stage, the project had advanced beyond typical "pen-pal" exchanges in that students had a clear focus on both the goals and substantive nature of the collaboration.

Learning to Sort

Before the classes headed to their school libraries, teachers at both schools were careful to define the terms the students needed to undertake the project. Together, they created a simple data-collection form for the students' use in sorting the books, with columns for the students to indicate the gender, ethnicity and profession/occupation of the person described in the biography. The teachers at Almond Avenue brought their classes together in a series of practice sessions in one of the classrooms to explain why a common data-gathering instrument

The exploration of books in the classroom, school, and community libraries led students to read more and to talk more about books. A native English-speaking student and a native Spanish-speaking student compare impressions of a book they have both read.

would be helpful and to give the students guided practice in using the form to classify biographies.

The students were intrigued by the premise of the investigation and that there might be differences in the way different groups were represented in the schools' biography collections. Children resonated right away with the concept of "fairness" and anticipated discovering which kinds of people were included in the library books and which groups were "left out." The students pored over the biographies that the teachers had brought to the classroom for them to practice with and soon they clamored to add a new category to the investigation. "They were most interested in knowing if the person described in the biography lived around them, was here now, and they were quite surprised that most of the people were dead. The children created a new classification: 'Dead or alive'" (Patti McLain, personal communication, October 29, 2002). The biographies that the children had authored and added to the classroom library were all about people who were very much alive. In contrast, the biographies from the school library appeared to include a preponderance of people who had died. The teachers guided the students in adding new columns to their data-gathering forms to include this important information.

The sorting tasks weren't straightforward for the 6-, 7- and 8-year olds. As Patti noted, "It became apparent that the children had really never heard of most of the people in the books." Until third grade, the students read stories, folktales, and fiction, and were not "scheduled" to read much nonfiction until the upper elementary years. The teachers saw the project as an excellent opportunity to expose students to, and create interest in, the important genre of nonfiction books. They also saw opportunities to introduce the students to new skills they would need in the upper grades

Resources

Connecting Math to Our Lives/Conectando las Matemáticas a la Vida Project Website: www.orillas.org/math. The CMTOL webpages include a range of project examples conducted by K–12 students to investigate equity issues and to connect math to their lives, and an online tour explaining the project's link to collaborative critical inquiry.

Teaching Math across the Curriculum: Peterson, B. (2005) Teaching math across the curriculum. In E. Gutstein & B. Peterson (Eds.), *Rethinking mathematics: Teaching social justice by the numbers* (pp. 9–15). Milwaukee, WI: Rethinking Schools. This is an excellent article on teaching mathematics from a cross-disciplinary and critical perspective. Author Bob Peterson writes, "'Number numbness' among students has its roots in a curriculum that rarely encourages students to link math and history, math and literature."

when doing research in nonfiction books, such as taking notes and scanning for information. They noticed that the students were relying primarily on picture clues—clues that sometimes didn't give enough information or proved misleading. Relying on picture cues to determine "what the person was famous for," or even for the deceptively simple category of "gender," led the students on occasion to jump to the wrong conclusions:

> For example, a biography about Jimmy Carter had a picture of him working in the Habitat for Humanity Project. The children first guessed that he was a builder. I also remember the kids looking at someone with a wig—Benjamin Franklin—and thinking it was a girl. I remember the wig so vividly. They thought for sure he was a girl who was a beautician. (Patti McLain, personal communication, October 29, 2002)

The teachers saw a "teachable moment" for directing the students' attention to other kinds of clues to the content, and for teaching students to scan the text of the book in search of specific information. The students appreciated how much they could discover by skimming a biography, its table of contents, and its chapter headings for names, places, dates and other textual clues to the identity of the person.

The questions raised during the sorting process led to other new learning as well. In contrast to the simple sorting tasks many primary students perform, these students were grappling with the difficult decisions that social scientists make, such as how to create good data-collection instruments and how to represent categories of data that are not mutually exclusive. This project raised new questions about classification that don't always come up when students are taught sorting and graphing skills using a math text and classroom manipulatives. Typical graphing tasks for young children include sorting colored blocks or creating graphs based on simple surveys on such topics as the children's favorite flavors of ice cream. Most exercises ask young students to classify objects with obvious and discrete qualities, with activities such as placing the blue blocks in one pile and the red blocks in another, then counting them. Or they might use a Venn diagram to show overlap between two or three categories.

Children working in cooperative teams use both textual and picture clues to investigate the biography collections.

Sorting natural and social phenomena is much less straightforward, the students discovered.

> The children found that some people were more than one thing. For example, Leonardo da Vinci was an artist, inventor, and writer. They were not sure how to keep track of this, yet it seemed to be very interesting information to the children. It seemed to fit with "When I grow up I want to be a . . . ," to which children of this age relate. The discussions helped broaden the children's thinking about what they want to do and be when they grow up. (Patti McLain, personal communication, October 29, 2002)

The children also thoughtfully discussed how to categorize a person's race or ethnicity. Each new exercise in categorizing the biographies raised new and provocative topics for classroom dialogue.

The students struggled with what terms to use when discussing and categorizing race and ethnicity. Patti McLain remembers the students commenting that "Martin Luther King was black, but was also African American." The commonly used terms *black* and *white* led the children first to explore skin color as a basis for categorizing the people they found in their books. Yet when they examined the range of skin tones in their own class and compared their colors of skin, they had trouble distinguishing white, light brown, brown, and so on. The children realized that skin color doesn't fall into neat or natural categories.

Another challenge the students faced in recording ethnicity is that they could often identify people of European descent or African American descent from the pictures and photos but they had difficulty determining the ethnicity of other people. Patti remembers that the children examined a series of biographies about baseball players and had no trouble identifying the ethnic background of Willie Mays or Babe Ruth.

> But when I added a book about Orlando Cepeda, they became confused. In California someone who looks like Orlando Cepeda might be a native speaker of Farsi, Tagalog, Spanish, or another language and could be from any of a variety of cultures or countries. (Patti McLain, personal communication, October 29, 2002)

Gathering data on ethnicity presented a challenge for young students, yet the teachers felt this was an important category to include. They reviewed with the students how to find information about ethnicity, along with other cultural and linguistic clues to the identity of the person, in the text of the biographies rather than from overreliance on the pictures in the books.

The teachers realized that the level of sophistication and complexity of not only the math and data gathering but also the discussions about equity would naturally depend on the developmental levels of the students. Nevertheless, they welcomed the opportunity to raise issues of equity and fairness with even the very young students at the school. Children are inherently interested in what's fair, the teachers concluded, as they observed their students' sustained interest in using math to explore issues of representation. The idea of being "left out" or excluded is one that related to the students' personal experience, and the children wanted to know whether entire groups of people might be "left out" of the books in the libraries. As the students progressed in the biographies investigation, they continued their discussion about "who gets included and who gets left out." "The children definitely thought that if you're going to make a library, the books should be about everybody, not just one group" (Patti McLain, personal communication, October 29, 2002).

Visit to the School Library

Finally, the students were ready to visit their school libraries to count and sort the biographies. With their revised list of categories in hand, the students scoured library shelves for biographies. Working in teams, they counted and classified the biographies to create their graphs. Analyzing each book was a multistep process. After filling out a form for each biography analyzed, the students added their data to large wall charts, placing mini-figures they had drawn to represent the people described in the biographies.

By making the procedures clear and the steps of the project concrete, the teachers found ways to "lower the threshold" for the young students into a sophisticated real-world analysis with some significant discoveries.

> For the youngest students, the step of physically placing a cut-out paper figure of a person on the large bar graph helped make the data analysis phase more concrete. The youngest ones didn't yet have a strong sense that the number 26 was double that of 13, but they could look at two columns of data on a bar graph they had created, one with 26 figures and one with 13 figures and state confidently that there were twice as many books about men than women. (Patti McLain, personal communication, October 29, 2002)

The children carried the charts back to math class to analyze the results. The data confirmed their predictions. Of the 227 biographies they found, 177 were about men and only 43 were about women. Furthermore, the overwhelming majority of biographies were about people who were no longer alive. Eager to share their findings with their partner classes at Fairmont Elementary, the students began discussing what they would include in a group letter.

A teacher asked, "Why do you think we found more biographies written about men than about women?" She added to the group letter the list of possible explanations offered by the students. For example, one young child commented, "Some women were scared to do things that men could do." Another nodded in agreement, declaring, "Men are braver." Other children, especially the girls, rejected the notion that men are inherently more courageous than women. "Maybe there are more men in the world than women" countered one student. Another student cited what she knew about history: "In the olden days men would keep the women in the house to clean and do chores."

Without delay, the students e-mailed their letter with their data to their partner class in San Francisco. That night, the teachers e-mailed a copy of the students' findings to all the classes in the Connecting Math to Our Lives (CMTOL) project, along with a note of explanation and invitation to join the discussions about the biographies project.

Reflecting on the Findings

The teachers at Almond Avenue School discussed the findings with other teachers in the CMTOL network as they pondered how to proceed with their students. Enid Lee, an antibias educator who provided valuable suggestions on the design of the CMTOL activities, stressed the importance of talking with students about what the data meant and suggested directions those discussions might take. The participating teachers and online coordinators also shared ideas and resources about antibias education for young students, and the Almond Avenue teachers considered what approaches would be most appropriate for their primary-level students.

Primary-level students display the data gathered in their school library using a pictograph. On the right, the teacher has captured student comments during a classroom discussion on gender equity: "Why do you think there were more biographies written about men than women?"

When girls have gone through books and found only a certain number of women doing "important things," what does that say to them about themselves and what does that say to boys about their own importance? We can expand on that when we ask what does it mean when very few of the people, men or women, are Latino, Asian, or African American. (Lee, 1998)

As teachers talked with students about the images they see each day in books and on television and the ideas that children form about themselves and other groups, it seemed important to take the project a step further. The real impact of any biographical bias could not be estimated without further data on whether this was an isolated case at Almond Avenue.

While waiting for a reply from their partner class, the students pursued the investigation in Livermore's public libraries. By now, the project had captured the attention of other teachers at the school as well as the children's parents, who accompanied students to various neighborhood libraries to continue the investigation.

At school, during science and social studies classes, the teachers took advantage of the students' interest in gathering more data to introduce terms and concepts that were part of the science and social science curriculum. When different groups of students collected data in different places, the teachers raised important questions about "interpreting" and "questioning" other people's data. They encouraged the children to question the "process" and thus the "validity" of the information.

Checking the local community libraries, however, didn't put the students' minds at rest. "Is it just here in Livermore that we have this problem?" the students wondered aloud. "Just how widespread is this problem?"

Deepening the Investigation

When the classes at Almond Avenue opened their e-mail, they discovered that the students at Fairmont Elementary School had responded. Computer resource teacher Diane Rosen helped organize class trips to the school and neighborhood libraries in San Francisco to collect data. The results of the investigation carried out by the partner class were strikingly similar, with disproportionately low representation of women and people of color at both schools and at neighborhood libraries. "We were just amazed; we were really surprised," wrote the students from Fairmont School.

The students' curiosity wouldn't be satisfied until they checked to see if these patterns held true at the largest public library in the area—the Main Branch of the San Francisco Public Library. Their teachers contacted the librarians at the San Francisco Main Library and arranged for a joint visit by children from the two schools to the Children's Section to count and analyze their biography collection.

Finally, after a number of meetings between the teachers and the librarians to plan the logistics, the big day arrived.

Subject: Library here we come!

Saludos de Patti Purcell McLain

Mañana is the day and all is set for the library. We have around 80 kids participating, along with approximately 30 adults, including parents and high school students whom we recruited. Interestingly in our initial visit we found in the whole library only two biographies for children written in Spanish. (Patti McLain, personal communication, March 12, 1998)

With the help of many wonderful parents, the classes from the two schools all arrived via public transportation. The students met face to face

Assessment and Identity Texts

When students engage in projects that are driven by their questions and curiosity, and when they feel they are contributing to making the world a better and fairer place, they invest themselves in their academic work, creating products they are proud to share. The biographies that the students authored at the beginning of the project based on interviews with their classmates are one example. The teachers helped the students share these "identity texts" by binding them and placing them on the shelves of their classroom library. This not only filled the students' own library with biographies that were more culturally and linguistically diverse but it also gave the children a sense of pride to see the texts that they had authored or that featured the stories of their lives read and reread by their peers.

The biographies investigation was a sustained writing, data gathering, and analysis project that students included in their school portfolios and published online, and for which they have received recognition and positive feedback from parents, community members, and other community leaders. With the reports that they have received from others who have read about their project, and who have been inspired to try similar projects in their schools, towns, or countries, the children see without a doubt that their work has had a significant impact and received wide validation as having importance.

for the first time on the lawn outside the library—an exciting moment! All activities in the biography section of the Children's Library were conducted bilingually in teams of four. Students were assigned one of four tasks for which they were responsible in their group: librarian (collects and re-shelves books); reader (reads the book for information); cartographer (charts group findings on wall posters); and writer (fills in the forms). Children rotated between these tasks based on their comfort levels with the skills. Parents, who also formed bilingual teams, monitored the activities. Students recorded information about gender, race, nationality, language, dead or alive, and what the person was famous for. This information was recorded on individual forms and then the relevant information for each book was recorded on large group charts and placed on the walls of the library. The results indicated that more than 70 percent of all books were written about dead white men. By now the students were not surprised (Patti McLain, personal communication, March, 13, 1998).

Taking Action Based on the Data

As the public librarians viewed the large graphs on the wall, which boldly highlighted the gaps in the biography collection, they commented that they had suspected that these patterns might hold true. Patti explains, "They told the students that they would be happy to show a student-authored letter detailing the findings to those involved in the purchasing decisions to see what they could do" (personal communication, October 29, 2002).

The students took this responsibility seriously. They returned to school and finished the "number-crunching" via the Internet and e-mail. The Web master for San Francisco Unified School District, Mike Fleischer, set up an online database so that the students in Livermore and San Francisco could add their data to a shared database, view the collective

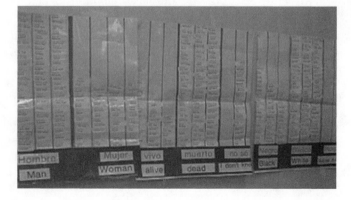

The bar graphs created by the students in the two partner classes during their investigation at the San Francisco Children's Library reveal big gaps in the biography holdings.

findings in a single table, and jointly analyze the data.

The children continued their discussions and reporting using a variety of computer applications that included:

- The new online database to record and display their collective findings;
- E-mail to coordinate the data entry and discuss the findings with their partner class;
- A mailing list and Web-based forum to stay in touch with the larger group of schools participating in the CMTOL Project;
- Word processing to compose and edit their letter and reports; and
- Graphing software to convert their data into attractively formatted graphs.

The next step entailed taking action based on the data collected. The students were anxious to share their data with the librarians in San Francisco and began composing a letter to the San Francisco Main Library, recommending future purchases for the library based on their research. "We spent days with the children discussing the data and deciding what should be said and to whom," Patti recalls.

The librarians had welcomed us and felt like allies in this project. One librarian took the time to explain to us and to the students that one

Community

This project encouraged interaction and cooperation within a sequence of nested, interlocking learning communities. First, the teachers carefully structured peer-to-peer interaction in their own classrooms, preparing easy-to-use data-collection forms for student use in their local school investigations.

Second, the students linked with a partner class that provided an authentic audience for their writing and a broader dataset for their investigation. The students were able to look for patterns in data (an important math skill as well as a social science skill) and to reach conclusions that were significant both mathematically and socially.

Third, family members accompanied the students to the San Francisco Public Library and acted as facilitators during the data gathering. The teachers carefully planned cooperative learning teams to maximize interaction, efficiency, accuracy, inclusion, and collaboration between the two groups of students and their families.

Fourth, the students shared their investigation and findings with distant peers through the global learning network, inspiring classes in other states and countries to investigate issues of representation and to take action to address inequities.

reason the students found the results they did was that the collection was a very old one, and included books that dated back many years. Until recent years, books about women and minorities were not always available from the publishers. She said that if we checked just the books published during the last few years she was sure the students would find a greater percentage of books about women and minorities. We could see that the San Francisco librarians really were making a good effort. Still, our data might help show what the effect of so many years of not purchasing diverse books meant for those involved in the purchasing decisions—that it really takes a great and sustained effort to create a collection that is more representative of the city. (Patti McLain, personal communication, October 29, 2002)

The children realized that when arguing for change and advocating a change from the status quo, mathematical, scientific, qualitative, and quantitative data lend weight to opinions. By including statistics with their observations, their writing acquired new significance and weight. The teachers reaffirmed, as a result of the project, that gaining communication skills is the ultimate purpose of language teaching, and that an important part of communicating effectively and persuasively in a broad range of contexts is knowing how to back up and substantiate one's opinions.

The project clearly supported students' academic learning in a number of curriculum areas and went beyond the school district's content standards. The teachers noted that the children had taken new interest in exploring their school and community libraries, and were now checking out and reading the biographies they had researched. Furthermore, the teachers were convinced that the students improved their math skills; after investigations at several libraries they became expert at presenting their data in graphs and making mathematical statements about the data. The students had learned a number of new scientific terms and spoke more fluently about "validity," "generalizing," and "hypotheses." In addition, they had gained valuable practice writing to their partners in English and Spanish, and composing more formal letters. But the children also learned something more. Patti explains:

The students realized—and this was the biggest message—that they had the ability to get information that could be given to somebody, and that with the correct information, things could be changed. Because when they wrote that letter they knew that what they were doing was telling some very big people—telling them in a nice way—that maybe they better look at things differently. I don't know that the children had ever before seen themselves as capable of gathering information like that.

That was the part that was really exciting. They felt so empowered. (personal communication, October 29, 2002)

Conclusion: The Power of Information

The school year ended, but projects concerned with equity continued as other students in Connecting Math to Our Lives now read on the project's website about the Fairmont and Almond Avenue students' investigation. Like their California counterparts, math classes in Puerto Rico, Romania, Catalonia (Spain), and several states in the United States have all investigated issues of representation in their libraries or in the media in their localities, and several have taken action to make their libraries more inviting places for children and their parents.

Patti McLain and her colleagues, by using their teaching expertise in this innovative, cross-disciplinary project, helped show that teachers can be much more than rote instructors of reading, math, or science. Using their larger influence, they taught their students to discern fairness, to promote a spirit of fairness at the school, and to become aware of their power to influence change. The Almond Avenue faculty demonstrated that teachers can provide students with guided opportunities to think critically, to pursue dialogue and inquiry, and to focus these cognitive skills on a much larger world than 6- to 8-year-olds are usually encouraged to consider. Rarely do students have the opportunity to advocate for change in their world. "When they do, they understand the power of having information" (Patti McLain, personal communication, October 29, 2002). The courageous and inspired work of the teachers and students at Almond Avenue and Fairmont schools in the CMTOL Biographies Project continues to inspire others, reverberating in classrooms, libraries, and communities around the world.

Discussion Questions for Study Groups

1 The children in this portrait used math skills to investigate issues of representation in the books in their school library, and in this way contributed to greater equity at their school site. What ideas do you have for students to use their data-gathering skills to investigate issues of equity? In thinking about this question, consider the perspective of anti-racist educator, Enid Lee, who suggests that "until every person regardless of racial background is experiencing equality in the areas of respect, rights to self-determination and full humanity, representation and resources we still have a job to do" (Lee,

2002b, p. 404). As you think about the schools you have visited, where do you see inequities in the "4R" areas discussed by Lee (respect, rights, responsibilities, and resources)? What issues do you think students at the grade levels you teach or will teach would be interested in investigating? What role might technology play?

2 Bob Peterson, fifth-grade classroom teacher and editor of the *Rethinking Schools* publication, proposes that schools should have "math across the curriculum" comparable to "writing across the curriculum" (2001, p. 84). Peterson writes, "Kids need every tool they can get to make this world—their world—a better place. Mathematics is one such important tool" (p. 88). What ideas do you have for teaching math across the curriculum? What role might parents and families, the broader community, or a distant partner class play?

3 The children in this project used the study of biographies as a means to learn math and science skills. The project leader highlights the specific skills (classification, validity, etc.) the students gained. In what ways could the biographies project be used in the teaching of history, English, spelling, art, or physical education?

4 In which specific ways does the biographies project promote critical thinking skills? How are these skills transferable?

5 In this project the children were encouraged to make use of an online partnership with a sister class as a way to share their biographical findings and in the process learn about math. How could online partnerships be used to facilitate the learning of other subjects in the curriculum?

6 Educational researcher Stephen Krashen (2004b) argues that an important factor in improving student reading is access to books. Students in the biographies project asked the question, "Who is represented in the books in our classroom, school, and community libraries?" What other questions might students and teachers investigate relating to access to books and opportunities to read widely? What other ideas do you have for designing projects and activities that would help provide students with greater access to books and would encourage them to read more? What role do you feel that computers and other technologies play in either taking time and resources away from reading, or in promoting more reading?

Endnote

1. The Connecting Math to Our Lives/Conectando las Matemáticas a la Vida project was organized by the global learning network project De Orilla a Orilla and the Pacific Southwest Regional Technology in Education Consortium in collaboration with the International Education and Resource Network (iEARN).

The biographies activity described in the CMTOL project announcement was inspired by Bob Peterson, fifth-grade teacher and an editor of *Rethinking Schools.*

CHAPTER 9

Nuestro Diccionario/ Our Dictionary

Student Lexicography

Dictionary use is often associated with the frustration of trying to read texts, in either a first or second language, that are beyond students' current language abilities. Looking up words slows down the search for meaning and, for many students, turns what should be a pleasurable activity into drudgery. But what if students could create their own dictionaries, drawing both on their prior cultural and linguistic knowledge and their own active inquiry? The projects reviewed in this chapter show that young students can use technology to create multimedia and multilingual dictionaries that enhance language awareness and motivate them to inquire further into the magic and mystery of language and how it affects all of our lives.

Professor Ruth Bennett, a California State University at Humboldt researcher, launched an investigation with the simplest of premises: Third- to eighth-grade Hupa and Yurok Native American students living on the northern California coast could benefit academically from building what she called "bilingual natural history dictionaries," using computers as tools to express their own, their families', and their tribes' unique insights as they defined and illustrated the flora and fauna that animated their ancestral homelands (Bennett et al., 1985). In the process, the students would also be helping to revitalize their native languages and cultures. The project began in 1985, at a time when the graphics-based interface that made such an endeavor possible had become available just months before on Macintosh computers. Professor Bennett was years ahead of her time as a pioneer in the field of community lexicography, or collaborative dictionary building, that would gather strength years later, and only after many advances in computer technology. The communal knowledge that the students' dictionary would encode—and would dignify in the process of children defining their natural world—was in one sense ageless while in another in danger of disappearing forever.

These elementary and middle school students found themselves working cooperatively among peers, experiencing positive collaboration across grade levels, and constantly consulting parents, extended families, and community elders as they became seasoned lexicographers, seeking to get their tribes' words "just right." As the academic year progressed, evidence poured in that convinced Professor Bennett and the future teachers who were her collaborators in the dictionary research project that important new educational ground was being broken in northwest California:

- Students worked with unflagging interest all year long on the project, and showed a marked preference for cooperative activities like the dictionary project, compared with more competitive academic tasks.

- Cross-age groupings, with older and younger students collaborating on definitions, generated the greatest variety of language use. Older students volunteered their help more often in these groupings, and younger students sought assistance more frequently, resulting in less stilted and more abstract and detailed definitions.

- Oral language and written academic language were linked in ways that affirmed native oral traditions while expanding vocabulary and writing abilities in both native languages and English (Bennett, 1987).

From a twenty-first-century perspective, the technical tools employed for this project seem humble enough. Researchers were able to design a font for the phonetic alphabet they had created as a writing system for Yurok and Hupa, formerly not written languages. Students then could edit their definitions with a bare-bones word processor, by today's standards, and they employed a rudimentary drawing program to illustrate their definitions. Yet it is clear that what drove this pioneering project was neither advanced technical expertise nor sophisticated technological resources, but a simple, compelling activity structure—*community*

Cognition

The development of students' competencies with dictionaries as reference is sometimes limited to lower-order skills, such as looking up lists of vocabulary items. Too often, dictionaries are underutilized in classrooms and school libraries. Students report that they resort to using them as little as possible, and complain of finding definitions that are circular and hard to understand. By way of contrast, collaborative dictionary building projects, like the one described in this portrait, permit the refinement of higher-level vocabulary knowledge. Writing the definition of a noun requires the explanation of its relationship to other similar nouns and the precise description of characteristics that set it apart. The process of writing a good definition must strike a balance between brevity and completeness, thus providing students with valuable experience in another high-level cognitive skill: summary writing, widely considered an essential academic skill in many states' learning standards.

Tools

Dr. Jacek Iwanski has developed a suite of programs for building dictionaries. The flagship software, Verbs & Nouns, is described in this portrait. Lookup is a companion program that brings together dictionaries and allows users to find items among several dictionary databases. Word List Maker is a multipurpose program for generating frequency rankings of words in any text, highly useful when educators want to determine key terminology for specific content areas. It can be used to isolate words by their parts of speech; to make anagrams, word-frequency lists, indexes, and spelling lists; to analyze words by their endings; and for many other tasks. These low-cost software programs are available for Macintosh computers, and Dr. Iwanski is currently designing Windows-based versions. Available at http://users.netmatters.co.uk/dandaforbes/typelist.html.

dictionary building in cooperative learning groups—fueled by a recognition of the value that familial and communal knowledge can play in academic learning.

Nearly two decades later, teachers and students in another California school, this time in Fresno, are once again using computers to build bilingual dictionaries. And in a way, this community is also engaged in a project of language rescue and cultural identity. Ann Leavenworth Center for Accelerated Learning, an elementary school, began its two-way bilingual immersion program, Estrellas (Stars) in 1997. In Estrellas, about half the children in each grade are from families whose dominant language was Spanish in kindergarten, and the other half come from homes where English is spoken. Instruction is provided by team teachers who, while bilingual themselves, model one and only one of the two target languages. Parents enroll their children in these programs—and make a commitment to continue in the program until sixth grade—with the goal of enabling their children to attain full bilingual literacy, and then moving on to advanced instruction in both languages in middle and high school.

In what ways are the families and students of Estrellas rescuing language and culture?

■ For half the students, those from Spanish-speaking families, parents realize that the language of the home will gradually fade for their children, as it has for so many generations of immigrants before them. When home languages are lost during the elementary school years, it is all the more difficult for parents to guide their offspring through the turbulent adolescent years when they face the specters of gang involvement, teenage pregnancy, and drugs, as well as more difficult academic learning challenges.

- Over half the parents of the English-speaking families are of a Latino heritage, often with aunts, uncles, cousins, nieces, nephews, or grandparents who still speak Spanish and provide a link to the family's language roots. For them, Estrellas holds a promising answer to the intergenerational question, "Will the circle be unbroken?" They see in Estrellas, and in their children's emerging Spanish skills, a way to break the cycle of language loss in their families and the inevitable erosion of cultural identity that follows.

- For monolingual English-speaking parents Estrellas offers their children the advantage of bilingualism in an increasingly diverse and multilingual world. They see this as an economic, cultural, and personal opportunity.

When they are working on their lexicography project, which they call *Nuestro Diccionario (Our Dictionary)*, students work in pairs, an English-dominant student partnered with a Spanish-dominant classmate. They use a versatile dictionary-building program called Verbs & Nouns, developed by a Polish physicist, Dr. Jacek Iwanski. They are the first

Tools

Another class of useful software tools are computer programs that "harvest language" by producing concordances. A concordance is an alphabetical listing of words in a text of any size that is designed to show vocabulary in the context where it is used. These programs can be invaluable to teachers and students who not only want to know which words are important for a particular content area but also to gain insight into how those words are used. Concordances can even be quickly produced that show the most common "collocations" of two-, three-, four-, or more words in order. This can be extremely help-ful to teachers and students in analyzing how phrases are built for a specific domain of vocabulary. One concordance-building program of special interest to educators was designed by a young programmer, Matt Fahrenbacher, who recently received his teaching credential as a secondary mathematics teacher: the free, open-source ConcorderPro for Macintosh OS X. It can be found at http://homepage.mac.com/fahrenba/ concorderPro/concorderPro.html. Other Windows-based concordancing programs can be found by searching the Internet with the keyword Concordance.

elementary school students in the world to work with Verbs & Nouns, according to Dr. Iwanski, since all previous dictionary modules had been built by university students and their professors for studying a number of foreign languages including English, Finnish, French, German, Greek, Hungarian, Italian, Japanese, Portuguese, Russian, and Swedish. These dictionary modules had been built by students and their professors from around the world and are now available for free on Iwanski's website along with other dictionary-building software (see *Tools* sidebar).

After consulting with their teachers to develop a list of important terminology on their current unit of study that will be included in *Nuestro Diccionario,* partners begin the key process of selecting a word and developing its definition in Verbs & Nouns. They consult a number of reference works on their Bilingual Reference Shelf, which contains several comprehensive monolingual Spanish school dictionaries, a number of bilingual picture dictionaries, and a classroom encyclopedia in Spanish. The ground rules are simple: They may consult any reference work, but they may not have it open while they are jointly writing their definition. "That would be copying," explain the lexicographers to visitors.

In their discussions of each definition's nuances, it is plain that Estrellas students are linking academic oral language with sophisticated vocabulary development (see *Cognition* and *Assessment* sidebars). Jeffrey Thornton, an African American student, was working with Jéssica Valdez on the definition of *canal* for their geography unit. He saw that many English definitions used the term *man-made,* but Jéssica informed him that "no se dice así en Español" (that's not how you say it in Spanish), that the Spanish cognate "artificial" sounded better. Both these children were very familiar with canals in Fresno, where irrigation canals carry water many miles from the melted snow of the Sierra Nevada mountains to the orchards and farms outside the city. But as they developed their definition, Jeffrey felt that they shouldn't just talk about irrigation canals; what about the canals in Panama and east of the Mississippi that they had read about in previous social studies and history units? Their final definition: *"Un canal es un río artificial que conduce agua o barcos por una ruta específica"* (A canal is an artificial river that conveys water or boats over a specific route). Here was an economical definition that could be read in schools in Fresno and beyond. Estrellas students showed their sense of "ownership" and pride in their definitions by signing each one and reading their "signatures" as they made their recording, much as the pioneering lexicographers who wrote the *Oxford English Dictionary* a century before would add their initials to their work.

But there is more to building an entry in *Nuestro Diccionario* than successfully writing a cogent definition. Next, partners needed to provide vital information for each entry in the Word Editor of Verbs & Nouns, which included the word's English translation, its gender (whether masculine or feminine), and the word's stem and the endings for spelling its singular and plural endings. For example, *canal* is a masculine word that uses *-l* or *-les* to indicate its number, singular or plural. Verbs needed to be properly inflected in the Word Editor, too, so that their conjugations would appear with the right spellings whenever the verb was looked up. And so the students were engaged in a process with an intense focus on language forms that would aid their academic performance, both in classroom work and on standardized and standards-based testing.

Perhaps the last three stages of completing a definition held the most excitement for students. Partner lexicographers were provided lists of Internet sites with copyright-free graphics of drawings, photographs, or video clips that could illustrate their definitions, attaching them to that entry. When they found websites that were relevant to their definition, they included its Internet address in the entry since Verbs & Nouns

---

Community of Learning

This portrait describes one community of students at the elementary level building bilingual dictionaries to promote their own learning of academic vocabulary. Their ability to make definitions that include pertinent Internet links to World Wide Web resources has led them beyond dictionary building to the threshold of a more encyclopedic knowledge base. For older students and educators, the Web-based Wikipedia project provides a springboard into building a knowledge database with thousand of others united by the Internet into a community of learning. Drawing on the expert knowledge of thousands of voluntary contributors and monitored by peer reviewers to assure "quality control," Wikipedia aims at nothing less than the development of a free, universally available multilingual encyclopedia with rapid look-up capabilities and a wide-ranging scope. Currently, there are nearly 500,000 articles in the encyclopedia's Web-based holdings. Teachers are always looking for outlets for their students' academic efforts. Wikipedia provides learners everywhere with a chance to participate in collaborative knowledge generation. http://en.wikipedia.org/wiki/Main_Page. For other languages, visit http://meta.wikimedia.org/wiki/Complete_list_of_language_Wikipedias_available.

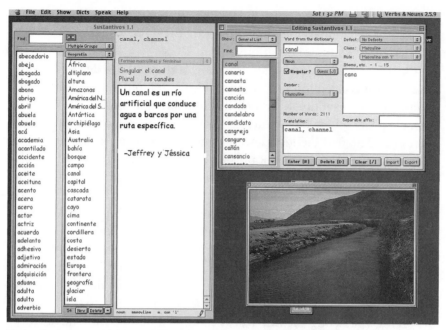

Verbs & Nouns provides tools for electronic dictionary building and for looking up words. This screen shows an entry for "canal" in the module for nouns (sustantivos). The left-hand column shows all entries, the middle column provides words grouped thematically, and the last column gives the student partners' definition. Clicking on a word activates an audio file, recorded by students, and displays a graphic they selected. The Editing box is used for translations and to specify word stems to which inflections are automatically added for singular and plural nouns.

allows dictionary users to click on links, converting dictionaries into encyclopedias by harnessing the World Wide Web. Now everything was set for the pair of lexicographers to record, in their own voices, their completed definition. While one student read the definition, the other would stand by until the end to "sign off" on their work. And so Jeffrey read his and Jéssica's definition ending with "por Jeffrey Thornton," and she chimed in "y Jéssica Valdez." It seemed only fair, they explained, after working so hard together that both should be known as the lexicographers behind their definition. Evidence of pride in their work is abundant; there are not many schools where students rush to the reference corner to show their friends their favorite dictionary definitions. When students work on *Nuestro Diccionario* at Ann Leavenworth, these moments happen every day.

Estrellas students were especially looking forward to merging their dictionary with one being developed 150 miles away at Osborn School with a two-way program like theirs. They know that they are the founders of a dictionary-building project that will one day include schools in other cities, states, and nations.

Clearly, their insiders' understanding of dictionaries departs from the common conception of a comprehensive reference tool written by experts, serving as ultimate arbiter of acceptable standard usage. Yet these young lexicographers have much in common with dictionary pioneers of other eras. The first dictionaries, indeed, were *bilingual* dictionaries that arose soon after the advent of printed books in order to meet the commercial and cultural communication needs of multilingual societies living in close contact. These efforts were stimulated by the pressing need for *translations* between vernacular languages to more effectively conduct their relations. Monolingual dictionaries would not appear until almost a century after the introduction of the printing press in Europe, and were designed to educate the public not about "every" word in a language, as dictionaries later would attempt, but rather to focus on defining the "hard" words. In this sense, *Nuestro Diccionario* is similar to the earliest dictionaries, selecting the key words that need definition to advance students' learning.

The objective of the first dictionary builders was one of democratization: to assist "children, women, and foreigners . . . and generally speaking all categories of people who had no access to the more traditional means of education" (Béjoint, 2000) in the learning of difficult, often Latin-origin vocabulary. These "hard" words often owe their eventual integration into everyday vernacular language to dictionary builders and their readers.

Assessment, Identity Texts

Vocabulary development is often evaluated with multiple-choice questions on standardized tests and standards-based assessment. In this portrait, we find another example of a student-generated product—a bilingual dictionary—providing unmistakable evidence of deep conceptual learning not easily assessed by current high-stakes testing batteries. While definition writing appears in the elementary school standards in many states, it is a high-level cognitive skill that can only be displayed by engaging in the definitional process itself and producing actual entries. Moreover, collaboratively constructed dictionaries provide multiple opportunities for students to share evaluative feedback on classmates' definitions that helps to shape and refine the learning process. Finally, parents recognize in a computer-based dictionary constructed by their children with audio, video, and Internet links a convincing example of successful technology-based learning.

Dictionaries were also tools that broke down gender barriers to literacy. Miller and Swift (1979) point out that "motivated girls lacked even a basic tool to use in teaching themselves until dictionaries were available." Dictionaries were conceived as self-teaching tools for the improvement of social and economic status. Indeed, a large measure of the success of Samuel Johnson's *Dictionary* can be ascribed to the urgent demand by an aspiring English bourgeoisie for a book designed to enhance its owners' "cultural capital" of words, a useful purchase to be studied for self-improvement, since the ideal of universal public education had yet to be embraced. The historical record is clear that the earliest lexicographers, from John Wesley and the Chambers brothers in England to the Grimm brothers in Germany and Pierre Larousse in France, were all explicitly populist in their orientation toward writing and publishing commercially successful dictionaries with an overarching goal of democratizing learning (Béjoint, 2000).

Verbs & Nouns takes this early democratizing potential of dictionary use and extends it into the very process of building dictionaries themselves. Dr. Iwanski describes the development of his software tool that began in 1994. He became interested in the potential of computers to serve as multimedia tools that would facilitate the laborious lookup process of dictionary texts. And rather than simply providing simple one-word entries, he wanted to explore the computer's ability to provide all the inflections for nouns as well as thorough conjugations of verbs. He began with Polish. "Polish has an extremely rich and difficult inflection and conjugation system and no paper dictionary can explicitly list all inflected forms for every word because of the space limitations," he explains. Once he had completed the Polish dictionary, he set himself a new challenge. "I thought that it could be an interesting project to write a very flexible program allowing the set up of the inflection rules for every language and every part of speech. This is how the idea for 'Verbs & Nouns' and its name emerged." This proved to be a daunting challenge, since languages are inflected in such differing ways, but Iwanski notes that by "systematically improving the program I've managed to make it flexible enough to support inflection even in such distant languages as Japanese and Russian. Because one program can be used to access many dictionaries, the user can learn just a single interface and use it for all languages and parts of speech" (personal communication, February 20, 2003).

Dr. Iwanski has created a dictionary-building tool that allows communities of learners to take ownership of how they define their words and their worlds, and to share, compare, and merge their insights with other communities around the world. His is the latest of computer tools like the ones Dr. Ruth Bennett first explored with Hupa and Yurok students, placing lexicography in the hands of teachers, students, and their communities.

Book Club   Discussion Questions for Study Groups

1. Geography is a topic of study in several grade levels. Write definitions of the words *glacier* and *earthquake*. Feel free to consult reference works as you write your definition, as professional lexicographers would do. What cognitive skills do you find yourself employing as you complete your definitions?

2. Dictionaries are complex documents usually composed by teams of lexicographers who meet frequently to share their work. How would working with others collaboratively differ from writing definitions in isolation as you just did?

3. This chapter discussed the fact that students do not often use dictionaries, and when they do, they often find them difficult to comprehend and frustrating to use. As an educator, how might you introduce stu-

dents to such a lexical exercise? How might you "warm up" students to the idea of dictionary use?

4. What are the inherent challenges of doing a dictionary project? What are some of the strategies you might use to overcome these challenges?

5. As an educator, what additional activities or projects related to exploration of words might you develop to promote critical literacy and bilingual abilities?

6. As an educator, how might you convince your colleagues and immediate supervisor of the value of such a project?

7. What skills, in addition to expansion of word knowledge, are likely to be developed by the students in such a lexical project?

CHAPTER 10

Closing the Digital Divide around the World

To what extent might computer technology enable students and communities in less affluent parts of the world to gain access to knowledge and resources that could reduce the digital divide between rich and poor countries? Is it even feasible to propose hi-tech solutions in contexts where there may not even be a reliable source of electricity? The two projects profiled in this chapter open up intriguing possibilities and suggest that human ingenuity might succeed in extending the intellectual tools that computers represent to communities that have struggled to meet even basic educational needs. What is less clear, however, are the social impacts of access to the "global village" among communities that have followed traditional lifestyles for centuries.

Available Only by the Million: MIT Media Lab's $100 Laptop Computer

In July 1997, the Media Laboratory at the Massachusetts Institute of Technology (MIT) and the 2B1 Foundation convened a conference in Cambridge, Massachusetts, that brought 200 educators from developing countries "who work with children and computers to break down world barriers of race, age, gender, language, class, economics and geography" (MIT News Office, 1997). The MIT Media Lab, well known for its many technological innovations that have facilitated educational computing and networking, was founded and is directed by Carlos Negroponte, author of *Being Digital* (1995). According to its vice-chairman, Seymour Papert, who wrote *Mindstorms: Children, Computers and Powerful Ideas* (1980) and who invented the educational programming language, Logo, the mission of the 2B1 Foundation "[is] aimed at preventing a growing economic and information abyss between the 'digital haves' and the 'digital have-nots.' We see the children of the world as central to achieving this goal." Papert explained the twofold goal of the July 1997 conference as focusing "not only on what the digital world can offer the world's children, but also what children provided with appropriate computing technology and connectivity can give to the world" (MIT News Office, 1997).

Unlike many conferences, this one yielded a tangible and ambitious result: a massive undertaking to produce and distribute by the hundreds of millions a "$100 laptop" computer for educational purposes, capable of operating under the most adverse climactic conditions. Negroponte described its design before its first production run of a million computers in 2006 by Taiwan-based Quantas, the world's largest manufacturer of computers:

> The $100 Laptop will be a Linux-based, full-color, full-screen laptop, which initially is achieved either by rear projecting the image on a flat screen or by using electronic ink (developed at the MIT Media Lab). In addition, it will be rugged, use innovative power (including wind-up), be WiFi- [networkable] and cell phone-enabled, and have USB ports galore. Its current specifications are: 500MHz [processor speed], 1GB [hard drive], 1 Megapixel [screen resolution]. (Media Lab Press, 2005)

The software on the laptop is entirely "freeware"—that is, it is not for profit and "open source," which means it is modifiable by programmers to permit multilingual computing adaptations. Thus, the $100 laptop is the equal of most $1,000 computers available in economically developed countries, with the exception of its hard drive capacity. Negroponte explained that since the computers are designed to make a peer-to-peer mesh network (a widely copied innovation developed by the Media Lab), children can save their work on a computer that is dedicated for storage, and can make copies of their work by sending it to yet another computer hooked up to a printer at school. An electronic slide show illustrating the design process for the $100 laptop can be viewed at www.dcontiuum.com/content/show.php?id=4.

More radical than its technological design is the plan for distributing and supporting the $100 laptops. These computers will never be available for purchase individually. Rather, they will be produced in quantities no smaller than a million for ministries of education around the world, with software preloaded for national languages and dialects. Negroponte and his wife, Elaine, through the 2B1 Foundation, have personally supervised beta testing at a school they founded in Cambodia,

Tools and Resources

To close the digital divide, functional, well-designed, and inexpensive hardware is not enough. It must be coupled with operating systems that are free or low-cost and open-source (that is, modifiable) and similar software that produces documents that can be read by computers everywhere.

Linux, an alternative to Windows and Macintosh operating systems, is indispensable in this regard. To learn more about Linux, explore the website at www.linuxiso.org/viewdoc.php/introtolinux.html.

Tools and Resources

Without question, the Microsoft Office suite of programs, including the word processor Word, the spreadsheet Excel, and the PowerPoint presentation software, are the application programs that have assumed preeminence on both the Windows and the Macintosh computer platforms. However, there is an open-source alternative to these predominant application programs called Open Office that is available in more than 40 languages: www.openoffice.org. There are also many freeware programs for education. One of several websites offering many links to other resources is www.merlot.org.

and negotiations have been launched with numerous governments to distribute the computers, including the People's Republic of China with 220 million students. The 2B1 Foundation has since morphed into a not-for-profit organization called OLPC—"One Laptop per Child"—that is funded by $2 million from Google, Advanced Micro Devices, Red Hat Incorporated, News Corporation, and Brightstar.

Perhaps the most controversial element of the plan to distribute the $100 laptops is the insistence by the Media Lab and OLPC that participating ministries of education adhere to the principle of "every child—one computer." Critics have maintained that this requires governments to make choices between developing education through technology innovation or attending to more basic economic necessities. According to some critics, community-access centers are a more feasible alternative to computers for each individual child. Negroponte counters, "One does not think of community pencils—kids have their own. [Pencils] are tools to think with, sufficiently inexpensive to be used for work and play, drawing, writing, and mathematics. A computer can be the same, but far more powerful" (Media Lab Press, 2005).

Seymour Papert adds that there are few societal problems that are not ameliorated by the raising of consciousness encouraged by education (MIT News Office, 1997). Many governments are in agreement with the MIT Media Lab and OLPC that children, when given the technology resources taken for granted by their peers in developed economies, will change not only the face of educational computing but also the economic development of their nations. This sentiment was echoed by United Nations Secretary General Kofi Annan at the World Summit on the Information Society held in Tunisia in November 2005, where the first prototype was presented:

The $100 Laptop holds the promise of major advances in economic and social development. This is not just a matter of giving a laptop to each child, as if bestowing on them some magical charm. The magic lies within—within each child, within each scientist, scholar, or just plain citizen in the making. (quoted in Van Herrin, 2005)

The Jhai Foundation:
Technology for Development and Reconciliation

Another approach to bridging the divide between digital haves and have-nots has its origins many decades ago. After a tour of duty in 1966 as a Navy bomb loader during the Vietnam War, Lee Thorn cofounded the national Veterans for Peace organization that was to play such a large role in the burgeoning antiwar movement of the time. Thirty years later, in 1997, he cofounded with Bounthanh Phommasathit, a Laotian refugee, another organization called the Jhai Foundation, which takes its name from the word in Lao that means "hearts and minds working together." Thorn writes:

> The Jhai Foundation is about reconciliation. We focus on relationships. We start with the relationship of Bounthanh Phommasathit and her family and myself. Bounthanh's family is from the Plain of Jars in Laos, per capita the most bombed place on Earth. I participated in that bombing directly. In each relationship we try to see the humanity in the other. We overcome our denial, tell our stories, mourn, make amends as appropriate, and do what we can to strengthen our friendship. We like self-help. We are interested in impact. We are most interested in relationships. We are demonstrating how, after such a devastating war, people from opposite sides can reconcile by working side-by-side. We call this the reconciliation process of development. (Jhai Foundation, Formerly Project Hearts and Minds, no date)

Currently, Jhai Foundation is working in 13 villages in Lao People's Democratic Republic (PDR) on community development, organic fair-trade farming initiatives, and technology projects. Two technology projects in particular have far-reaching educational implications. The first project was the establishment, with the assistance of Schools Online, of four Internet Learning Centers in Laotian high schools. Students and teachers in the first of the four Internet Learning Centers describe the impact of the Jhai Foundation technology project on their lives:

> We brought the first Internet learning center to Laos at Phon Mi High School. This center is unique. It is rapidly becoming self-sustaining.

The whole community feels it owns it. It teaches both kids and adults. And it is initiating a collaborative, project-based learning project that is unique in the world. Its project is to collaborate with schools in similar latitudes and in the U.S. to discover ways to experiment with local organic cash crops for local and international markets. From the beginning kids make money, their parents find ways to keep their kids home, and the school gets new community resources—parents who are farmers, agriculture extension agents—that they never had before. It is a win/win/win. (Jhai Foundation, Technology, no date.)

That initiative won the 2001 Stockholm Challenge Award and was also named a "premier project" by the Technology Empowerment Network that year.[1]

The second Jhai Foundation effort, called the Remote Villages IT Project, has attracted even more international attention. Jhai Foundation consulted five rural villages, asking what they needed to advance their children's prospects in the world of the future. Their response:

■ First, weather reports to anticipate growing conditions;

■ Second, up-to-date pricing information to help them price their crops competitively for sale in neighboring markets, where they were often cheated out of fair value for their produce and livestock, having no idea what conditions awaited them once they set out from their remote villages for the major town markets; and

■ Third, a means of communication with the world, especially the distant members of the Laotian diaspora, spread around the world but concentrated in the United States.

The Jhai Foundation Board could clearly see that the wide-ranging concerns voiced by the villagers pointed to a technology solution, one that would connect their remote villages to the Internet, linking them to information and communication resources they were currently denied in their distant settlements deprived of electrical power, let alone advanced technology. The foundation proposed an audacious solution: the invention of a device that did not then exist—a rugged computer that could survive monsoon rains and tropical temperatures, that would be human-powered, not relying on electricity and phone lines, and one that would nevertheless connect (via wireless technologies) the five villages to the Internet. The goal was to help these communities to leapfrog centuries in linking technology to their agrarian economies and in giving them the potential to communicate once again with relatives torn from their families in Laos in the aftermath of the U.S. bombing of the Plain of Jars.

Obviously, this would take some doing. Thorn turned to Lee Felsenstein, a fellow activist in the Anti-War and Free Speech Movement of the 1970s, perhaps better known as the engineer who invented *both* the first stand-alone desktop computer, the Sol-20, and the first portable computer, the Osborne, both on permanent display in the Smithsonian Institution in Washington as key artifacts in the history of personal computing. Felsenstein assembled a team of 25 engineers working on a *pro bono* basis, including a technology specialist based in Laos, Vorasone Dengkayaphichith; Anousak Souphavahn, a Laotian refugee in the United States, who rewrote Linux operating system code to make a user interface readable in Lao; and Mark Summer, a wireless computer networking specialist. Together they designed what they called the Jhai PC. Its features include the following:

- It is pedal-powered, running on a battery charged by a stationary bicycle.

- It is built with off-the-shelf computer components that can be readily obtained in major towns and the capitol of Laos, Vientiene.

- It connects to the Internet via an industry-standard wireless 802.11b card, beaming communications up to roof tops, on to tree-top antennas, and then to similar mountain-top antennas until connecting with telephone and Internet service at a hospital in the town of Phon Hong.

- It utilizes a Lao-language version of Linux, the free open-source operating system that can be re-programmed and thus remain sustainable for years, unlike commercial operating systems that become obsolete quickly.

Lee Thorn summarizes this achievement: "Right now the villagers have no way of telling what the market is like in the big towns they sell their crops to, telling what the weather report is for their crops, and so on. This will absolutely change that. Plus, they will be able to talk to relatives in the United States, some of whom they haven't seen in decades" (Jhai Foundation, Good News, no date).

As the Jhai Foundation has grown, it has focused not only on locally based sustainable projects internationally but also on projects within rural communities in the United States that are confronting similar challenges. For example, a significant new venture is its work in creating a "Navajo PC" for the Window Rock United School District within the Navajo Nation. It has also worked with other organizations to develop an "Indian PC" for use in South Asian countries (Jhai Archives, no date).

1 There are many examples throughout this book of networking projects involving students around the world. They point to the multiple learning opportunities that occur when cultures come in contact using networking technology. The low-priced and community-controlled technologies outlined in this chapter expand the promise of educational computing in geometric proportions. How do you think computers in schools will be transformed when hundreds of millions of students are communicating with their peers around the world, from both developing and developed nations? Will the information exchange benefit their communities, or will it distract attention from more pressing needs?

2 Once computing resources are more widely available, how will we overcome the language barriers that may be presented? For example, Cambodians who speak and write Khmer will certainly welcome opportunities to develop educational liaisons with Khmer speakers in other parts of the world, including California. Yet students in the U.S. immigrant communities may not know enough Khmer to collaborate effectively. What could each side do to enhance communication? Think this question through—there may be answers that you did not at first suspect!

3 Do you agree with Negroponte's idea of "one child—one computer"? Explore your answers fully, providing reasons on both sides of the debate.

4 Some might argue that supplying $100 laptop computers to developing countries should not be a priority in the context of poverty where the necessities of life are insufficient. What might you say in support of and in opposition to this?

5 To what extent might the introduction of widespread computing and Internet access to students in developing countries undermine indigenous ways of life and introduce desires for expensive consumer goods that are neither attainable nor useful in their situations? Could the $100 laptop represent a Trojan Horse for many communities in developing countries?

Endnote

1. Interestingly, the schools in India that are collaborating with the four Jhai-Schools Online Internet Learning Centers in Laos also worked with bilingual students from California in the FRESA (Strawberry) Project (see Chapter 6) on mutual agricultural concerns.

Part 3   Imagining Educational Futures

Framing Directions for Change

D uring the past 25 years, schools have undergone multiple changes. Globalization on the world stage has expressed itself locally in urban schools in the form of rapidly increasing linguistic and cultural diversity. Technological changes occurring almost daily have far outstripped the capacity of educators to integrate these technological tools into their classroom instruction. And "literacy crisis" rhetoric is constantly pumped out by a compliant media as a cacophonous reminder to educators and the general public that schools require radical surgery (perhaps even privatization) if the nation is to survive as a dominant economic power.

The preceding chapters have exposed the problematic nature of current educational directions. In the first place, No Child Left Behind (NCLB) ignores social determinants of academic achievement, with the result that there has been minimal focus on the empirical evidence suggesting that improvements in the living conditions of low-income children might represent a more cost-effective set of interventions than school-based interventions. Second, through its Reading First mandates and high-stakes assessment requirements, NCLB has strongly promoted a programmed learning approach to literacy instruction that has increased the pedagogical divide between schools serving low-income as compared to higher-income students.

Not surprisingly, these policies show no signs of improving the academic achievement of low-income and culturally diverse students. By contrast, the case studies that were presented in earlier chapters show clearly that low-income and culturally diverse students *can* engage in powerful learning when the pedagogical orientation shifts from behaviorist forms of direct instruction to transformative approaches that address issues of power and identity. The case studies demonstrate ways in which technological tools can be harnessed to promote students' literacy engagement and enable them to become generators of knowledge rather than just receivers of information.

We present in this chapter a two-part framework for understanding the failure of schools to educate certain groups of students. The first part of the framework highlights the social determinants of achievement and the second part focuses on the instructional determinants. In both cases, classroom interactions orchestrated by teachers are seen as having the potential to challenge and reverse coercive relations of power.

Introduction

The projects reviewed in Part II illustrate the kind of technology-supported instruction that can, in principle, be implemented in any school context, regardless of the income level of the community or the linguistic and cultural backgrounds of the students. All of these projects generated extensive literacy engagement on the part of students. Students not only read more and wrote more than is typical in transmission-oriented classrooms but they also experienced strong positive affect associated with these literacy practices. There is also evidence in the case study descriptions that students processed meanings at a deep rather than superficial level. Elementary school students in Project FRESA, for example, gained a multidimensional understanding of economic realities associated with agribusiness and expressed their understanding in a variety of authentic literacy activities ranging from writing poems, creating graphs, and writing letters to the governor of California and representatives of agribusiness.

In Chapter 4, we articulated a set of design criteria for evaluating technology-supported instruction that derive directly from the scientific research on learning and literacy development. Within virtually all of the projects described in Part II (and the appendix), the technology-supported instruction

- Provided cognitive challenge and opportunities for deep processing of meaning;

- Related instruction to prior knowledge and experiences derived from students' homes and communities;

- Promoted active self-regulated collaborative inquiry;

- Promoted extensive engaged reading and writing across the curriculum;

- Helped students develop strategies for effective reading, writing, and learning;

- Promoted affective involvement and identity investment on the part of students.

These projects also challenged predominant pedagogical assumptions regarding low-income and culturally diverse students. For example, students engaged in generating knowledge rather than answering closed and factual questions, they created literature and art rather than internalizing scripted content, and they acted on social realities rather than receiving systematic and explicit phonics instruction. Furthermore, they invested their identities in these projects in ways that contrast with the "virtually affectless environment" (Sirotnik, 1983, p. 29) of traditional drill-and-practice activities.

The image of the student that emerges from these projects is dramatically different from the image that emerges from typical NCBE-mandated instruction. As Sirotnik expressed it more than 20 years ago, low-income students are increasingly subjected to instruction that implicitly teaches "dependence upon authority, linear thinking, social apathy, passive involvement, and hands-off learning" (1983, p. 29). The recent escalation of high-stakes testing has reinforced the likelihood that low-income and culturally diverse students will experience these instructionally constricted learning environments.

The image of the teacher within the projects we have described also contrasts with the teacher envisaged by NCLB. The teachers who have initiated these sister class or other technology-supported projects have analyzed the deep structure of the curriculum with respect to students' academic learning and their cognitive and personal development. They do attempt to cover curriculum standards but not by means of a superficial lock-step sequential approach that ignores students' prior knowledge and cultural backgrounds. They define their roles as *educators*—professionals whose imagination, talent, and commitment are essential to nurture student learning. By contrast, one-size-fits-all scripted programs, explicitly designed to be teacher-proof, position teachers simply as readers of the "scientific" script. One-size-fits-all applies both to teachers and students.

> The escalation of high-stakes testing has reinforced the likelihood that low-income and culturally diverse students will experience instructionally constricted learning environments.

Obviously, very different societal images are also reflected in the projects we have described as compared to traditional transmission-oriented instruction. These projects explicitly focus on equity by challenging the subordinate status assigned to culturally and linguistically diverse students. By affirming the value of students' home language (L1), teachers are challenging the devaluation of students' language and culture in the wider society. The interpersonal space they orchestrate with their students in the classroom articulates the obvious fact that societies need all the multilingual talent and intercultural awareness they can get. When teachers challenge low-income and culturally diverse students to stretch their intellectual and linguistic resources to the maximum in order to grapple with issues and solve problems that are relevant to their lives, they also challenge the inferior intellectual status assigned to students by those who claim that linguistic and cognitive deficits (e.g., lack of phonological awareness or delayed vocabulary development) must be remediated by direct instruction before students can be encouraged to read or think (e.g., Mathes & Torgesen, 2000).

In this chapter, we synthesize the essential instructional elements that are implied by the research literature we have reviewed in Part 1 and by the case studies described in Part 2. Our goal is to provide a framework for school-based discussions of educational change. In contrast to the nonnegotiable "scientifically proven" statements that circle the wagons around NCLB, the framework we articulate is intended as a starting point for discussion among educators. Teacher agency, choice, and critical inquiry are central to the implementation of the framework we articulate in contrast to the compliance envisaged within NCLB. We see the articulation of a theoretical framework as a dialogical process. Our goal is not to present a static set of "scientifically proven" propositions but to articulate a perspective within which educators can examine and discuss their pedagogical choices. The framework *is* consistent with the empirical research but it aims to serve as a tool for rational educational change rather than as a statement of absolute "truth."

The framework is also multilayered in the sense that there are multiple access routes to its core components. Some educators may prefer to approach the issue of pedagogical choices from the perspective of Bransford and colleagues' (2000) discussion of how people learn. Others may find the New London Group's (1996) multiliteracies framework a useful starting point. Still others will draw on Paulo Freire's (1970) critical pedagogy. Just as some software (e.g., the Linux operating system) is designed as "open source," capable of being modified and adapted by any user, we envisage our framework as accessible to all and modifiable by all—an open source for generating language policy at the level of the school. In the spirit of this approach, we have used several theoretical perspectives to present the core ideas within the framework in an attempt to convey the dynamic nature of the constructs and the productive overlap among different perspectives.

Our instructional framework assigns a central role to the ways in which societal power relations in the wider society are either replicated or repudiated within the school context. These power relations interact both with the instructional choices that teachers make and with the modes of cognitive and personal engagement envisaged for students. We consider in the next sections how these power relations affect patterns of student achievement.

Societal Power Relations Are Relevant to Student Achievement

Poverty and Power

Evidence for the relevance of power relations to educational achievement is evident in the well-established relationship between socioeconomic status (SES) and achievement (see Chapter 1). In their influential National Research Council report, *Preventing Reading Difficulties in Young Children*, Snow and colleagues (1998) report correlations of .68 between poverty-related variables and reading development compared to average correlations of around .45 between reading development and phonological awareness. In other words, social determinants of achievement are more fundamental than cognitive or linguistic variables viewed in isolation. Other studies (e.g., Hoover, 2000) have shown even stronger relationships between poverty and achievement. These relationships include the combined impact of the economic situation of families and the unequal funding for schools serving impoverished as compared to affluent students within the United States.

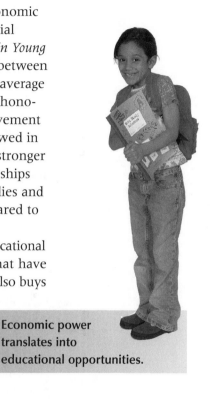

It is not hard to see how economic power translates into educational opportunities: money buys houses in affluent neighborhoods that have better-equipped schools and more experienced teachers; money also buys medical insurance, better nutrition, books, computers, and tutoring when required. The relevance of these nonschool variables is also evident in the research suggesting that improvements in families' economic and social prospects translates into improved school performance. In fact, non-instructional interventions that focus on improving the lives of low-income children and families may be as powerful in boosting academic achievement as any form of instructional intervention (Anyon, 2005; Rothstein, 2002).

> Economic power translates into educational opportunities.

Racism and Power

Intersecting with the influence of poverty is the influence of racism. We are using the term *racism* to refer to the exercise of discursive, economic, or physical power against individuals or groups defined on the basis of skin pigmentation or other physical features. More generally, we can talk about the exercise of coercive relations of power by dominant groups over subordinated groups. For example, racism, sexism, and homophobia all represent examples of coercive relations of power.

Nigerian-born anthropologist John Ogbu's work provides a useful starting point in understanding how coercive relations of power influence students' academic engagement and achievement. Ogbu (1992) distinguishes between voluntary or immigrant minorities, who tend to succeed academically, and involuntary minorities who tend to experience academic difficulties. The former have immigrated to the host country with the expectation of a better life and generally have a positive orientation to the host community and no ambivalence or insecurity in regard to their own identities. Involuntary minorities, by contrast, were originally brought into the society against their will—for example, through slavery, conquest, colonization, or forced labor—and were often denied the opportunity for true participation in or assimilation into the mainstream society. The four major groups in the United States (African Americans, Latinos/Latinas, Native Americans, and Hawaiian Americans) that have experienced intense racial discrimination over generations also manifest disproportionate academic failure and clearly match the profile of involuntary minorities.

However, Ogbu's distinction is undoubtedly oversimplified. It fails to explain the underachievement of some immigrant minority groups in the Canadian context (e.g., Afro-Caribbean, Portuguese-speaking, and Spanish-speaking students). Similarly, it does not account for considerable within-group variance in academic achievement nor the effect of variables such as socioeconomic status. It is also likely that refugee students constitute a separate category that cannot easily be subsumed within the *voluntary–involuntary* distinction (Vincent, 1996).

In spite of its inability to account for the complexities of dominant-subordinated group relationships, Ogbu's distinction represents a useful starting point in conceptualizing the causes of underachievement among subordinated group students. It highlights important patterns of how coercive power relations operating in the broader society find their way into the structures and operation of schooling. The distinction must be conceived in dynamic rather than static terms. The status of groups may change rapidly from one generation to another in ways that a rigid dichotomy cannot accommodate.

For these reasons, we prefer to discuss the issues in terms of a continuum ranging from coercive to collaborative relations of power. This continuum encompasses the important distinction that Ogbu has made but is more useful in analyzing how power relations in the broader society get translated into educational failure within the schools, and, most important, how this process can be resisted and reversed.

Challenging Coercive Relations of Power

Figure 11.1 proposes that relations of power in the wider society (macro-interactions), ranging from coercive to collaborative in varying degrees, influence both the ways in which educators define their roles and the types of structures that are established in the educational system. "Coercive relations of power" refer to the exercise of power by a

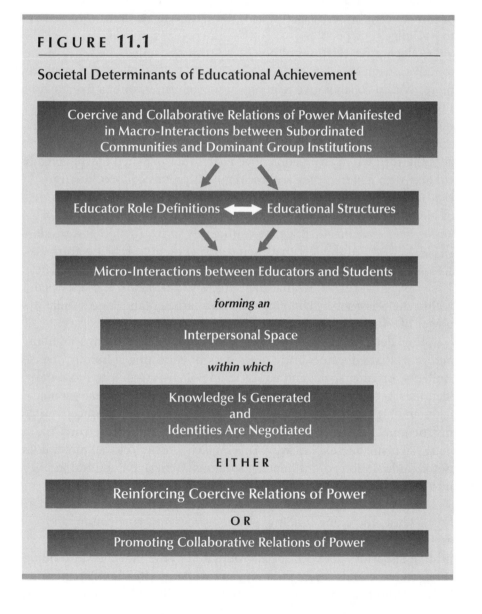

FIGURE 11.1

Societal Determinants of Educational Achievement

Coercive and Collaborative Relations of Power Manifested in Macro-Interactions between Subordinated Communities and Dominant Group Institutions

Educator Role Definitions ⟷ Educational Structures

Micro-Interactions between Educators and Students

forming an

Interpersonal Space

within which

Knowledge Is Generated
and
Identities Are Negotiated

EITHER

Reinforcing Coercive Relations of Power

OR

Promoting Collaborative Relations of Power

dominant individual, group, or country to the detriment of a subordinated individual, group, or country. For example, in the past, dominant group institutions (e.g., schools) have required that subordinated groups deny their cultural identity and give up their languages as a necessary condition for success in the mainstream society. For educators to become partners in the transmission of knowledge, culturally diverse students were required to acquiesce in the subordination of their identities and to celebrate as "truth" the perspectives of the dominant group (e.g., the "truth" that Columbus "discovered" America and brought "civilization" to its indigenous peoples).

Collaborative relations of power, by contrast, reflect the sense of the term *power,* which refers to "being enabled" or "empowered" to achieve more. Within collaborative relations of power, *power* is not a fixed quantity but is generated through interaction with others. The power relationship is additive rather then subtractive. The more empowered one individual or group becomes, the more is generated for others to share, as is the case when two people love each other or when teachers really connect with children they are teaching. Within this context, the term *empowerment* can be defined as the collaborative creation of power. Students whose schooling experiences reflect collaborative relations of power participate confidently in instruction as a result of the fact that their sense of identity is being affirmed and extended in their interactions with educators. They also know that their voices will be heard and respected within the classroom. Schooling amplifies rather than silences their power of *self*-expression.

Empowerment can be defined as the collaborative creation of power.

"Role definitions" refer to the mindset of expectations, assumptions, and goals that educators bring to the task of educating culturally diverse students. Broader social and educational policies attempt to mold the identities or role definitions of teachers. For example, the reading mandates and high-stakes testing of NCLB attempt to impose a conception of instructional effectiveness that is limited to transmitting the curriculum in a systematic and explicit way. This implicit teacher role definition does not include notions of influencing students to engage in critical inquiry into social realities.

"Educational structures" refer to the organization of schooling in a broad sense, including funding, policies, programs, curriculum, and assessment. Coercive power relations are evident in both the huge income disparities between social groups and in the much lower funding received by schools serving low-income students (Biddle & Berliner, 2002). Although educational structures generally reflect the values and priorities of dominant groups in society, they are not by any means fixed or static. As with most other aspects of the way societies are organized and resources distributed, educational structures are contested by individuals and groups.

Educational structures, together with educator role definitions, determine the micro-interactions between educators, students, and communities. These micro-interactions form an interpersonal space within which the acquisition of knowledge and the formation of identity is negotiated. Power is created and shared within this interpersonal space where minds and identities meet. As such, these micro-interactions constitute the most immediate determinant of student academic success or failure.

Micro-interactions between educators, students, and communities are never neutral; in varying degrees, they either reinforce coercive relations of power or promote collaborative relations of power. In the former case, they contribute to the disempowerment of culturally diverse students and communities; in the latter case, the micro-interactions constitute a process of empowerment that enables educators, students, and communities to challenge the operation of coercive power structures.

The case studies of technology-supported instruction show clearly how the interpersonal spaces created in the micro-interactions between teachers and students helped students acquire academic content and generate new knowledge. Consider, for example, how much the Project FRESA students learned about biological processes, mathematics, and using language in powerful ways. The framework presented in Figure 11.1 suggests, however, that these projects generated high levels of student engagement primarily because they validated and extended students' experiences and affirmed their identities as intelligent, imaginative, and linguistically talented individuals. Student empowerment, understood as the collaborative creation of power, resulted from, and fueled, their academic engagement. In other words, the instructional effectiveness of these projects derived from their challenge to coercive power relations in the broader society.

We shift now to a focus on the instructional dimensions of the framework and, in particular, to an examination of how language and literacy practices intersect with identity negotiation in the classroom.

The Development of Academic Expertise

The case studies reveal a pattern whereby teacher–student interactions generate a high level of both cognitive engagement and identity investment on the part of students. Teachers also help students understand language and critically analyze content either through various forms of English-language support (or scaffolding) or through use of students' L1. In addition, there are examples of teachers explicitly demystifying how the language code works but also extending this instructional focus to examining how language intersects with societal power relations. Finally, students are given ample opportunities to use language to generate new knowledge, create literature and art, and act on social realities.

These dimensions of the instructional environment are expressed in Figure 11.2. This framework highlights and "unpacks" aspects of what we have termed the "micro-interactions" between teachers and students in Figure 11.1. Thus, the instructional environment is framed within patterns of societal power relations and the highlighted dimensions express ways in which power is collaboratively created between teachers and students. These dimensions can also be unpacked in much greater detail, depending on the context and purpose of the discussion. For example, an elaboration of the Focus on Meaning component would involve several of the design principles discussed in Chapter 4 (e.g., promoting deep processing of meaning and relating content to students' prior knowledge). Finally, the framework is explicitly intended to express a transformative orientation to pedagogy. A critical dimension is incorporated in all three of the focus areas (e.g., critical literacy, critical awareness of language, and acting on social issues).

The central sphere in Figure 11.2 represents the interpersonal space created in the interactions between teachers and students (and among students either within the classroom or in networked environments). Within this interpersonal space, knowledge is constructed and identities are negotiated. In other words, teacher–student interactions can be viewed through two lenses: (1) the lens of *the teaching–learning relationship* in a narrow sense, represented by the strategies and techniques that teachers use to promote literacy, numeracy, content knowledge and cognitive growth; and (2) the lens of *identity negotiation* reflected in the messages communicated to students regarding their identities—who they are in the teacher's eyes and who they are capable of becoming. The framework proposes that an optimal learning environment, virtual or "real," requires that both cognitive engagement and identity investment be maximized.

In contexts of cultural, linguistic, or economic diversity, these interactions are never neutral: They either challenge the operation of coercive relations of power in the wider society or they reinforce these power relations. For example, if students' home languages are ignored or actively repudiated within the classroom, then the message to students

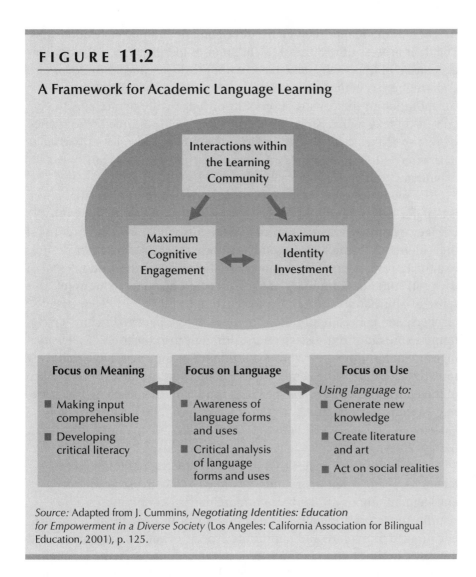

FIGURE 11.2

A Framework for Academic Language Learning

Source: Adapted from J. Cummins, *Negotiating Identities: Education for Empowerment in a Diverse Society* (Los Angeles: California Association for Bilingual Education, 2001), p. 125.

regarding their cultural and linguistic backgrounds reinforces the negative messages their communities often receive within the broader society.

Within the interpersonal space of teacher–student interactions, the more students become engaged cognitively, the more academic progress they are likely to make. If students are involved primarily in rote memorization in the classroom, only a fraction of their cognitive capacity is engaged in learning.

The interpersonal space represented in Figure 11.2 extends Vygotsky's (1978) notion of the *zone of proximal development* beyond the cognitive sphere into the realms of affective development and power relationships. The dual process of reciprocal negotiation of identity and collaborative generation of knowledge take place within this *knowledge construction zone* and are seen as being intimately related to each other. Teacher–student collaboration in the construction of knowledge will operate effectively only in contexts where students' identities are being affirmed. The framework also makes clear that the *construction zone* can also be a *constriction zone* where student identities and learning are constricted rather than extended.

The relevance of identity investment derives from the fact that affect is a major determinant of the extent to which students are likely to engage cognitively and academically. Students will be reluctant to invest their identities in the learning process if they feel their teachers do not like them, respect them, and appreciate their experiences and talents. In the past, students from marginalized social groups have seldom felt this sense of affirmation and respect for language and culture from their teachers, and consequently their intellectual and personal talents rarely found expression in the classroom. Although the construct of identity investment has not received much attention in the cognitive psychology research literature, it has emerged as a significant explanatory construct in the educational anthropology and second language learning literature (e.g., McCarty, 1993, 2002; McCarty & Romero, 2005; Norton, 2000; Pavlenko & Norton, 2006; Peirce, 1995; Pittway, 2004; Toohey, Manyak, & Day, 2006).

This perspective implies that in considering the potential of technology-supported instruction or projects to increase academic engagement among students from marginalized communities, two significant factors are likely to be (1) the extent to which students are encouraged to explore and appreciate aspects of their own cultural and linguistic heritage and (2) the extent to which they come to see themselves as intelligent and capable human beings in the process of carrying out these projects.

With specific reference to academic language learning, the framework proposes that instruction should focus on *meaning, language,* and *use*. Each of these foci is discussed next.

Focus on Meaning

The framework highlights the fact that effective instruction in a first or second language must focus initially on deep understanding of meaning or messages. Virtually all applied linguists agree that access to sufficient comprehensible input in the target language is a necessary condition for language acquisition. As noted in previous chapters, with respect to academic language learning in both L1 and L2, an abundance of research shows a strong positive relationship between extensive reading and the development of reading comprehension (see Cummins [2001] and Krashen [2004b] for reviews).

The Focus on Meaning component in Figure 11.2 argues that the interpretation of the construct of *comprehensible input* must go beyond just literal comprehension. Depth of understanding of concepts and vocabulary as well as critical literacy are intrinsic to the notion of comprehensible input when referring to the development of academic language proficiency. This implies a process whereby students relate textual and instructional meanings to their own experience and prior knowledge (e.g., activate their cognitive schemata), critically analyze the information in the text (e.g., evaluate the validity of various arguments or propositions), and use the results of their discussions and analyses in some concrete, intrinsically motivating activity or project (e.g., making a video or writing a poem or essay on a particular topic). These processes are clearly consistent with the principles of learning articulated by both Bransford and colleagues (2000) and Guthrie (2004).

Focus on Language

The Focus on Language component in Figure 11.2 attempts to put controversial issues, such as the role of phonics in reading instruction and the appropriate time and ways to teach grammar and spelling, under the "umbrella" of *language awareness*. The development of language awareness includes not just an explicit focus on formal aspects of the language but also the development of *critical language awareness* that encompasses exploration of the relationships between language and power. Students, for example, might carry out research on the status of different varieties of language (e.g., colloquial language versus formal "standard" language) and explore critically why one form is considered by many educators and the general public to be "better" than the other. They might also research issues such as linguistic code switching and the functions it plays within their own lives and their bilingual communities. Or they might analyze letters to the editor on controversial issues such as immigration and examine how the language used in these letters positions and potentially stereotypes minority group learners such as themselves and their parents. To be effective, these activities and projects need to be anchored in problems or issues identified by the students in collaboration with their teachers or other adults, and grow out of their wishes to understand those problems better. The partner class investigations by Italian students of dialect and folk culture in Mario Lodi's Cooperative Education movement, mentioned in Chapter 5, are illustrative of an explicit focus on language with transformative possibilities for education.

In short, the framework proposes that a focus on formal features of the target language should be integrated with critical inquiry into issues of language and power. Also, to be effective, a focus on language must be linked to extensive input in the target language (e.g., through reading) and extensive opportunities for written and oral use of the language (e.g., oral or written discussion of controversial issues).

Focus on Use

The Focus on Use component in Figure 11.2 is based on the notion that L1 and L2 acquisition will remain abstract and classroom bound unless students have the opportunity to express themselves—their identities and their intelligence—through language. In order to motivate language use there should ideally be an authentic audience that encourages two-way communication in both oral and written modes. Clearly, computer-mediated sister class projects provide such an audience. The three examples of language use presented in Figure 11.2 (generate new knowledge, create literature and art, and act on social realities) are intended to illustrate important components of critical literacy. Language must be used to amplify students' intellectual, aesthetic, and social identities if it is to contribute to student empowerment. Unless active and authentic language use for these purposes is promoted in the classroom, ELL students' grasp of academic (and conversational) aspects of their second language is likely to remain shallow and passive.

There is little question that technology can provide many of the essential components required to stimulate active written language use. Collaborative sister class projects, publication of student work on classroom or school webpages, or simply the use of computers to lay out and print newsletters or other forms of publication all facilitate access to wider audiences than would otherwise be possible. Communications technology can dramatically expand the communities of inquiry to which students have access and provide immediate outlets for communicating the results of stu-

Technology can provide many of the essential components required to stimulate active written language use.

dents' intellectual and artistic work (e.g., through school or class web-pages) (see, for example, Brown, 2000; Cummins & Sayers, 1995; de Klerk, 1998; Skourtou, Kourtis-Kazoullis, & Cummins, 2006).

The Role of Identity Texts in Developing Academic Expertise

The products of student work carried out within this pedagogical frame-work can be termed *identity texts* insofar as students invest their identities in these texts (written, spoken, visual, musical, or combinations in multimodal form) that then hold a mirror up to students in which their identities are reflected back in a positive light. When students share identity texts with multiple audiences (peers, teachers, parents, grand-parents, sister classes, the media, etc.) they are likely to receive positive feedback and affirmation of self in interaction with these audiences. Chow and Cummins (2003), for example, note that students who created dual-language books often sent copies of these books to friends and relatives in their countries of origin. They also contacted these friends and relatives by e-mail to direct them to the Dual Language Showcase website (http://thornwood.peelschools.org/Dual/) where their dual-language book was displayed.

The case studies and vignettes discussed throughout this book illustrate the concept of *identity text*. The Project FRESA website is a good example, as is the project on immigrant workers' rights carried out by students at the International High School at LaGuardia Community College in New York City (see Chapter 3; www.whatkidscando.org/index.asp). The concept of *identity text* has also been elaborated in a Canada-wide research project entitled *From Literacy to Multiliteracies: Designing Learning Environments for Knowledge Generation within the New Economy* (Early et al., 2002). This project has developed a description of *multiliteracies pedagogy* based on the dual-language literacy practices observed in classrooms with high concentrations of bilingual students. The description involves the following components that clearly map onto pedagogical dimensions highlighted within the academic expertise framework:

- Multiliteracies pedagogy constructs an image of the child as intelligent, imaginative, and linguistically talented; individual differences in these traits do not diminish the potential of each child to shine in specific ways.

■ Multiliteracies pedagogy acknowledges and builds on the cultural and linguistic capital (prior knowledge) of students and communities.

■ Multiliteracies pedagogy aims explicitly to promote cognitive engagement and identity investment on the part of students.

■ Multiliteracies pedagogy enables students to construct knowledge, create literature and art, and act on social realities through dialogue and critical inquiry.

■ Multiliteracies pedagogy employs a variety of technological tools to support students' construction of knowledge, literature, and art and their presentation of this intellectual work to multiple audiences through the creation of identity texts.

As noted, multiliteracies pedagogy draws on transmission, social constructivist, and transformative orientations to teaching and learning. The description is consistent with the New London Group's multiliteracies instructional framework (Chapter 2) but attempts to express the pedagogical dimensions in such a way that human relationships and identity investment are highlighted explicitly as central to effective pedagogy.

Although the framework we have presented is entirely consistent with the empirical research on how people learn, it represents a radical departure from the normalized assumptions that characterize the majority of classrooms serving culturally and linguistically diverse students. Specifically, as outlined in Chapters 1 through 4, the following assumptions and practices have become normalized in ways that constrict both the identity options for culturally diverse students and their cognitive and academic engagement:

■ Literacy is assumed to equal English literacy.

■ There is minimal acknowledgment or promotion of students' cultural/linguistic/imaginative capital.

■ The involvement of culturally and linguistically diverse parents is limited and passive.

■ Technology use is sporadic and unconnected to coherent pedagogical philosophies and practices.

These normalized instructional assumptions and practices were common prior to NCLB but they have become entrenched much more rigidly as a result of the mandate for systematic and explicit phonics instruction from kindergarten through grade 6 (Lyon & Chaabra, 2004) and the ubiquity of high-stakes testing.

Conclusion

In this chapter we have presented an approach to conceptualizing school improvement and literacy development that differs in significant ways from other frameworks for educational reform. Although virtually all school improvement frameworks claim to be "evidence based," they differ significantly in what kinds of evidence they regard as relevant and scientifically credible. One major distinction is the extent to which the theoretical frame focuses narrowly on individual cognition (and associated instructional interventions) or admits the relevance of social determinants of school achievement. The reports that laid the groundwork for NCLB (Snow, Burns, & Griffin, 1998; National Reading Panel, 2000) did not explicitly deny the relevance of social variables; they just failed to consider them in any coherent and systematic way (Gee, 1999, 2000). Three assumptions contributed in varying degrees to the neglect of social determinants. The first two assumptions are based on interpretations of what constitutes scientific research and/or can be usefully investigated, whereas the third is explicitly ideological in orientation:

- Social determinants are acknowledged as relevant but educators have no control over them and so it makes sense to focus on what *can* be changed—namely, the quality of instruction. Within this view, classroom instruction should be based on scientific data that compare the efficacy of alternative approaches. The report by Snow and colleagues (1998) exemplifies this assumption.

- The only research that qualifies as "scientific" and contributes to knowledge is experimental- and quasi-experimental-controlled comparisons of alternative instructional approaches or interventions. This assumption automatically excludes sociologically oriented and anthropologically oriented research because these disciplines usually analyze the influence of variables that cannot readily be quantified within an experimental research paradigm. The National Reading Panel report falls into this category.

- It is ideologically unacceptable to spend tax dollars to raise the living standards of impoverished communities or to equalize school funding. Therefore social determinants of achievement are of little interest and can be ignored. Achievement can be raised by implementing scientifically proven instructional methods in low-income schools. This ideological viewpoint is implicit in the actual implementation of NCLB.

The refusal to consider social determinants of school achievement has resulted in the emergence and enforcement of a framework for literacy instruction that is highly transmission oriented and constricts teacher and student identities in classroom interactions. Furthermore, as we have argued, the orientation to literacy instruction that has been enforced and justified as "scientifically proven" clearly violates the scientific consensus from cognitive psychology regarding how people learn. These instructional approaches simply reinforce the subordinated status of low-income and culturally diverse students. The alternative approaches to literacy instruction that are illustrated in the case studies we have reviewed and in the current theoretical framework are much more consistent with the cognitive science literature than the scripted drill-and-practice virtually mandated by NCLB.

When social variables are admitted into the discussion of school improvement, it is hard to escape the obvious relevance of historical and current power relations. Power differentials between social groups result in home and school conditions that fail to provide a minimal basis for healthy academic growth. Thus, one obvious direction for raising academic achievement is to provide the minimal conditions for physical, cognitive, and academic growth by investing in low-income schools and communities. As Anyon (2005) and Rothstein (2002) have pointed out, there is persuasive evidence that such investment pays academic dividends.

Attention to the role of social determinants and the psychological dimensions of coercive relations of power also opens up pedagogical insights. If the devaluation of identities within school and society contributes to students' mental withdrawal from academic effort, as suggested by extensive anthropological research (e.g. Fordham, 1990; Ladson-Billings, 1995; Ogbu, 1992), then it is reasonable to hypothesize that pedagogical approaches that affirm the identities of culturally and linguistically diverse students may promote greater academic engagement and achievement. Again, there is considerable empirical research to support this hypothesis (see review in Cummins, 2001).

The academic expertise framework that we have proposed incorporates a similar emphasis on critical literacy, active learning, deep understanding, and the importance of building on students' prior knowledge that is incorporated in a number of other frameworks (e.g., Bransford et al., 2000; Guthrie, 2004; The New London Group, 1966). However, it also argues for the centrality of *identity negotiation* and *identity investment* in any conception of effective instruction for low-income and subordinated group students. Learning will be optimized when teacher–student interactions maximize both cognitive engagement *and* identity investment.

The framework attempts to express in a very concrete way the kinds of instructional emphases and language interactions required to build students' academic expertise. Optimal instruction will include a *focus on meaning*, a *focus on language*, and a *focus on use*. The focus on meaning entails the development of critical literacy rather than surface-level processing of text. The focus on language involves promoting not just explicit knowledge of how the linguistic code operates but also critical awareness of how language operates within society. If students are to participate effectively within a democratic society, they should be able to "read" how language is used to achieve social goals: to elucidate issues, to persuade, to deceive, to include, to exclude, and so on. The Focus on Use component parallels the New London Group's transformed practice but expresses in much more concrete ways what this might look like within the classroom context. It argues that optimal instruction will enable students to generate knowledge, create literature and art, and act on social realities.

The academic expertise framework also makes explicit the fact that classroom instruction always positions students in particular ways that reflect the implicit (or sometimes explicit) image of the student in the teacher's mind. How students are positioned either expands or constricts their opportunities for identity investment and cognitive engagement. The nested pedagogical orientations in Figure 2.1 (Chapter 2) represent a continuum ranging from relatively constricted to more expanded opportunities for identity investment and cognitive engagement.

The final chapter discusses in more detail how educators, individually and collectively, can articulate and implement pedagogical choices that will promote literacy engagement and higher levels of literacy achievement. In contrast to the constriction of teacher choice within NCLB, we argue that educators should systematically and explicitly articulate their pedagogical options and make informed pedagogical decisions that reflect their own identities and their aspirations for their students.

Discussion Questions for Study Groups

1. In this chapter, the concepts of coercive and collaborative relations of power are described. Think about how these two types of power enter into your own life. List three examples each of coercive and collaborative relations of power that you have experienced or observed during the past few days. As an educator, how might you promote collaborative relations of power in your school or classroom?

2. *Identity negotiation* is proposed as a central component of the framework discussed in Chapter 11. Think about the interactions you have had in the past few days with family and colleagues. How have identities been negotiated in these interactions? What similarities and/or differences exist between identity negotiation in social interactions with friends and colleagues as compared to the interactions teachers have with their students in the classroom?

3. In your own classroom or school context, what kinds of learning activities typically generate the greatest identity investment from students? How do these activities differ from those that generate little identity investment?

4. There is little question that technology can provide many of the essential components required to stimulate active written language use. What kinds of projects can you think of that would harness technology for "active written language use"?

5. In this chapter, dual-language books written by students are used as an example of identity texts. What other kinds of identity texts might be feasible to explore with students and communities in your school context?

6. When social variables are admitted into the discussion of school improvement, it is hard to escape the obvious relevance of historical and current power relations. How do social variables affect (either positively or negatively) the literacy engagement and academic development of students in your school?

224

Implementing Change

A very simple, but also empowering, message runs through this final chapter: School improvement is too important to leave in the hands of politicians or school administrators—teachers must take the lead in initiating change. Working with communities whose children are currently marginalized by the school system, teachers can articulate, and act on, the wide range of choices they face every time they walk into their classrooms. This process involves imagination—the process of envisaging options and alternatives—and a commitment to social and educational justice.

We have seen throughout this book the dramatic change in students' lives and educational prospects that individual teachers brought about when they focused their imagination on expanding students' cultural, linguistic, and intellectual resources. Rather than acquiesce in the exclusion of students' talents from the one-size-fits-all classroom, these teachers initiated projects and learning activities that enabled students to construct knowledge and gain insight into social realities. Students thought more, read more, wrote more, and learned more. The interactions these teachers orchestrated constructed an image of their students as intelligent, imaginative, and linguistically talented, and simultaneously challenged the devaluation of students' identities in the wider society.

Clearly, in an era of prescribed curriculum and high-stakes testing there are many constraints on teachers' choices and actions. Yet, educators are never powerless. Individually and collectively, educators have choices

- In how they interact with students;
- In how they engage students cognitively;
- In how they activate students' prior knowledge;
- In how they present and discuss textbook content;
- In how they use technology to amplify imagination;
- In how they involve parents in their children's education; and
- In what they communicate to students regarding their home language and culture.

In this chapter, we discuss strategies whereby educators can take on the role of change agent. To acknowledge and articulate pedagogical choices entails both responsibility and opportunity. Educators take on the responsibility to expand rather than constrict students' intellectual horizons and their engagement with literacy. But in taking on this responsibility, educators are also given the opportunity to stretch their own horizons as educators and to nurture human possibilities, which is why most educators entered the profession in the first place.

Alternative Routes to Change

The model of top-down, centrally mandated educational change implemented in the United States through No Child Left Behind (NCLB), and to a lesser extent through the National Literacy Strategy in the United Kingdom (U.K.), represents only one option for large-scale educational reform. Much more enlightened (from our perspective) is the educational reform strategy initiated in the Australian state of Queensland in the late 1990s. Allan Luke, one of the authors of the New London Group's (1996) *Multiliteracies* blueprint, was appointed Deputy Director General of Education with the mandate to initiate new approaches to curriculum, pedagogy, and assessment that would address the challenges of new community cultures, new forms of knowledge and technologies, and globalized economies (Luke, 2002). We first outline the Queensland experience and then articulate the related foundations on which we base our own reform agenda. Finally, we present a concrete "choice template" that might be used by educators within schools to discuss the range of options they have with respect to improving the effectiveness of their own individual and collective teaching.

The Queensland Experience

Luke (2002) contrasts the approach to evidence-based reform adopted in Queensland with the U.S. and U.K. approaches where the basic strategy involves specification of target outcomes, standardization of teaching by means of centrally mandated programs and instructional approaches, and monitoring of outcomes on standardized tests. The Queensland approach to reform was equally committed to an evidence-based approach. However, its view of "evidence" was much broader than the "scientifically proven" spin that continues to dominate U.S. discourse on educational reform. Queensland's approach was based on local, school-level analyses of community literacy needs, audits and local mobilization of available teacher professional expertise, and the study of community linguistic and cultural profiles. A number of research studies were commissioned that contributed to *Literate Futures* (Luke, Freebody, & Land, 2000), a policy document that was adopted by the state government and is currently under implementation.

The empirical data that informed the development of policy included an analysis of pedagogy in 1,200 classroom lessons over a three-year period and extensive consultation with key educational stakeholders in the state (e.g., parents, teacher educators, etc.). The development of policy was also influenced by the work of New Literacy theorists (e.g., Barton, Hamilton, & Ivanic, 2000) who argue that literacy is always situated in particular times and places and thus cannot legitimately be viewed as an autonomous set of skills. Thus, skills are not fixed but change according to the social context and students' modes of participation in these contexts.

Literate Futures focused on four core strategies:

1. *"Balanced approaches."* The *four resources* model of reading instruction (Freebody & Luke, 1990) was adopted as a means of avoiding the either-or dichotomy between a code-focus or a meaning-focus to the teaching of literacy that has characterized the "reading wars" in numerous countries. This model specifies that students need to access four dimensions of what it means to be literate. These dimensions are code breaker, text participant, text user, and text analyst. *Code breaker* involves being able to decode and encode language at an appropriate level of proficiency and it incorporates phonics and the use of accurate spelling and grammar, along the lines of what we have termed "discrete language skills" (Chapter 2). *Text participant* involves using background knowledge and knowledge about language (e.g., vocabulary) to understand and compose texts. *Text user* involves using written language appropriately according to context, audience, and content for particular real-life purposes. *Text analyst* involves critical analysis of the ways texts are used to convey ideas and influence people. These dimensions are not sequenced in a linear order and there is no assumption that there is one best (or "scientifically proven") method that will apply to all communities.

2. *Whole-school planning.* Schools were required to develop whole-school plans that included analysis of local community linguistic and cultural resources, audits of teacher expertise, and community involvement. Progress toward meeting achievement goals were assessed in relation to "distance-traveled" performance targets benchmarked against "like-schools" of similar community demographic and socioeconomic backgrounds. Schools were encouraged to discuss and negotiate progress with stakeholders and the school communities but there was no publication of "league tables" that compare schools with other schools from very different socioeconomic and demographic communities.

3. *Multiliteracies.* Each school was encouraged to focus on blending information technologies and traditional print literacies such that the "new literacies" required by online communication, mass media, and digital cultures would be integrated with the four resources model.

4. *Professional development.* There was a recognition that much of the expertise needed to systematically improve literacy was already in the schools but that it was dispersed and not sufficiently recognized. Thus, the audit of staff expertise was intended to identify existing resources within the schools but also to re-focus them in more effective ways.

Luke (2002) notes that this strategy contrasts sharply with a compliance approach that targets short- and medium-term improvement of test scores via the standardization, monitoring, and control of teacher classroom behavior and methods. It is based on the premise that teacher learning and professionalization, rather than deskilling and centralized control have the potential for more flexible and sustainable approaches to these problems.

Furthermore, the Queensland strategy was explicitly intended to have "a strong social-justice orientation for dealing with the economic consequences of new conditions, and for preparing students for new economies, technologies, and cultures" (Luke, 2002, p. 193). Luke (2006) notes that since the inception of the policy, test scores have shown upward trends but he cautions that these positive outcomes cannot be directly attributed to the policy changes. More important from his perspective is that "the suite of reforms beginning in 2000 led to major and ongoing pedagogic dialogue amongst teachers and among teacher-educators across the state" (p. 10).

The Queensland reform differed significantly from that in the United States in its approach to the relationship between poverty and literacy. As in other contexts, it was found that poverty and location were "the strongest predictors of low test scores, high dropout rates, and poor overall achievement" (Luke, 2002, p. 192). However, in contrast to NCLB, the Queensland policymakers viewed this fact as relevant to the kinds of solutions that might be envisaged. In the United States, researchers and policymakers viewed improvement of literacy outcomes essentially as a process of correcting student deficits in phonological awareness and ensuring that systematic explicit phonics dominated

Teachers and diverse communities are acknowledged as part of the solution rather than as part of the problem.

early literacy instruction. Thus literacy policy was constructed "as a short-term technocratic, readily manageable 'fix'" (Luke, 2002, p. 193) rather than as a more medium-term set of educational and social initiatives that respond to the real complexity of the issue.

We are highlighting the Queensland strategy not as an exemplary approach to educational reform but simply as an alternative that illustrates that evidence-based reform *can* address traditional, linear, text-based literacies while still recognizing teacher professionalism and community linguistic and cultural resources. Simply put, teachers and diverse communities are acknowledged as part of the solution rather than as part of the problem.

In the next section, we summarize the foundations of the change process we are proposing in contrast to the process that has been underway in the United States.

The Foundations of Change

The educational reform process that is exemplified in NCLB and that draws on prior experience in states such as Texas is summarized here with respect to its assumptions about pedagogy, assessment, and how

The "Grade Expectations" Change Process	
Approach to change	Top-down, hierarchical, and coercive; schools that fail to meet achievement targets can be disbanded and states that refuse to participate lose major federal funding.
Diagnosis of problem	Student deficits in phonological awareness and inadequate early reading instruction.
Solution	Phonological awareness training and systematic explicit phonics instruction.
Evidence	Experimental and quasi-experimental research showing effects of phonological awareness and phonics instruction on decoding; *however, policy ignored scientific evidence regarding (1) social determinants of reading achievement and (2) the absence of effects on reading comprehension beyond grade 1 for normally achieving and low-achieving students.*
Pedagogical philosophy	Direct instruction/behaviorism; skills hierarchies are taught in a sequential scripted manner moving from least to most complex.
Outcome goals	Increase in standardized test scores.
Monitoring of progress	Adequate yearly progress as measured by standardized tests with minimal accommodations for ELL and special needs students.
Results to date	Minimal evidence of test score improvement in states that have implemented this approach during the past decade (e.g., Texas and California).

The "Great Expectations" Change Process

Approach to change	Educators and communities are major stakeholders who should be given responsibility and opportunity to identify promising directions for school improvement that fit local conditions and community aspirations.
Diagnosis of problem	Underachievement is rooted both in societal inequities and inadequate educational provision. Causes of achievement gaps are multiple and thus interventions must be multidimensional and address both instructional and noninstructional factors.
Solution	Address social inequities in health care, nutrition, housing, and library provision that affect low-income students' readiness to learn and their opportunities to engage with literacy; identify and support programs, such as those described in this book, that generate high engagement with literacy among low-income students and that conform to the scientific evidence about how people learn.
Evidence	A range of scientific evidence from multiple disciplines is relevant to understanding and addressing underachievement. Variables related to socioeconomic status show the strongest and most consistent relationship with achievement, suggesting that social as well as educational interventions are needed to increase achievement. Variables related to opportunity to read and amount of reading show strong and consistent relationships to reading comprehension, and thus a major focus of school-based interventions should be to increase the amount of reading and discussion of books that students carry out.
Pedagogical philosophy	Instruction should be based on the scientific evidence regarding how people learn (Bransford et al., 2000); this implies building on students' prior knowledge, promoting strong cognitive and personal engagement, and encouraging active self-directed student learning. Furthermore, instruction should address the changing nature of literacy in an era of globalization and rapid technological expansion. This requires an emphasis on multiliteracies and the development of critical literacy.
Outcome goals	Increases in various dimensions of literacy, including the critical literacy necessary to participate in a democratic society.
Monitoring of progress	Some uses of standardized tests to assess basic literacy outcomes at a national or state level, as in the NAEP, but also development of portfolio and other performance measures that can assess a much broader range of literacy and cognitive outcomes. Serious assessment of these outcomes will also encourage their incorporation into curricula and instruction.
Results to date	Multiple case studies showing high levels of literacy engagement among low-income students when the pedagogy affirms their identities and enables them to express their intelligence, imagination, and multilingual talents.

change is best effected. We then contrast these assumptions with those that underlie the analysis in this book. The contrast is essentially one between "grade expectations" and "great expectations"—between a focus on increasing lower-level literacy skills through rigid instructional prescriptions as compared to promotion of a much broader range of literacy and cognitive skills that all students need for social and economic participation.

Articulating Choices

Planned change in educational systems involves *choice*. Administrators make choices at a broad system level, school principals make choices at the level of individual schools, and teachers make choices within their classrooms. Choices at each of these levels are aimed at increasing the effectiveness of instruction and improving student learning. At each level of decision making, choices are constrained by the realities of politically imposed curriculum and assessment policies, funding, teacher availability and expertise in particular curricular areas, as well as by student and community characteristics such as poverty, knowledge of the language of instruction, and so on. However, within the limitations imposed by these realities, there are always degrees of freedom that permit educators to make choices on a continuing basis. Even when educators do not consciously frame their instructional actions as "choices," they have nevertheless chosen these instructional actions (e.g., to simply teach directly from the textbook) from among potential alternatives that they may not have consciously articulated. Paradox-ically, choice is not an option—there is no choice but to choose from a range of instructional alternatives.

In short, individual educators are never powerless, although they frequently work in conditions that are oppressive both for them and their students. Although they rarely have complete freedom, educators do have choices in the way they structure the micro-interactions in the classroom. They determine for themselves the social and educational goals they want to achieve with their students. They are responsible for the role definitions they adopt in relation to culturally diverse students and communities. Even in the context of high-stakes testing and English-only instruction, educators have options in their orientation to students' language and culture, in the forms of parent and community participation they encourage and in the way they implement pedagogy and assessment. Relevant to the choices that educators make is the inescapable reality that, in the words of U.K. educational theorist Terry Wrigley (2003, p. 2), school "improvement should be an ethical project, not just a technical one." The issue is not just about raising test scores, but about defining ourselves as educators.

Figure 12.1 presents a simple grid that can be used as an entry point for discussions of the range of choices educators actually have. We highlight six concrete aspects of curriculum and instruction—Tools,

Content, Cognition, Assessment, Language/Culture, and Parental Involvement—that can be readily identified in any school situation.

We label these dimensions "Instructional Options" to emphasize that educators and policymakers have choices with respect to how they conceptualize and use these aspects of curriculum and instruction in their schools and classrooms. These choices will reflect educators' identities or role definitions as well as the underlying pedagogical orientations that drive their instruction (i.e. transmission, social constructivist, transformative).

The initial focus of the inquiry, either for an individual educator or for teachers collectively within a school, is on "Where We Are." In other words, with respect to the six instructional options, what kind of practices are teachers currently engaged in and what pedagogical assumptions underlie these practices? For example, with respect to assessment, a teacher may have instituted a portfolio assessment process to complement standardized test scores and to provide an alternative perspective

FIGURE 12.1

A School-Based Choice Template for Planning Literacy Instruction

Instructional Options	Where We Are	Where We Want to Be	How Do We Get There?
Tools			
Content			
Cognition			
Assessment			
Language/Culture			
Parental Involvement			

on students' progress. Perhaps the teacher instituted this policy on the grounds that assessment should reflect the full range of instructional goals and provide affirmative feedback to students who carry out imaginative or high-level conceptual work.

"Where We Want to Be" initiates discussion on what educators' individual or collective vision of education is—why are they in the classroom? What are their goals for the students they interact with for 25 hours every week? What kinds of instruction would be consistent with their own image of themselves as educators? What kinds of instruction will enable their students to express and develop their intelligence, imagination, and multilingual talents?

Finally, "How Do We Get There?" focuses on strategies for bridging the gap between where teachers are instructionally at this time and where they want to be. It articulates the range of choices educators have and their power to undermine oppressive and counterproductive policies that limit students' educational potential and personal growth as educators.

In critically examining one's own individual and collective practice, teachers can usefully employ Guthrie's (2004) "literacy engagement" framework as a tool to assess the efficacy of current practice and the potential impact of any changes that might be made. For example, in assessing the adequacy of "Where We Are," we can translate this into the question: "Does the teacher's current practice result in high levels of literacy engagement on the part of his or her students?" We can consolidate Guthrie's indicators of engagement (see Chapter 2) into three dimensions:

- Amount and range of reading and writing;

- Use of effective strategies for deep understanding of text; and

- Positive affect and identity investment in reading and writing.

Guthrie notes that in all spheres of life (e.g., driving a car, doing surgery, playing golf, cooking gourmet meals, etc.) participation is key to the development of proficiency. He notes that "certainly some initial lessons are valuable for driving a car or typing on a keyboard, but expertise spirals upward mainly with engaged participation" (2004, p. 8).

The range of choice options can be appreciated by examining the choices that educators currently make in relation to each of the six instructional options in Figure 12.1.

Tools

Tools are the implements people use to carry out a variety of tasks. Within schooling, tools range from pencils, pencil sharpeners, and chalk, to calculators, cameras, computers, and projectors. In recent years, the continuing revolution in digital technologies has dramatically expanded the potential to use tools, such as the Internet, for instructional purposes. However, as noted in Chapter 4, this has not been an unproblematic process and there is a clear pedagogical divide in the way these tools are employed in low-income as compared to higher-income schools.

In carrying out an audit of how digital technologies are used in schools or classrooms, we might consider how much access students have to computers or other forms of technology, what activities they carry out on computers (drill-and-practice programs, games or simulations, word processing, use of presentation software, sister class projects, etc.), and what they are learning from these activities. What underlying pedagogical orientation is operating in their use of technology? Is there any tangible output of their work with these technologies? (Worksheet? PowerPoint presentation? Identity text?) What kinds of feedback on their accomplishments do they receive from significant others in their lives (e.g., peers, teacher, parents/grandparents)? Is there evidence that the time students spend working with technology entails high levels of literacy engagement?

In asking "Where We Want to Be" teachers might wish to consider examples of creative uses of digital technologies that they have come across (or read about in books such as this one) and ask themselves whether moving in this direction is feasible at this time. If not, then why not? If current uses of technology are predominantly transmission oriented, do educators want to expand this orientation to include social constructivist or transformative orientations? If so, what might these look like for students in a particular school context?

Finally, teachers may want to consider how they move in directions that they would see as representing powerful forms of instruction for particular students. What are the obstacles to moving in these directions and how can those obstacles be removed? For example, if access to technology is seen as a problem, one might ask, "Are there ways I can use my current classroom computers more effectively?" Remember, that Célestin Freinet initiated a network of 10,000 schools that engaged in sister class projects long before computers were available in any schools. Or teachers may be able to work with community groups or businesses to secure funds for particular projects. When educators articulate their goals clearly and discuss them with colleagues and community members, possibilities frequently emerge that were not originally apparent.

Content

Content refers to the texts (broadly defined) that are included in the curriculum or that students are encouraged to read or view. This content is conceived either as what students should learn or as a means of promoting certain forms of development (e.g., thinking skills). With respect to content, one could ask, "To what extent does the content connect with students' prior knowledge?" "Whose perspectives are reflected in the text and whose are omitted?" "What social functions do the inclusion and omission of particular texts and perspectives serve?" In other words, content is never ideologically neutral (in any country or education system). The content of the curriculum reflects choices that have been made by people and groups at various levels of the educational and societal hierarchy. Educators in schools and classrooms also have choices with respect to how they use the content that is handed down to them.

Thus, in relation to "Where We Are," teachers can critically examine the textbooks or other resources used within their classrooms. If a particular set of textbooks for teaching reading is mandated, then examine the strengths and weaknesses of these textbooks and the instructional approaches they incorporate. This examination will inevitably merge into discussion of "Where We Want to Be" and "How Do We Get There?" For example, if educators are locked into a highly scripted set of reading materials that provide little opportunity for real discussion of texts, are there opportunities to generate discussion and critical inquiry in other areas of the curriculum? In social studies, for instance, might it be possible to have students carry out projects such as creating a social history of their neighborhood or interviewing elders in the community and producing a report on the "Voices of Our Elders"? Or, within math, can the limited pedagogical vision underlying the reading program be compensated by having students carry out projects such as those illustrated in the Biographies Project (Chapter 8)? There may even be some degrees of freedom within the reading program itself. Some texts may allow for discussion or alternative interpretations that go beyond the script. In other words, teachers can frequently resist the mandate that they become slaves to the script (see vignette on page 245).

Cognition

Cognition refers to the type of cognitive engagement that particular forms of instruction evoke. Typically, cognitive engagement has been viewed in terms of a continuum ranging from higher-order thinking involving analysis and synthesis of information to lower-order thinking involving rote memory and direct application of information. Cognition also incorporates the construct of imagination that, as noted in Chapter 2, represents one of the "most powerful and energetic intellectual tools children bring to school" (Egan, 1986, p. 18). We have presented many examples of students' capacity for imaginative intellectual work in this book. Imagination may find expression in writing, art, music, or multimedia productions where students make some original intellectual contribution to the world of ideas.

In examining the levels of cognition that are evoked in the tasks set for student, there is usually a clear distinction between the kinds of cognitive engagement evoked in transmission orientations to pedagogy as compared to social constructivist and transformative orientations. In examining "Where We Want to Be" and "How Do We Get There?" brainstorming among colleagues will frequently generate creative ideas for transmitting skills or meeting curricular goals or standards by means of constructivist or transformative instructional approaches. In math, for example, students can practice calculating percentages and, at the same time, be engaged in critical inquiry by applying math to understanding social issues in the world around them. Grade 5 teacher, Bob Peterson, outlines one example of how this process can unfold:

> We use information from UNICEF (www.unicef.org) to compare our lives with those of children from around the world. For example, 20% of the children in "developing" countries are not enrolled in primary school, 71% of households in developing countries have access to safe water, and 42% have access to adequate sanitation. Like any other description of poverty, it is important for students to look at root causes and to ask the hard questions of why affluent governments, corporations, and people aren't doing what is necessary to change such situations. (2001, p. 90)

Assessment

Assessment is intended to evaluate the learning that has occurred. Typically, assessment focuses on the achievement of individual students rather than on the learning that groups or communities of students have engaged in collaboratively. Much current high-stakes testing is oriented to assessment of what students have (and have not) learned rather than to assessment designed to guide learning. Unfortunately, not all learning outcomes are equally easy to assess. Specifically, lower-order cognitive functions and learning outcomes can be assessed in relatively efficient ways (e.g., through standardized tests), whereas more complex learning outcomes reflecting higher-order thinking and use of more sophisticated learning tools are often more challenging to assess in a timely and cost-effective manner. As noted in Chapter 3, there is no alternative but to complement standardized tests with some form of portfolio or performance assessment if teachers are to assess adequately the full range of literacy outcomes reflected in curriculum standards and in descriptions of twenty-first-century literacy practices (e.g., Leu et al., 2005). Promising directions for electronic portfolio assessments have already been developed (Stefanakis, 2002) and these will undoubtedly be refined in the future.

In examining their current practice, teachers may find themselves in a situation where they feel compelled both to inflict extensive test practice on their students and also to narrow the curriculum in order to teach to the test. If teachers feel frustrated with this mandate, they might consider some of the research that validates their feelings of frustration. For example, Guthrie (2004) estimates that teaching to the test is likely to contribute only about 10 percent to test scores. In other words, "10% of the variance in test scores (differences among learners) can be explained by the extent that teachers provide specific lessons relevant to the surface structures of tests.... This may help a few children with a small portion of their test scores, but it will not help most children with most of the high competency they need to achieve" (2004, pp. 7–8).

In this situation, educators might ask whether there are ways of preparing students for high-stakes standardized tests that do not require months of mindless drills to be inflicted on students. By brainstorming with colleagues, teachers might arrive at test preparation strategies that reflect social constructivist pedagogical orientations rather than transmission orientations. For example, one way to involve students actively in demystifying the construction and social functions of standardized tests is to provide opportunities for them, working in groups, to construct their own tests on topics with which they are familiar or on which they have carried out research. For example, the teacher might explain how multiple-choice items are constructed (e.g., the role of distractors) and the different test-item formats that appear in typical tests. Groups might initially construct a set of five items on topics with which they are familiar such as baseball, popular music, television programs, popular slang, and so on. The teacher could then incorporate these items into a 25-item test that all students (including the teacher!) take.

When students have become familiar with the conventions of multiple choice tests, this could become one of the standard ways of assessing students' learning across the curriculum. For example, during the week each group might research aspects of a particular topic (e.g., the American Civil War, the European arrival in North America, endangered species, long division, etc.) and construct items based on their research. Groups could also construct items that focus on vocabulary they have explored or on a unit of study that has just been completed. At the end of each week, these items are incorporated into a student-generated, multiple-choice test using formats that mirror "real" tests. All students take these tests and the group that performs best gains some form of reward (e.g., points to be accumulated toward some goal).

Within this conception, standardized tests are viewed as one particular genre of language. Students need to be familiar with the conventions of this genre if their academic worth is to be recognized. In generating multiple-choice items, students are developing language awareness in the context of a highly challenging (but engaging) cognitive activity. This type of strategy conforms much more closely to what is known about how people learn insofar as students are engaging their prior knowledge, self-regulating their academic work, and processing meanings deeply in order to generate questions and distractors rather than just to answer questions. Students are also more likely to be intrinsically motivated to carry out this task than if they are simply required to do test-preparation practice. A strategy such as this would likely develop test-taking skills (and a lot more) far more effectively than current drill and practice approaches.

This example illustrates how options that teachers may not have been aware of can emerge once they articulate the fact that they do have choices and begin to discuss these choices with colleagues actively and critically. Again, the criterion of whether any approach is "scientifically based" is whether it results in active literacy engagement on the part of students. Based on that criterion, we would argue that filling out test-preparation worksheets is likely to entail considerably less literacy engagement than a fun and cognitively challenging activity of creating multiple choice test items to inflict on peers.

Language and Culture

As noted in Chapter 11, most schools serving culturally and linguistically diverse students operate with certain normalized assumptions about students' language and culture. They assume that "literacy" refers only to English literacy, despite the fact that students may be engaged in a wide variety of L1 literacy practices outside of school. With the exception of bilingual or dual-language programs, there is typically minimal acknowledgment or promotion of students' cultural or linguistic capital within the school. This unfortunate reality represents a choice that educators, individually and collectively, within these schools have made. It involves the (usually implicit) assumption that students' oral proficiency and literacy in their home languages are irrelevant to their education and life prospects. The rapid loss of home language abilities experienced by most ELL students born in the United States (or Canada) during the elementary school years is typically viewed as of little educational concern (Wong Fillmore, 1991).

At a more theoretical level, the normalized default option represents a choice to use monolingual instructional strategies to teach bilingual students rather than exploring bilingual instructional strategies. Clearly, in schools with multiple languages the options for formal bilingual instruction may be quite limited but there are many opportunities to use bilingual instructional strategies within the multilingual classroom even when English is the language of instruction, and perhaps the only language that teachers speak. These bilingual instructional strategies involve teaching for transfer across languages (from students' L1 to English and from English to students' L1). They also communicate to students that their L1 proficiency is an important accomplishment that is acknowledged and appreciated within the classroom. Some of the choices that can be pursued within monolingual instructional contexts are as follows:

- ■ *Focus on cognates.* As noted in Chapter 2, the academic language of English is derived predominantly from Latin and Greek sources. As such, it has many cognate relationships with other Romance languages. Drawing students' attention to cognate relationships and encouraging them to search their internal lexical database for similar meanings as they read is one strategy that is particularly useful in helping students from Spanish-speaking backgrounds to transfer L1 knowledge to English. For example, if the student comes across the low-frequency word *encounter* in an English text, he or she will soon connect it to *encontrar,* which is the Spanish (high-frequency) word for meet or encounter.

■ *From kindergarten on, students bring in L1 words to class to explore with peers and teacher, and they incorporate these words into technology-supported bilingual/multilingual dictionaries.* These words can be discussed in the class and entered into Internet search engines to find images that depict the meanings. Students can also look up the words in electronic dictionaries and create their own multimedia glossaries (print, image, audio) to reflect their "language detective" work.

■ *Students write creatively in L1 and L2 and amplify these identity texts through technology.* Audio can also be integrated into the texts and they can be displayed on the school's website so that parents and possibly relatives in other countries can access them.

■ *Students create movies, audio CDs, and/or webpages to communicate the outcomes of their projects aimed at generating new knowledge, creating literature and art, and acting on social realities.* Durán and Durán (2001) and Hull and Schultz (2001, 2002) have described how low-SES minority students in the United States created various kinds of multimedia resources on substantive topics of relevance to their lives in the context of after-school technology-mediated initiatives.

■ *New arrivals (immigrant students) write in L1 and work with peers, teachers, older students, community volunteers, and technology (e.g., Google or Babel Fish translations) to create bilingual identity texts.* For example, a newly arrived student in grade 5 might write a story or a personal account of some aspect of his or her experience in L1. Students and/or the teacher can then cut and paste this text into Google or Babel Fish for automatic translation into one of the school languages. The resulting translation will likely be somewhat garbled but sufficiently comprehensible to give the teacher (and other students) the gist of what the new arrival is trying to communicate. A group of students can then be assigned to work with the newly arrived student to edit the school language version of the text. Then the dual-language text can be entered into the class or school website as a bilingual identity text. Thus, the newly arrived student very quickly attains the status of a published bilingual author.

■ *Students engage in technology-mediated sister class exchanges using L1 and L2 to create literature and art and/or to explore issues of social relevance to them and their communities.* Multiple examples of these sister class exchanges are outlined in this book. Ideally, they provide opportunities for students to use the full range of their cognitive and linguistic talents.

All of these options are consistent with social constructivist and, in many cases, transformative approaches to pedagogy. However, they are unlikely to appear in curriculum guidelines and certainly not in scripted programs. Thus, a major choice that educators face is whether to follow the prescribed curriculum despite the fact that it frequently doesn't lead to literacy engagement for bilingual and ELL students (partly because they can't fully understand the language) or step outside the curricular box and explore pedagogical options that connect with students' background knowledge and engage them in active self-directed literacy activities.

Parental Involvement

Parental involvement is universally endorsed as important for students' academic development and is frequently cited as a factor in the relatively strong academic achievement of more affluent students. Parents of low-income and culturally diverse students are often unfamiliar with how the school system operates; they may not feel welcomed within the school because of cultural or language differences; or both parents may be working long hours at minimum wage to survive economically. In many cases, when parents do not show up for parent meetings or teacher conferences, teachers may conclude that parents are not particularly interested in their children's education.

In contrast to this common view, there are many examples where culturally diverse parents participate actively in their children's education when the structures for participation are changed so that their languages and cultural expertise are recognized. Many examples can be found in the book *Authors in the Classroom* (2004) written by Alma Flor Ada and F. Isabel Campoy and in *Multilingual Education in Practice: Using Diversity as a Resource* (2003) edited by Sandra Schecter and Jim Cummins. Ada and Campoy discuss how children, teachers, and parents can become authors and write in a variety of genres resulting in an anthology of creative writing expressing experiences and insights. They describe how teachers can include parents in this process:

> Many teachers have chosen to include their poem alongside the poems written by the students in a *Where I Come From* anthology to be sent home to the families. Then they have asked the parents or caretakers to write similar poems to create a parents' anthology. Some teachers have chosen to make the anthology with contributions from all three sets of authors: teacher, students, and parents. (2004, p. 248)

(The implementation of this approach by Judith Bernhard and her colleagues in the Miami Dade school district is described in the vignette "Authors in the Classroom" in the appendix.)

A similar project was carried out by educators in Thornwood Public School in the Toronto area (see "Dual Language Bookmaking" vignette in the appendix). Elementary school students created dual-language books, initially writing in English and then working with parents or older siblings or peers to create L1 versions of their stories. Parents' linguistic resources were crucial to the success of the project and several parents were also able to supply word processing in the home language (e.g., Arabic, Korean, Chinese) to help make the dual-language books more professional in appearance.

These examples again illustrate the power of choice, particularly when it is propelled by a clearly focused imagination. These projects are transformative in pedagogical orientation because they challenge prevailing assumptions about the engagement of low-income and culturally diverse parents in their children's education.

Conclusion

The starting point in our examination of how schools can more effectively promote students' literacy abilities is to acknowledge that in every pedagogical situation, there are choices, or degrees of freedom, with respect to how teachers use a variety of technological tools, how teachers present and inquire into the content of instruction, and the type of cognitive engagement teachers' instruction attempts to evoke. Educators also have choices in the ways they assess students' intellectual and academic progress and in the extent to which they attempt to affirm students' language and culture within the classroom and school context. Choice is also apparent in how teachers aspire to involve parents as active partners in their children's education.

The exercise of choice is not easy. There is no guarantee that a teacher will get to the instructional spaces he or she would like to reach. But that teacher can be guided, and perhaps inspired, by narratives of travelers who have already explored these routes and by the shared commitment of fellow travelers who are determined to nurture the emergence of intelligence, imagination and multilingual talents.

1 A central theme in Chapter 12 is that educators always have choices, even though these choices may be constrained by various factors. What choices can you identify in your own teaching situation? What external constraints would you like to remove or reduce if you could?

2 Most schools serving culturally and linguistically diverse students operate within certain normalized assumptions about students' language and culture. What assumptions about students' language and culture can you identify in your own school situation?

How do they compare to the assumptions articulated in this chapter? How are these assumptions manifested in the classroom?

3 With a partner, carry out an audit of your own school situation with respect to "Where You Are," "Where You Want to Be," and "How You Get There?" using the chart on page 233. Focus on at least three of the categories (Tools, Content, Cognition, Assessment, Language/Culture, and Parental Involvement) that seem most relevant to your situation. Are there any additional categories that you would add to this list?

APPENDIX

VIGNETTES

"Media Assassins" at the 99th St. Elementary School

For years, extremely low test scores made the 99th St. Elementary School among the lowest-performing schools in its district and in California. To turn things around, fourth-grade teacher Salina Gray and several other teachers who are concerned not only about test scores but also about how the school's program failed to encourage critical thinking are implementing a social-justice curriculum that uses technology to bring more of the world into this inner-city school.

The school sits on the border of Watts and Compton in South Central Los Angeles. Sixty percent of the students are Latino; the remainder are African American. Salina states, "Our school is located in an area with high rates of gang activity and the students have been dealing with the challenges common to young people growing up in the inner city." Like many other urban/inner-city schools, 99th St. teaches regimented basic skills via a mandated curriculum, with classroom instruction that is largely decontextualized and disconnected from the students' lives.

In 2002, Salina and several colleagues began participating in a local university program to explore critical social-justice pedagogy in urban schooling contexts.[1] The kinds of pedagogy they subsequently implemented in their classrooms demonstrated to them that by layering media analyses onto existing state mandates, content standards, and scripted-language arts curriculum, they could engage students in deeper critical inquiry and writing, with promising academic results, including higher test scores.

Salina, now in her sixth year of teaching, has always held high expectations for her students but, she notes, "I literally had to be just like 'tough love' to get it out of them. Once I started learning about critical pedagogy, it helped me step my game up."

The mandated reading program divides the school year into six-week thematic units and prescribes tests, writing assessments, and reading assignments. It is a challenge to connect the curriculum to student interests and encourage critical inquiry. In addition, the prescribed texts are often above the reading level of English language learners. Salina's response has been: "To get my kids interested, I bring in as much outside literature and information about the outside world as I can in the form of film and Internet articles."

During the fourth-grade Mystery to Medicine unit, before starting a story with high-level vocabulary about the first open-heart surgery, Salina downloaded several short video clips of open-heart surgery from the University of Southern California website. Her students watched with fascination, copying the URL so that they could share the videos at home. As the class discussed the videos, Salina introduced new technical and scientific vocabulary that they would later find in their text. "I wanted them to start the unit engaged, saying 'I know that word'," she explains.

Prior to the assignment of a four-paragraph essay about the "common cold," a required but low-interest writing assessment, Salina divided her class into small groups to conduct online research about diseases that affected their communities, such as AIDS, diabetes, hypertension, and asthma. The groups reported on these health issues and their social and political implications. Students read avidly, discussed findings with their teammates, and wrote far more complex reports than were required. Salina guided the teams through the process of starting with a topic, identifying resources, taking notes, converting notes to complete sentences, and developing a report. "They now know how to write an expository paper, a research paper. I was very confident that they would have no problem writing their little article on the common cold."

That year the Mystery to Medicine unit coincided with the longest-running grocery workers' strike in U.S. history. Salina linked this current event to the medical unit by showing her class *John Q,* a film starring Denzel Washington as a struggling factory-worker—and more broadly depicting the effects of socioeconomic status on health-care access. Each day, the class watched another 10 to 15 minutes. Students became concerned about the young child who was denied a heart operation because his father lacked adequate medical insurance. Salina explains, "We discussed it as realistic fiction. We studied the characters and we made predictions."

At the same time, Salina's students read current newspaper articles and did Internet research about the striking grocery workers. She says, "They found more facts about what workers wanted, getting different perspectives about the strike."

Students were quick to see the link between *John Q* and the striking grocery-store employees who hoped to preserve health benefits. "The students were appalled to learn that health insurance was not free, or at the very least, accessible, to all," says Salina. "We had many conversations where kids would say 'How come the president is making us go to war and they're paying the army but there are kids dying here who can't go to doctors?'"

By the end of the unit, the students had not only read the stories, passed their common-cold writing assessment with high marks, and mastered the skills required by the unit, but they had also written reports and opinion pieces on other diseases about which they had read.

The students' level of engagement soared. When Salina reached the end-of-the-unit reflection questions, the students weren't ready to stop. She recalls, "They were still so excited. My question to them was, 'What do you want to do about it?'"

She continues, "The students decided to write articles to add their voice to the chorus of people worldwide who are demanding equal health-care access for all. A reply came from the governor of California, thanking them for raising those questions and saying that they were good citizens and that they were the kind of citizens that he hoped would grow into adults who would do great things, and that was very empowering. The kids really felt like they had a voice."

That year, Salina's fourth-grade students won many awards for exceptional progress. At the school awards assembly, of the 25 fourth-graders from four classes who received awards for being proficient or advanced in math or language arts on the CAT6, nearly 50 percent were in Salina's class. She reports, "I had a lot of kids who went from 'far below basic' to 'proficient.' Even my lowest kids are doing well in the fifth grade this year. That was the first year I actively and explicitly brought in so many different things and it really did work."

Salina continues, "Far too often, scripted reading programs take the power away from the teacher to be creative and decide what is best for students. I resent the fact that often teachers are not treated as professionals. Districts and administrators tell teachers that they need to have high expectations if they want their students to succeed. Well, I say the same thing to them—that they need to have high expectations of teachers and allow us to do what we need to do."

Salina uses the term "Media Assassins" to describe how she brings new forms of media into the classroom to engage her students in critical inquiry. First, she encourages her students to watch and read with a critical eye, "to deconstruct images that perpetuate limiting visions of who they are, who they should be, and what the world is." Second, she brings in media that counteract misinformed notions that the children might have, such as the idea that access to health care is equitable, and she helps them analyze issues

Letter to Public Officials from a Student in Salina Gray's Class

4th Grade
99th Street Elementary School
April 20, 2004

I am a 4th grader at 99th Street Elementary School in Watts, California. We have been studying a unit called "Mystery to Medicine." It made me think about people that don't have equal access to health care. Think about the children that don't have health care. There are kids who could have broken legs or arms, but can't see the best doctors because their parents don't have health insurance. What if you were someone with children and they were sick or hurt, wouldn't you want to be able to get good health care for them?

Here in L.A. grocery workers were on strike because they were asking for more money for health care. It was sad because I once was going to Ralph's grocery store with my mom, and there was a woman on strike that was wearing a t-shirt with a picture of a little boy on it. He had a broken leg or something, and it made me sad because I knew that she probably needed better health insurance for him. It made me think about a movie our teacher showed us called *John Q*. He was a man that didn't have enough health insurance to get his son a heart transplant. I think that's why people were on strike. It is a fact that everyone does not have equal access to health care.

Something needs to be done so that all people, even poor people, can have the best doctors and the best medicine. It's not fair that people have jobs and work hard but still they don't make enough to get good insurance for their families. I think that everyone should have health care so that they can be healthy.

of equity. Finally, she encourages her children, as critical thinkers and young citizens, to produce media—by writing or using images when and where they can—in the cause of social justice.

For Salina Gray and other teachers at the 99th St. School, the media provide an ideal context in which urban classroom teachers can develop students' academic and critical literacies, including reading and writing for empowerment.

ENDNOTE
1. The 99th St. School Teacher Inquiry Project was organized by UCLA's *Institute for Democracy, Education and Access (IDEA)* and facilitated by Dr. Jeff Duncan-Andrade, who was then Director of Urban Teacher Development and Post-Doctoral Research Fellow at UCLA.

RESOURCES

http://tcla.gseis.ucla.edu/voices
Teaching to Change LA (TCLA), an online journal of UCLA's Institute for Democracy, Education and Access, addresses educational conditions in Los Angeles schools and creates a unique environment from which urban students, parents, and teachers can be heard beyond their local classrooms. Contributors use computer-generated maps, photographs, graphs, video, and audio to communicate the complex ideas, stories, and other data that are relevant to their own communities and schools.

http://tcla.gseis.ucla.edu/rights/background/salina.html
Transformation Through the Students' Bill of Rights: An Interview with Salina Gray.
Salina Gray speaks about the effect the Students' Bill of Rights has had on her teaching practice and on her students.

http://tcla.gseis.ucla.edu/reportcard/features/5-6/curriculum.html
Implementing a Social Justice Curriculum in an Inner City School
Laurence Tan, another 99th St. teacher, discusses how he created a social justice curriculum by using everyday practice and pedagogy.

http://tcla.gseis.ucla.edu/reportcard/features/5-6/toyguns.html
No More Guns: 99th Street Students Boycott the Ice Cream Truck
Teachers Laurence Tan and Kim Min reflect on the growing awareness and activism of the second- and fifth-graders as the students organize to boycott the sale of toy guns by a local ice cream truck.

The Algebra Project

Robert Moses has helped make history twice. During the 1960s, he was a civil rights activist, a leader in the movement to transform into living reality the democratic principle that then received only token lip service, but today seems an unquestionable legacy: "one person, one vote." United in its focus to achieve this common goal, the civil rights movement unleashed a maelstrom of resistance in the state of Mississippi, where only 5 percent of the African American population were registered to vote, despite their majority status among citizens in the state.

To succeed in their efforts, Moses asserts, the common goal embodied in the slogan "one person, one vote" needed an organizing principle, what he calls a "crawl space"—an agreed upon "protected environment" that the community recognizes as justified, feasible, and defensible. In Mississippi, that crawl space was the voter registration drive made possible by the 1957 Civil Rights Act, passed under the Eisenhower administration. The community organizing efforts of Robert Moses and his colleagues there helped shape the groundswell of national support that led to the passage of the Civil Rights Act of 1964 and the Voter Rights Act of 1985.

In the 1980s, Moses was making history again when he founded the Algebra Project, a seeming far cry from his civil rights activist background. Not so, he has argued in a book coauthored with Charles E. Cobb, Jr., *Radical Equations* (2001). Like the democratic principle embodied in "one person, one vote," the national birthright to free public education from kindergarten to twelfth grade was unquestioned. Moreover, by the mid-eighties the citizenry generally shared the view that all children can learn and deserved the kind of education that would realize their potential. Moses defined the "crawl space" of the Algebra Project in the logical, mathematical terms of an "if, then" statement: "If we can teach students algebra in the middle school years, then we should do it" (Moses & Cobb, 2001, p. 93). Just as the industrial age had created the need for a workforce that could read and write, and helped fuel the drive for free public education to achieve this end, the educational needs of the contemporary workforce are focused on technological skills, and hence require high levels of mastery of mathematics and science, in addition to literacy.

The goal of the Algebra Project—that every student should complete a college preparatory mathematics curriculum—seems as quixotic as the goal of universal voter registration in Mississippi: Today, only 11 percent of high school students are successful completers of college preparatory mathematics programs. Moses knew in the 1980s what has become more generally recognized now: Algebra is the "gatekeeper course" to the college preparatory mathematics curriculum, and, like literacy skills, holds the keys to unlock—or lock down—every student's potential for personal growth and economic attainment.

Moses' own children brought home the need for the Algebra Project. In 1982, Maisha Moses was in eighth grade at Martin Luther King, Jr. School in Cambridge, MA, and, as a result of her parents' tutoring, was more than ready for algebra; however, her school offered no options for middle-school study of algebra. Maisha's teacher approved a plan for her and three other students to study algebra with Moses that year, and all but one passed the citywide algebra test in the Spring, the first in their middle school ever to do so. The Algebra Project was born, and in the following years added both seventh- and eighth-graders to their ranks with such success that the Cambridge School Committee named the project as an official component of their math program in 1985. Soon, other Boston area public schools joined the King school in adopting what was emerging as the "Algebra Project Curriculum."

One of the core principles of the Algebra Project Curriculum developed from Moses' doctoral studies at Harvard University with Professor Willard Van Orman Quine, a proponent of the view that abstract mathematical concepts are best approached when linked to everyday experiences and language. As the Algebra Project expanded to include students from the upper elementary grades, it became increasingly important to discover and share such "pre-algebra" experiences and the language to describe them. This effort resulted in what came to be known as the "Transition Cur-

riculum," and one of its central elements was a "learning trip." The concept of the learning trip came to Robert Moses serendipitously during a field trip of Algebra Project students as they took the Red Line MTA subway from Harvard Square to Park Street in Boston, and back to Cambridge. Later, in class, the students moved naturally into what Moses terms "People Talk" about their round-trip journey and the stops along the way, which led naturally to "Feature Talk," where Moses helped them understand their trip as analogous to positive and negative movement along a number line, describing each subway stop in terms of its mathematical features and directional relationship to other stops along the way. Finally, students had been readied to negotiate "Symbolic Representations," making use of standard mathematical formulas to express more abstractly their experientially grounded insights into number systems. As the Algebra Project received recognition and funding from foundations and expanded to a national effort, the basic structure of the "Transitions Curriculum" remained unchanged, although learning trips might take place on bus routes or simply through classroom excursions on foot through the neighborhood (see note on page 250).

Classroom technology was an early and central component contributing to the Algebra Project's ability to reach young people. In particular, Moses makes note of the graphing calculator as an important tool in communicating about mathematical concepts with youth who otherwise find schooling abstract and bookish.

> My students, like many of their generation, do not read as much as they should. Most of what they learn they learn from pushing buttons and seeing how images change. Their modalities of learning have been attuned to this image-making process. If you use these graphing calculators, you arouse their interest. The kids will take time to try to figure out how the calculator works, how those buttons make images come and go on the screen. They learn something and will show you what they have learned. They would never do that with a book. Students do not open a math book and say, "Let me show

you what I know from this page," but they will show you what they know about a single button on a graphing calculator. (Moses & Cobb, 2001, pp. 116–117)

However, Moses notes that using technology in this fashion poses new challenges for educators:

I think you have got to go where the kids are. And that place is different from the place where teachers have been taught to be. Our graphing calculators completely reorganize the subject. The exercises in the chapters at the end of mathematics textbooks depend on the chapters at the beginning. With graphing calculators you can move around in innumerable ways; it's a non-linear way of presenting information. You need teachers who are comfortable taking the subject apart and putting it back together again on the spot in response to questions of children. And this is a real difficulty. (Moses & Cobb, 2001, p. 117)

Once again, effective classroom technology use depends on the ability of teachers to improvise, to respond in timely ways to "teachable moments." This improvisational skill should not be viewed as antithetical to reaching established learning goals such as those set forth in state-mandated standards for mathematics, or any other area of instruction. The Algebra Project, to be sure, has been instrumental in multiplying the numbers of students from many diverse backgrounds who successfully complete college preparatory curriculum. But as Moses notes, there is a long way to go still: "We need a revolution in order to get the teaching of math up to where the technology and the students are" (Moses & Cobb, 2001, p. 117).

Note: The reader will note many parallels in the evolution of Robert Moses' Algebra Project and Célestin Freinet's École Moderne (see Chapter 5). In particular, the community "learning walk" as the experiential underpinning for more demanding academic activities is strikingly similar. Both approaches also make extensive use of classroom-based technologies, and stress structured yet often improvisational teaching approaches that provide practitioners with continuous feedback from students and colleagues to inform curriculum improvement.

RESOURCES

Moses, R. P., & Cobb, C.E., Jr. (2001). *Radical equations: Civil rights from Mississippi to the Algebra Project.* Boston: Beacon Press.

California Students Use Technology to Connect with Tsunami Survivors

When California teacher Joana de Sena heard how the December 2004 tsunami devastated South Asia and parts of coastal Africa, she decided to seize the moment and help her students think about the tragedy in a constructive way. Classroom discussions and projects could help them understand the human aspect of this disaster and maybe even connect with the children their age in the stricken countries.

Joana teaches a culturally, linguistically, and academically diverse class of fifth- and sixth-graders at Eliott Elementary, a public magnet school in racially mixed Artesia, near Long Beach. Students represent a variety of cultures, including Indian, Korean, Philippine, Vietnamese, Cambodian, Mexican, African American, and Portuguese/Azorean; many come from homes in which languages other than English are spoken. More than a third of the class have been identified as GATE, or high achievers; another third are in the Resource Specialist Program and have been identified as having mild learning disabilities.

Now in her twenty-fifth year of teaching at Eliott School, Joana welcomes the opportunity to teach in a heterogeneous classroom. She offers an enriched curriculum to all and creates an inclusive environment. She says, "We have one rule, which is that no one gets left out. A global world needs all kinds of people and everyone needs to contribute" (Joana de Sena, personal communication, 2005).

Joana, who is credentialed in special education and over the years has taught both "regular" and "special education" classes, rejects the notion that low-achieving students should focus on remediation, saying, "I truly believe that all students are capable learners. It's up to me to figure out the best practices for all students, whether they are high achievers or have serious gaps in their education." She adds, "I want all my students to become educated, productive citizens and to become life-time learners. If we bog any of them down with constant repetition, I don't think I'm being fair to them." Through enrichment, she has seen that she can help even the children with learning disabilities to compensate for their needs.

Joana discusses world issues with her students to help them to appreciate other cultures and values. She observes, "Too often what is heard on the evening news is distant from the realities of children in U.S. schools. This is particularly true in families struggling for their own survival and working hard to make ends meet. It's critically important that the victims do not become numbers, that we do not become numb when we hear about the plight of others."

Responding to Natural Disaster

On the first school day after Winter Break, the students were eager to discuss the devastation that had struck South Asia and Africa on December 26, 2004. Many of them had seen images of the disaster on television. The students asked about tidal waves and earthquakes, a discussion that soon turned to plate tectonics. The sixth-graders had already studied earthquakes and plate tectonics earlier that school year and Joana was pleased with how many connections the students made to their science curriculum. "The December tsunami gave them a visual image of what can actually happen in a large earthquake," she says.

Four computers in the classroom were invaluable for ongoing discussion. The class had an online subscription to the *Los Angeles Times,* so students were able to read updated information on the tsunami throughout the day. They saw that the damage was even more widespread than originally thought and that the death toll kept rising.

As the students viewed the news articles, they grew concerned about the children who had lost their homes and family members. They asked, "What happens to the children if their family dies? What happens to the families that are in the newspaper photographs?"

Joana remembers, "We talked about what it would be like to lose your parents and be left alone in the world and not have any other relatives." To help her students understand what the other children might be experiencing, she tried to have them tap into their personal situations. "Have you ever lost a grandparent or a pet?" she asked her students. "What is it like to go around the house of that person? And how does that feel?" The students responded, "It's lonely. It feels like someone hit me. I miss them. I feel emptiness." Joana comments, "They were relevant responses to feelings of such a loss. Then the students wanted to know, 'What can we do?'"

Eliott Elementary, a technology and global studies magnet school, helps its classes to connect with students in other countries through online projects. Yet very often countries that appear in the headlines don't have Internet access or a way for children to contact other children. Through a Santa Monica, California-based humanitarian medical organization, the International Medical Corps (IMC), Joana had previously contacted people who had emigrated from or traveled to countries in conflict or that had suffered natural disasters. That day, during the students' lunch period, Joana learned that her students could send messages to Indonesia with a local IMC volunteer,

Dr. Neil Joyce, who would leave that evening to meet with an international team to help set up public-health programs in Banda Aceh, in Indonesia's Aceh province.

That afternoon, Joana explained the role of international medical humanitarian organizations in natural disasters and described what Dr. Joyce would do in Indonesia. The students remembered Banda Aceh from their discussions earlier that day as one of the hardest-hit areas, with reports of many, many people dead or missing (eventually 110,000 people were known to have died, with a further 130,000 missing or lost in the province of Aceh). She recalls, "I told them that one of the things that Dr. Joyce would be doing would be to help make sure that the Indonesian children had something to eat and some place to live and that their health was taken care of so that they were not abandoned on the streets."

> There were so many questions. They really were interested in finding out what happens to the kids. It led to us deciding to send the artwork and the photographs because then they wanted to know, what can we do, how can we help? I asked, "Would you like to draw some pictures for the children there that might make them feel better? To let them know that you are here and that they are not alone in the world?" They were immediately engaged. (Joana de Sena, personal communication, 2005)

Joana allowed students to choose the groups with which they would work, with the caveat that no one be left out. She talked with students about their artwork as she walked around the classroom. The students realized that they didn't share a language with the children in Indonesia and would need to find ways to express their ideas through their drawings and images.

Each group talked about messages to convey and how to communicate ideas through pictures. One team, a GATE student paired with a "resource" student, used cut-paper techniques to create a bold design with three faceless children holding hands. One partner explained, "We care about the children and it doesn't really matter

When students in California realized that they didn't share a language with the children in Indonesia, they found ways to express their ideas through drawings and images.

what they look like. We care about them because they are human beings."

At a nearby table, a team drew maps of California and maps of the tsunami-affected area to show the origin and destination of the messages. The artists commented, "It doesn't matter where they live, it just matters that they are suffering and that they can overcome their suffering."

By the end of the school day, the children had used the class digital camera to take photos of themselves to include with their drawings. The package with the children's artwork was filled with messages of caring and concern: "We hope you are really safe." "We heard what happened and we are very sorry." "We care about you." "We feel your pain and hope you feel better." Each was illustrated with images created by the children, some with maps labeled "we are here," one with a diagram the students had labeled "plate tectonics," another with brightly colored butterflies carrying the message, "This paper is filled with hope."

That night Joana delivered their digital photos and artwork to Dr. Joyce who hand-carried them to Banda Aceh. Joana explained that even without knowing much about how their drawings and photos would be shared, "The students felt really good that they had contributed in some way."

Her class also played an important role in the school district's fund-raising drive for Red Cross tsunami relief, talking with other students at the school about the disaster and giving what they could of their own money. Joana reports, "Several children from the class gave their lunch money, saying, 'I don't need to eat today because I have everything I need.' They were very instrumental in convincing other children to donate. The outpouring of caring was amazing."

A Response from Indonesia

Two weeks later, an e-mail with photos attached arrived from a National Geographic photographer working in Indonesia. The students were thrilled. The photographer explained that he was working with the International Medical Corps team in Banda Aceh and had taken photographs at the refugee camp where the artwork was on exhibit. He wrote: "We showed your messages to the kids and explained. They were very happy and grateful.... They were so excited to see the drawings and hear about someone caring! It was such a joy to see them" (Chris Rainier, e-mail correspondence, 2005).

When the students received the e-mail they were amazed. They said, "What does it mean? Did the children like it?" I said, "Yeah, look at

A teacher at a refugee camp in Banda Aceh shares the student artwork and messages from California with Indonesian children who were separated from their families during the tsunami.
Copyright © Chris Rainier.

their faces. What do you think?" They were very curious about it. "Where is this? Where are the pictures posted?" We went to the map and I showed them Banda Aceh. I shared with them that their messages had reached children in a refugee camp, and that made the students even happier. I read aloud the e-mail in which the photographer communicated that the children there enjoyed viewing them. They were very happy that it made the children happy. (Joana de Sena, personal communication, 2005)

Joana's students continue to log on to the Internet regularly to read the newspaper reports about the tsunami-affected areas and reconstruction efforts, now with special attention to Banda Aceh. They hope that their messages have been part of a larger effort to help provide a sense of hope for the future.

The experiences of Joana and her students are vivid reminders that technology may give us images, but it takes sympathy and imagination to understand and respond to the human experiences behind those images. This veteran teacher hopes that from these kinds of global learning network projects her students will draw some

Fifth- and sixth-graders in California took photos of one another in include with their artwork in the package they sent ot Indonesia.

lessons that will be important to them in the future, such as:

- Important things happen in faraway places.

- It is nice to give of yourself.

- When people are down they need support.

- Cultures and customs may vary but all people are the same in some essential ways, as are their needs.

Clearly, global learning networks do more than teach geography. They also help children participate in community development and humanitarian aid, understanding the power of helping people to rebuild their lives.

Student-Generated Databases Using Knowledge Forum® in the Eastern Arctic

Grade 5 teacher, Elizabeth Tumblin, sits at one of the computers in her classroom in Joamie School in Iqaluit, located in Canada's Eastern Arctic Territory of Nunavut. She is attempting to draw graphics to represent the database that her students are creating on vertebrates and invertebrates. Noticing her less-than-expert computer drawing skills, one of her students says, "We can do that, Miss," and her students take over the drawing of the sky with the sun shining down, the land with a house representing human habitation, and the sea with a whale swimming contentedly. Elizabeth's students have no hesitation in taking on the role of artistic experts, willing to share their expertise in northern life and creating computer graphics with their teacher.

This reversal of roles has occurred in the context of a unique collaborative software environment called Knowledge Forum® (formerly called Computer Supported Intentional Learning Environment [CSILE]) that Elizabeth has been using with her students to enable them to record, share, illustrate, and comment on their topics of investigation and those of their classmates, much as a community of scientists would. Sandy McAuley (2003) introduced Knowledge Forum® to the school district and has worked for many

years with the Knowledge Forum® research team at the University of Toronto. Sandy points out that "the goal is the creation of a community of learners in which students actively and collaboratively build knowledge about curriculum topics" (2001, p. 9).

The program starts with an empty database. Students and their teacher collaboratively decide on the topics they want to explore. McAuley describes the process as follows:

A Knowledge Forum® unit begins with students creating a communal database by entering initial notes with questions and thoughts derived from the whole-group brainstorming process. They identify what they want to learn and develop a plan to learn it. Plans often involve working with books, encyclopedias, and Internet, but they equally involve contacting and interviewing local resource people or, because Knowledge Forum® is Internet-aware, having remote resource people contribute to students' developing database. (2001, p. 10)

Students can also search the database to see what others have discovered and they can comment on and ask questions about each other's work. McAuley (1998) likens Elizabeth's teaching in the Knowledge Forum® environment to "watching someone conduct an orchestra." She initially orients students by reviewing the range of things they will be working on in the next 40 minutes, answers any questions they might have, and then they're off.

Most students pull out special folders, which they use to keep track of their progress. Five students head to the computers, which are arranged along the side of the room. There they log in to Knowledge Forum® and begin browsing the database for new contributions or enter their own. Another small group heads to the collection of resources they have assembled on indigenous peoples, the topic they have chosen to study. Another group heads to a map and begins noting information about where various indigenous groups live. Other students work independently at their desks. There is a steady buzz of conversation, but if you eavesdrop you learn that most of it is related to the work at hand.

Elizabeth moves from group to group, asking and answering questions, checking progress, refocusing the few who have drifted off task. This is a remarkable performance, given that six months earlier most of the students had used computers only for playing games, if at all, and the kind of school work they were accustomed to was filling in the blanks. It is even more remarkable considering that for most of them it's their first year in a classroom where the majority of the instruction is in English rather than Inuktitut (1998, p. 12).

The indigenous people's unit started with students brainstorming and categorizing their questions about indigenous peoples. Then they broke up into small groups and each group selected a particular people to research. The database revealed that the students didn't confine themselves to their own work:

> A note from a member of the group working on Mohawks elicits a story from a student in another group whose mother had met Mohawks in Montreal. A note on the writing system of the Cherokee prompts a comment that the writing system resembles the syllabics used to write Inuktitut. That prompts another comment that the Cree use a similar system. The end result: an investigation into the origins of the syllabics used by a number of North America's first peoples. (1998, p. 13)

While this brief sketch illustrates the potential for Knowledge Forum® to promote student inquiry, McAuley is frank about the challenges involved in implementing such a radical shift from traditional transmission-oriented classrooms to collaborative knowledge-building communities:

> It hasn't always been easy—the successes have taken considerable commitment, strong belief that students can take a more active and responsible role in their education, and a willingness to collaborate. Without these three elements success is much less likely. (2001, p. 11)

RESOURCES
More information on Knowledge Forum® can be obtained at www.learninginmotion.com.

Educational Video Center

For more than 20 years, the Educational Video Center (EVC) has been teaching urban youth how to produce documentary videos that explore community issues central to their lives, ranging from too-easy access to handguns by adolescents to teenage suicide and the juvenile justice system. One team produced a video on children in foster care, and another team nine years later interviewed the original participants to track the impact of the foster care system on their lives. All of these documentaries were designed by teams of students themselves who received training from EVC staff in all aspects of documentary production, including planning, research, interviewing, shooting, editing, and postproduction. Every documentary has been publicly presented in a community forum where its producers fielded questions about the implications of their media work for social action. One EVC production was nominated for—and received—an Emmy.

Steven Goodman has eloquently outlined the history of EVC from its beginnings in New York City in his *Teaching Youth Media: A Critical Guide to Literacy, Video Production, and Social Change* (2003). The noted philosopher and educational theorist Maxine Greene writes in the preface:

> Most adults are aware of the degree to which today's young people (especially those who are poverty-ridden) are enmeshed in a visual and oral media culture rather than the print-based culture long associated with literacy. Few, though, have confronted the degree to which this change has created a language gap—what Goodman calls a disconnect between the experiences of the young and the print culture prevailing in high schools. This ground-breaking book not only explains the consequences thereof, but also presents a view of critical literacy that may well close this gap. (p. ix)

Greene concludes, "This is a brilliant and exciting book. It may transform some corners of the world."

After more than two decades of teaching adolescents the intricate ins-and-outs of documentary production, Goodman summarizes what he has learned from his students: "I believe that these young video makers have important lessons to teach us about how to more effectively use media technologies and cultural traditions to build upon students' skills of visual and oral expression as stepping-stones, instead of stumbling blocks, to learning" (p. 38).

Teaching Youth Media describes the three overarching principles of the Educational Video Center. They can be summarized as:

1. ***Student-led inquiry is at the heart of the process.*** Learning how to pose evocative questions to emotionally involved participants around difficult social issues is key to producing a successful documentary. Editing responses into a coherent message is equally challenging.

2. ***Presentation of the documentary to community audiences confers importance and appreciation to the videomakers' work.*** Students have the opportunity to speak up about what they've learned and offer suggestions on how the community can respond. Previously passive observers become active participants in social change efforts that they themselves helped launch.

3. ***Documentaries are evaluated publicly as students present portfolios of their work at roundtables, which include parents, students, teachers, interviewees, researchers, other producers, and artists.*** Portfolios are a vehicle for self-reflection by student producers and can include a variety of "best work" examples for constructive commentary by roundtable members.

Goodman describes the outcomes from this threefold EVC approach to media education in straightforward terms: "Among the most effective strategies for teaching critical literacy is for students to create their own media. Then they can begin to understand through their own experience the multiple layers of data that make up the television or videos they watch and the magazines they read" (p. 6). There are obvious parallels in Goodman's approach to media education and the pedagogy of Mario Lodi, discussed in Chapter 5.

The Educational Video Center is also involved in several promising initiatives to bring youth media education not only into after-school programs but into the official school curricula. For details, search for "Educational Video Center" or visit www.evc.org.

Authors in the Classroom:
"The Early Authors Program"

Conducted in the 2003–2004 school year, the Early Authors Program (EAP)[1] was a large-scale, early literacy program that involved 32 child-care centers, 800 families, and 1,000 children, who, with their teachers and parents, produced more than 3,000 books in English, Spanish, and Haitian-Creole. Piloted in Miami–Dade County, one of the nation's most diverse urban centers, the project aimed to help address poverty and illiteracy among Miami's culturally diverse communities and to help close the achievement gap (Bernhard, Winsler, & Bleiker, 2004). The EAP was designed in collaboration with children's book authors/ scholars Alma Flor Ada and Isabel Campoy and based on principles articulated in their book, *Authors in the Classroom* (2004). Ada and Campoy (2004) point out that "writing can transform us into authors, from followers of other people's agendas to shapers of our own ideas" (p. 4).

This ambitious program established a family literacy project at each preschool, and invited children, teachers, and parents to jointly write, illustrate, and publish books. As a result, children would learn to read and write not only from commercially published books but also from their own very personal literature.

Building on the premise that literacy involves much more than the mechanics of reading and writing, the Early Authors Program departed from the teacher-led, structured, phonological awareness approach of many early literacy interventions that focus on component skills. The more holistic approach of the Early Authors Program, which aims to nourish children's sense of self-worth and identity as readers and writers, has been able to demonstrate its worth in a federally funded evaluation, which we review here. Our discussion is based on the project evaluation report (Bernhard, Winsler, & Bleiker, 2004) and papers that have been published about the project (Bernhard,

Winsler, Bleiker, Ginieniewicz, & Madigan, 2005; Bernhard, Cummins, Campoy, Ada, Winsler, & Bleiker, in press).

Making Books:
Every Class a Publisher

Every EAP classroom had a publishing station with a computer, color printer, digital camera, and laminating machine, and became a publishing house for books authored by teachers, parents, and children. Using the *Authors in the Classroom* model, the EAP began by inviting teachers and parents to put their life experiences into words and to write their own stories to share with one another and with the children. By the time the preschool children began making their own books, they were already part of a community of authors at home and at school, and had seen many books authored by people they knew, including their teachers and their own parents.

Teachers and parents began the bookmaking process with the preschoolers by taking digital photos of the children engaged in their favorite activities and teachers scanning in family photographs shared by the parents. Looking at the photos, the children narrated their stories to their teachers, who typed the children's words into the computer. When the home language was different from the school language, teachers helped the children create a bilingual version of the book to share at home and at school.

The teachers then printed, laminated, and bound the pages into books that were filled with photographs, drawings, and stories about children's families and classmates, plus their own experiences and observations of the world. The books featured such titles as, *I Can . . . , The Story of My Name, Our Families' Hopes for Our Children,* and *Where We Come From.* Technology made much of this possible:

Without the digital cameras it couldn't have been done. Also, . . . typing the students' and parents' words was important. We were able to have the writing look very professional. At [the preschool age, kids] don't like it to look scribbly and messy. They received a lot more positive feedback because it looked like a true book. (Judith Bernhard, personal communication, March, 16, 2005)

The process allowed the preschoolers' emerging speech to take on the prestige and permanence of print. Interviews with the literacy specialists, conducted as part of the project evaluation, revealed the impact on the children. One EAP literacy specialist observed that "there was a lot of pride when the book was finished . . . when they got their final book, they shared it with the class and they just beamed. They were so excited to show their book and they felt so proud" (Bernhard et al., in press).

Through the process of dictating, transcribing, and publishing, the children began to see the connection between speech and print. An EAP literacy specialist fluent in both Haitian-Creole and English noted,

They all saw the connection, pretty much except for the babies, because . . . they could understand that [anyone could read] the words we'd written, [that] we had recorded what they had said, and that we were writing down what they had said. (Bernhard et al., 2005, pp. 26–27)

The literacy specialists also noticed marked improvement in the children's expressive ability:

They definitely became more verbal. In the beginning, some of them were just saying one word or two words when they were looking at their pictures. By the end, some of those kids that were just giving us a word or two were saying full sentences. (Bernhard et al., 2005, p. 26)

The books were a catalyst for language growth, which could be attributed to the children's growing sense of self-worth and affirmation of their ethnic, cultural, and linguistic identities.

A preschool child from the Early Authors Project is captivated by a classroom-authored book featuring him and his family.

These [books] were more personal because they included the photos of the children, and the children were able to see themselves in the book, which was one of the main points of the program—for it to have meaning for the child because the child was the main character of the book. (Bernhard et al., 2005, p. 27)

In African American, Latino, and Haitian neighborhoods in some of Miami–Dade's poorest sections, EAP preschoolers took a new interest in all types of books. They often reached first for the self-published bilingual books, which stood side by side with commercially published books on classroom shelves and in home libraries. The lead project evaluator noted the significance of this constant reexamination:

The children asked for these books to be read over and over again. . . . They would take the books home and the aunt and the grandmother and everyone would make a big fuss. Some might say that the children weren't really reading, but they were certainly turning the pages; they were certainly figuring out that those little squiggles there were "what I said when my picture was taken." They were learning all those reading skills. (Judith Bernhard, personal communication, March 16, 2005)

Teachers and literacy specialists alike felt that the many hours that went into producing and reading the books helped the children develop important early literacy skills. Project evaluators made a more formal determination based on quantitative measures of students' language and literacy progress, drawing similar conclusions.

From Theory to Reality: The Transformative Literacy Model

Authors in the Classroom, the pedagogical approach upon which the EAP is based, builds on the principles of transformative education. Ada and Campoy (2004) stress the power that authorship has to develop a sense of voice and agency, ultimately to transform one's life and bring together classes and cultures to create a more humane and democratic society. Their *Authors in the Classroom* approach stresses that teachers, parents, and children can create books that explore family and cultural strengths, hopes and dreams for the future, the importance of dialogue and community, and the necessity of acting for a better, more equitable world in which everyone's experience is valued.

Ada and Campoy move from theory to action using simple but generative writing prompts and story structures for creating such books, which young children, and even parents without much formal schooling, can complete. The writing activities, which can be presented in one parent meeting or class session, provide a springboard for discussion around key themes related to the processes of awakening voice and a sense of identity and agency. *"I am"* books and stories about children's names help affirm self and strengthen self-identity. *"I can"* books help students discover capacities and strengths. *"Where I come from"* poems and childhood memoirs are designed to help understand the past and to create the future. Collectively authored books (such as *A Person in My Life, ABC Books,* or *Counting Books*) help build relationships and a sense of community.

The model uses a three-pronged approach in which teachers, students, and parents or relatives all write. When teachers write books based on their personal experiences, they not only serve as models for authorship to their students and the students' families but they also connect more deeply with their students' families and create new relationships between home and school, based on the sharing of human experiences where both teachers and parents are considered experts.

Ada and Campoy emphasize that in a highly literate society writing conveys leadership and power. Their work has shown that technology tools can play an important role in democratizing written expression, when embedded in a process that emphasizes the development of voice. This theme is also taken up in Cheryl Winkley's (2005) participatory research project on authorship as a pedagogical tool to develop voice:

> Two threads weave through the pedagogy of authorship. One is the story—the story is the author's own and reflects the author's values, culture, heritage, and perspective. The other is the act of publishing . . . whether as a self-bound book, or a book published using modern technology. (p. 5)

The act of publishing lends the author's words a permanence that the oral word does not always have, and increases the possibility that these words can be more widely shared.

Parents and Teachers as Partners in Literacy

The EAP challenged the notion that families from immigrant and underserved communities lack literacy skills useful to their children's academic progress. EAP encouraged parents to be actively involved regardless of whether they were formally educated or spoke English.

The process of providing advice and sharing experiences helped the parents identify ways in which they could support their children in school, and also helped them develop their own sense of voice. Project facilitators remember that at the outset, most project participants viewed them as "the experts who were going to tell the parents how to bring literacy to their children." At one of the first parent meetings, at a Haitian Creole Community Center, it became apparent that these assumptions would be changed by the invitation to the parents to become authors, by the many examples of books written by other parents that were shared, by the guided writing activities, and by the supportive environment in which parents were encouraged to speak out in their own language:

> The parents took over ... they started doing acrostics, telling about the wishes they had for their children, and the room was transformed, from them just sitting there listening, to them participating and sharing the excitement ... with their children. It was really quite powerful. (Judith Bernhard, personal communication, March 16, 2005)

The project also helped raise the status of the parents in the eyes of the teachers. Literacy specialists and project organizers saw that the parents were able to participate fully in all the bookmaking activities and in lively discussions about how they chose their children's names or where the family came from, or in creating acrostics describing their children's positive qualities. One of the project evaluators commented, "The teachers realized that the parents are not illiterate at all but rather that there are degrees of literacy ... and that the parents were more than able to participate" (Judith Bernhard, personal communication, March 16, 2005).

Evidence of Success

A rigorous federally funded evaluation entitled *The Early Authors Program: A Miami–Dade Early Literacy Initiative* confirmed the growth that the teachers, parents, and literacy specialists saw in the children's language skills.[2] Participating preschoolers grew academically at a faster rate than children who received other literacy interventions: "Children who participated in the EAP intervention showed greater gains than control children in language and literacy development, according to all measures of expressive and receptive language" (Bernhard et al., 2005 p. 29).

The evaluation also documented high levels of satisfaction with the project on the part of all involved, and many positive changes in the learning environment that are consistent with literacy development. Interviews with the literacy specialists gathered evidence of

- A positive impact on identity and self-esteem;
- Increased motivation on the part of the students; and
- A greater understanding of transformative education on the part of teachers.

Teacher questionnaires provided evidence of improved classroom environments, conversations between teachers and children about books, more books in classrooms, and book areas attractively arranged.

The program evaluators concluded that the project effectively supports young children's literacy, including those children whose families speak languages other than English. They argue that it offers an attractive alternative to deficit-based family literacy programs: "In the search for alternatives or additions to the skills-based approaches that are dominating the landscape of early readiness, the Early Authors Program holds out hope of a more meaningful path to literacy" (Bernhard et al., 2004, p. 82).

Although the EAP received funding for just one year, everyone involved had a great sense of satisfaction and wanted to continue the project: "The greatest success of this program might have been in its accessibility. Almost all who participated said they believed in it, enjoyed it, and felt that it was ending too soon" (Bernhard et al., 2004, p. 83).

Ada and Campoy held an EAP closing session entitled *How to Continue the Legacy*. Project participants, pleased with the strong positive outcomes, expressed the desire for the project to continue. Parents and teachers planned how to continue even after the EAP funding stopped. The computers and digital cameras remained in the preschools and the parents and teachers were committed to continue to write and publish books together.

Writing and Authorship: Emerging Voices across the Country

Ada and Campoy have helped establish *Authors in the Classroom* programs across the U.S. as well as in Eastern Europe and the Pacific Islands, transforming hundreds of classrooms into publishing houses. The Miami-Dade implementation and consequent formal evaluation confirmed the many powerful personal testimonials these program developers have heard in a decade of using these strategies in schools around the country. For example, at a Los Angeles school where teachers, parents, and students participated in the *Authors in the Classroom* training, the principal decided, at the suggestion of a fifth-grade teacher, that during the fifth-grade graduation ceremony, each student would receive a book written by one of his or her parents, with the student's biography and the parents' hopes and dreams for their child. The school supported all the families in participating, regardless of their level of literacy.

Some parents wrote their books directly. Others got help from their child's teacher and the technology department, which helped the parents type and print their stories on computers. The parents illustrated the books, adding photos and illustrations and elaborate covers. At the graduation, parents of each student presented the book and read an excerpt. The presentations were videotaped so that each student could receive a tape of his or her parents reading the book they had written about their child's life and their dreams for his or her future. Alma Flor Ada, who visited the school and heard directly from the parents involved, remarked:

> One very poignant experience is worth sharing. A young mother, who had one of the most beautifully designed and illustrated books, was very hesitant to come up stage to show it to the group. When finally persuaded to do so, she surprised us all by saying: "This is my book. I cannot read it to you. I do not know how to read. But I will tell you what it says because it is *my* book. I am the author. Every word came out of my mouth, and then the teacher wrote it. This is the life of my son. This is what it says...." And, then, every so often, she would stop herself to reaffirm: "You see, I am not reading. But I am telling what it says. Because *I am the author."* (Alma Flor Ada, personal communication, December 12, 2005)

Ada commented, "We have been insisting that there is a great difference between writing (a mechanical process) and authorship (the ownership of knowing we have something to say,

and saying something that is uniquely ours). This mother gave the most valid example of this concept. And here, technology, in its multiple forms, has an extraordinary role to play."

ENDNOTES

1. The *Early Authors Program* (EAP) was sponsored by the Early Learning Opportunities Act, Child Care Bureau, the Canada–U.S. Fulbright Program, and the Early Learning Coalition of Miami-Dade/Monroe.

2. The EAP evaluation included a variety of measures, including interviews with the literacy specialists, standardized tests, questionnaires, observations, and other assessment instruments. A longitudinal design was selected to assess changes in students' language and literacy skills over time and to permit inferences to be made about the influences responsible for those changes. The pretest was completed in March 2003 and the posttest in April 2004.

Bernhard and colleagues (2005) describe the methodology used in the evaluation study: "The initial target evaluation sub-sample consisted of 325 EAP children, selected at random from the consenting children at EAP classrooms at the same 32 EAP centers, and 103 control chldren who were randomly selected from consenting families in classrooms at similar centers, serving the same population of families in the same neighborhoods, that were not participating in EAP. Participating EAP and control centers enrolled mostly children in poverty who received government subsidies for childcare" (p. 14).

Their report concludes: "Finding specific, theoretically-predicted, positive effects of early childhood interventions, not only on the classroom environment but also on independently assessed child outcomes with a pre-post, experimental-control group design with random selection of participants is very close to the 'gold standard' for scientifically rigorous evidence of efficacy in intervention research. The present study had all of those features, in addition to the inclusion of qualitative interview data with participants, as methodological strengths, lacking only random assignment to groups, to be considered the goal-standard for methodological rigor. Indeed, the present study provides strong support for the efficacy of the Early Authors Program with low-income, diverse preschoolers in a large, subsidized childcare setting" (p. 30).

Virtual Pre-K

Jenny Ramos, like many parents of preschool children, is excited and hopeful about her son Martín's upcoming year in kindergarten. She also wonders how she can best help Martín make a successful transition from his Head Start preschool program to their neighborhood school in San Bernardino. "I was very enthusiastic when I heard about the *Virtual Pre-K* program at Martín's preschool," she explained in Spanish. "What I especially liked was how it helped me see ways I could turn the everyday experiences we share at home into stepping stones for learning at school" (personal communication, March 15, 2005).

Virtual Pre-K (VPK) is a bilingual, interactive, parent involvement resource centered on ways that preschool teachers and parents can connect learning in the classroom with learning in the home and community. It began as an initiative of the Chicago Public Schools in 2001 under the directorship of Alicia Narvaez with the goal of employing a range of existing technologies now available in homes to build a bridge between parents of preschoolers and their teachers.

Twenty learning units were prepared in English and in Spanish around the following themes that were chosen because of their easy connection to home and community:

All about Me

1. Transitions
2. My Body
3. The Five Senses
4. My Feelings
5. I Can Do It!
6. First Steps to Reading
7. Giving Words Meaning
8. My Family
9. My Heritage
10. Starting School

Taking Care of Me

1. Fun with Fruits and Vegetables
2. Great Grains
3. Discovering Dairy and Protein
4. Terrific Teeth
5. Let's Move!
6. My Healthy Body
7. Safe Outside
8. Fire Smart
9. Safe at Home
10. Growing and Knowing

Each lesson is supported by a variety of learning materials for parents and children, ranging from "low-technology" print media in the form of activity cards to "higher-technology" media, including tapes for videoplayers and CDs for computers. Materials for parents and preschoolers are provided in a colorful lunchbox that includes activity cards and a choice of videoclip media. There is also an easy-to-navigate website for families with Internet access at home or at the preschool.

These materials and resources are intended not as a one-way transmission of school knowledge to home but as a two-way bridge to more effective collaborations between home, school, and community. For example, when parents come to schools and community centers to pick up the boxes, this is seen as an opportunity for parents and teachers to extend their connections by viewing the materials together and discussing how they can be used in the home. In addition, the project explicitly challenges the widespread assumption that "school readiness" means school readiness in English. Rather than being located in a "deficit" position due to the fact that they may not be fluent in English, parents' culture, language, and knowledge of the world are validated and the dialogue between parents and teachers reinforces the legitimacy and importance of Spanish use in the home. Parents are full partners in the project and technology is used to enhance that partnership.

The six-minute video lessons are divided into three parts. First, a Chicago public school teacher explains the importance of the lesson's theme, illustrated by an activity *in the classroom*. Next, parents of preschoolers demonstrate an activity to support their children's learning *at home*. Finally, suggestions are offered for extending the lesson's theme when the family is *out and about*, exploring community learning resources.

The lesson "My Body" on the "All about Me" videotape or CD, for example, begins with a teacher describing how children learn about the parts of the body through an activity called "Space Suit Bodies." The videoclip shows how children lie down on a sheet of colored butcher paper as their outlines are traced. They then draw a bubble around their heads (a space helmet), adding their facial features as well as gloves, boots, and other elements of their space suits, decorating them with glued-on buttons and 20-inch zippers. Next, the video presents a parent using dried and cooked pasta, glue, and construction paper to construct "Noodle Bodies" as the family prepares a spaghetti dinner. The closing sequence depicts a family visit to a park where recreational activities offer a chance to discuss how children use their bodies as they play. The Virtual Pre-K lunchbox also includes parent activity cards for "Noodle Bodies" as well as a recipe for making "Play Dough Bodies" with salt, flour, salad oil, and some food coloring.

For parents with Internet access at home or through the preschool, the Virtual Pre-K website (www.virtualpre-k.org) offers a number of features, available in English or Spanish, to support family involvement.

"My Success Chart" allows parents and children to see their progress by means of a checklist for completed activities and a notepad where a learning log can be recorded and retrieved. There are *discussion boards* where parents and teachers can share their experiences as they build home–school partnerships. In *the chat room* parents can join in scheduled discussions moderated by leading preschool and health educators. Preschool teachers who participate in the Virtual Pre-K project are also provided with a range of training and classroom materials. Lesson plans are aligned with national and Head Start preschool learning standards.

From its origins in the Chicago Public School System, Virtual Pre-K now reaches parents and preschoolers through publicly sponsored licensing arrangements for home–school partnerships in Dallas, Texas, in Washoe County, Nevada, and in five southern California counties where 65 percent of California's ELL students attend school. Thousands of other parents and educators around the country have become more engaged in preschoolers' learning through partnering arrangements for Virtual Pre-K resource materials.

The five-county California consortium is cosponsored by the California Association for Bilingual Education through a joint venture, Project INSPIRE. INSPIRE's mission statement captures the spirit that animates the Virtual Pre-K

project: "Through this collaboration our goal is to meet the on-going needs of teachers, parents, and students—in English and in Spanish—as they prepare for a successful academic experience for all students and their families" (www.virtualpre-k.org/help/aboutsocal.php). Jan Gustafson of the San Bernardino County Office of Education comments on how the relationships between parents and teachers have been expanded and become much more two-way as a result of the project:

> Parents go home and do a family tree, or family album, or go on a "smelly walk." They're simple activities but so enriching and really engage them in a wonderful way with their children that they're coming back to school and sharing their enthusiasm, and they're doing it in both languages, or in the language in which they feel most comfortable.

María Huizar, director of Project INSPIRE, highlights the fact that the Virtual Pre-K project is all about acknowledging and building on the cultural capital of students and parents and enabling parents to advocate more effectively for their children:

> The parents are so eager for knowledge that they can use to help their children and especially to advocate for ELLs in the schools and districts their children attend. Parents get really excited when they visit the page on the VPK website that has links to other sites in Spanish where they can get information they can use.

As Jenny Ramos puts it, "It makes me happy and proud to work with Martín's Head Start teacher so closely as we share in preparing him for this next important step in his life."

Note: The success of Virtual Pre-K has prompted expansion of the program to cover skills and concepts for kindergarten. Following the same format as the Virtual Pre-K resources in English and Spanish, Virtual Kindergarten was launched in 2005 with lessons on videotape and CD-ROM, printed activity recipe cards, and an educational website, www.virtualk.org. The ultimate goal is to continue the home–school partnerships that develop in preschool into kindergarten and beyond to promote life-long success for children and families.

Write the Truth

Bob Peterson is a fifth-grade teacher at La Escuela Fratney in Milwaukee, Wisconson. A probing question from one of his students launched an extensive Internet-based search by this teacher and the entire class as they sought to fill in important information gaps about the United States presidency that their social studies textbook had entirely glossed over.

Peterson was discussing the end of slavery in the United States in 1865 when a student astutely asked, "Well, which presidents were slave owners?" As a teacher, he immediately recognized the door opening into one of those "teachable moments" that are so important for organizing instruction that motivates students to dig deeper for knowledge and to think critically—important higher-level skills that too often are neglected in classrooms that limit themselves to the kind of superficial analysis measurable by standardized tests.

First, Peterson admitted to his students that he did not know the complete answer to their classmate's question, other than the fact that George Washington and Thomas Jefferson were slave owners. He asked them, "How can we find out?" Initially, the students suggested studying history books and searching the Internet. The teacher had already established a protocol for engaging students in teachable moments that he called Action Research Groups, "which in my classroom, means an ad hoc group of interested students researching a topic and then doing something with what they learn." Volunteers for this Action Research Group, to Peterson's surprise, included several boys willing to work through recess to get the project going. The project eventually would include the entire class.

The group investigated their school library, looking through dictionaries and encyclopedias, in both printed and CD formats, for information on U.S. presidents who owned slaves, yet they found nothing. Indeed, they searched through their entire social studies textbook and were surprised to learn that not only was no mention made of presidents who owned slaves, but the word *racism* never appeared.

The students discovered that the Internet was often sanitized, too. Even official websites on presidential history at the White House, the Smithsonian Institute, and the National Museum of American History made no mention of the slave-holding practices of U.S. presidents. Students began to ask themselves why reference sources and textbooks made no reference to this important historical question. Their responses: "They tell other things about presidents." "They don't want us kids to know the truth." "They think we're too young to know." "They don't know themselves." "They should tell the truth!"

Peterson did locate two books that were helpful: James Loewen's *Lies My Teacher Told Me* (Simon and Schuster, 1995) and Kenneth O'Reilly's *Nixon's Piano: Presidents and Racial Politics from Washington to Clinton* (Free Press, 1995). "Overall," Peterson concluded, "our best resource was the Internet." By using the *google.com* and *altavista.com* search engines and carefully tailoring their search strategies, the students were able to complete their investigation. Peterson explains,

> By the time we had finished our research, the students found that 10 of the first 18 presidents were slave owners. Those who owned slaves: George Washington, Thomas Jefferson, James Madison, James Monroe, Andrew Jackson, John Tyler, James K. Polk, Zachary Taylor, Andrew Johnson, and Ulysses S. Grant. Those that didn't: John Adams, John Quincy Adams, Martin Van Buren, William Harrison, Millard Fillmore, Franklin Pierce, James Buchanan, and Abraham Lincoln.

Peterson then integrated this social studies investigation into his ongoing mathematics lessons that were designed to help Action Research Groups answer the questions, What do the data tell us? and How can we construct new knowledge with the data? Through designing bar graphs and pie graphs, they learned to visualize what they were learning about U.S. presidents. He points out, for example, that students

> added up the total number of years in which the United States had a slave-owning president in office, and compared it to the years in which there were non-slave owning presidents in office. We figured out that in 69 percent of the years between 1789 and 1877, the United State had a president who had been a slave-owner.

Clearly, the teachable moment Peterson's student helped to launch had yielded many opportunities for high-level analytical and critical thinking in several curriculum areas. Yet the lessons that students would learn were far from completed.

They decided to act on their new knowledge. They wrote letters to the publisher of their social studies textbook. A white student, Michelle, explained to Donald Lankiewicz, vice-president at Harcourt School publishers, the results of the class's research and concluded, "All I'm saying is that you should put the word 'racism' in your social study books and explain why it's bad." Lankiewicz's reply to Michelle pointed out that the subject of unfair treatment of people was mentioned on page 467, and that many facts about presidents were not included owing to space limitations. Michelle's written response showed her awareness of the importance of the issues the class had raised in their action research.

> In a history book you shouldn't have to wait till page 467 to learn about unfair treatment.... Adding more pages is good for the kids because they should know the right things from the wrong. It is not like you are limited to certain amount of pages.... All I ask you is that you write the word "racism" in the book and add some more pages in the book so you can put most of the truth about the Presidents.

Michelle and her classmates never received a further reply from the publisher, but the learning opportunities that their probing questions produced had undoubtedly left an indelible mark on their critical thinking abilities and, equally important, had provided valuable lessons in taking action based on the knowledge they had generated collaboratively.

More information on this action research project can be found under "Write the Truth" at www.rethinkingschools.org/archive/16_04/16_04.shtml.

DiaLogos: A Sister Class Exchange between Greece and Canada

(coauthored with Vasilia Kourtis Kazoullis)

DiaLogos was an Internet-based sister class project carried out over two school years between elementary school classes (grades 4, 5, and 6) in Toronto, Canada, and on the islands of Rhodes and Kassos in Greece. The students in Greece were learning English as part of their regular curriculum while many of the Canadian students were of Greek heritage and were learning Greek in supplementary classes outside the regular school day. Students in Greek elementary schools receive three hours per week of English instruction. The DiaLogos students attended regular English lessons for two hours each week using the class textbook, and once a week the lesson was held in the DiaLogos computer room and focused on the sister class exchange. This brief description of the project is drawn from the 2002 doctoral dissertation of Vasilia Kourtis-Kazoullis.

Over the course of the project, numerous activities were carried out between the students. The Greek students were exposed to colloquial expressions in English that would never have appeared in their textbooks (e.g., *stuff like that, and stuff, chilling out, with a really big bang, we had a blast, whaz up,* etc.). The exchange also stimulated extensive creative writing and analysis of social issues. Two examples are outlined here. For more detail, see Kourtis-Kazoullis (2002) and Skourtou, Kourtis-Kazoullis, & Cummins (2006).

Creating Literature

Evgenios Trivizas, a well-known Greek writer of children's stories, gave the project permission to use an introduction to a story which he had just begun and had not completed. This introduction was translated into English and was circulated in Greek and English to all the schools via e-mail with directions to the teachers and students on how it could be used. The students were to continue the story in any way they wanted and were to decide on joint endings with students in their sister classes.

The story dealt with a grouchy man, Mr. Stripsidis, who sent away different animals who came to his home for protection. Thus, each time a new animal came into the story, there was repetition of vocabulary and grammatical forms in the dialogue. This repetition helped students construct their story endings by basing new dialogue they wrote on what had already appeared. There was also a problem to be solved. Finding an ending meant finding ways of negotiation between the man and the animals. Students were also required to collaborate with members of their sister class on a joint ending. The Greek students were encouraged to use the target language (English) but were free to use their first language when needed—or they could use both languages in the same text. Each class in Greece was divided into smaller groups of two or three students who jointly worked on the activity.

Over the course of the project, 80 different stories were written, 59 by the students in Greece (35 stories in Greek and 24 in English) and 21 by stu-

dents from Canada (9 in Greek and 12 in English). Some texts included both languages, reflecting students' attempt to use the target language. Because the students were so highly motivated, they made far greater efforts to use the target language than would have been the case in a typical classroom setting. The students from Canada also used words that the students in Greece would not normally come across in their English books (which contained only standard English) such as *zapped him*. It is interesting that the students learned the form of the target language that the members of their sister class were using. For example, when one of the students in Canada used the expression, *So, it is cool*, a student in Greece not only figured out the meaning of this expression but also used it in communication with the sister class.

Critical Interpretation of History

In response to a request by a Canadian student for information on Ancient Greece, students in Rhodes began a project to carry out research on the history of their own island. Students went to the archeology department and interviewed archeologists, visited the museum (many of the students for the first time) and a special exhibition commemorating the 2400-year anniversary of the establishment of the city of Rhodes, and they documented archeological sites in their village. Students were also given an electronic research sheet that guided them through different Internet sites that would be used to collect information. One activity involved taking an electronic quiz dealing with archeology on a U.S.-based archeological web magazine called *Dig Magazine*. A high mark on this quiz would give the students the title of "honorary archaeologist"—a title that they were eager to get as a result of the visit to the museum and their resulting interest in becoming archaeologists. As many of the questions on the quiz related to Greek culture, they were confident that they would do well. However, when the students answered the following question in this quiz, they were surprised to find that their answer was labelled incorrect:

2. The marble figures and sculptures from the Parthenon in Greece which have been owned by Britain since 1801, are called

   a. The Parthenon facts

   b. The Greek Relics

   c. The Elgin Marbles

   d. The Olympic Artifacts (*Dig Magazine,* 2000, quiz 6)

Most of the students answered (a), as they knew that the marbles were from the Parthenon. However, this response evoked the following feedback:

> Your answer for question 2, Parthenon, is WRONG!

> The answer is c, the Elgin Marbles. The marbles were taken by a British ambassador named Lord Elgin in 1801 when Greece was ruled by Turkey's Ottoman Empire

Students decided to research the topic and discovered that the fate of the so-called Elgin Marbles was still a highly contentious issue between Britain and Greece (which has been demanding their return). The students, with the help of their teacher, wrote to the editor and argued their point. This action may seem like a very small step; however, it was a major step for these 10-year-olds. As expressed by Vasilia Kourtis-Kazoullis (2002), "These *small* students from a *small* island in a *small* country, speaking a *small* language took a big step into the world far beyond their classroom to *battle* with the editor of a *large* educational magazine from a *large* country with a *large* language. They might never have taken this step if they had not felt that someone else was teaching them incorrectly about their *own* identity."

In their letter, the students outlined the history of the Parthenon and the Greek view that the marble statues had been plundered. They concluded their letter as follows:

> When you refer to these marbles on your web page, please do not refer to them as the Elgin Marbles. In reality, they are of Greek origin and should be called the Marbles of the Parthenon. Elgin profited by stealing them. He should not profit by having them named after him.

> We thank you very much. We would appreciate a reply from you with your own viewpoint on this matter.

> On behalf of the 6th grade class of the Kremasti Elementary School in Rhodes, Greece

Letters were received back from the editor and the "in-house" archaeologist of the magazine. These letters noted the complexity of the issue but also acknowledged the legitimacy of the students' concern.

In short, in the context of their critical inquiry, these students discovered that how others depict their own culture might be very different from how they view themselves. But more important, they discovered that they could take action and that this action could bring results.[1]

ENDNOTE

1. As Internet access has expanded across the globe, so too has the variety of collaborative projects that seek to build international understanding by engaging learners from many different countries in dialogue about crucial global issues such as the environment, peace, and human rights. One project of particular note is the Peace Diaries project (www.peacediaries.org) organized by the not-for-profit organization Knowledge iTrust Inc (KIT) (http://www.knowledgeitrust.org/). The Peace Diaries project is described as follows on their website:

> The Peace Diaries was launched in January 2002. The vision: To establish a forum where students of every background (race, gender, creed and religion) could gather to learn about each other and address issues on topics of human rights, community, family, culture, democracy, conflict and peace. Web-based education technology has brought together learners in classrooms in thirteen countries to collaborate on projects that have produced content for the Web, books and radio. English Language Writing supported by a web-based teacher/student literacy tool has attracted ESL

and EFL teachers and their students to the program to not only strengthen their global agency but also to practice and learn English.

A number of additional projects focus on developing partnerships among classrooms and schools to promote learning and collaboration:

- The International Educational and Resource Network (IEARN) is an educational network linking more than 100 countries that enables teachers and young people to use the Internet and other new technologies to collaborate on projects that enhance learning and make a difference in the world. http://www.iearn.org

- De Orilla a Orilla (Spanish for "From Shore to Shore") is a global learning network project that forms partnerships among classes within the U.S. and internationally with a focus on multilingualism, collaborative and critical inquiry, and social action. http://www.orillas.org

- Global SchoolNet provides a virtual clearinghouse for collaborative projects and a range of resources and project-based support materials to support shared learning. http://www.globalschoolnet.org/

Dual-Language Bookmaking

In Chapter 2, we discussed the three major principles that cognitive psychologist John Bransford and his colleagues (2000) articulated to capture the essential features of *How People Learn*. Bransford's synthesis of scientific research emphasizes that students should build on their preexisting knowledge, aim for deep understanding of issues and content, and be encouraged to self-regulate and take ownership of the learning process. Because ELL students' prior knowledge is encoded in their L1, students' L1 is obviously relevant to their learning. It is the cognitive tool that they have used and relied on up to this point. Bransford's principles imply that educators should explicitly teach for transfer of concepts and skills from L1 to English. It is hard to argue that we are teaching the whole child when school policy dictates that students leave their language and culture at the schoolhouse door.

Patricia Chow and her colleagues at Thornwood Public School, a K–5 school in the Peel District School Board in the Greater Toronto Area, were among the pioneers in exploring how students' home languages could be incorporated into the school as tools for overall literacy develop-

ment. More than 40 different home languages are spoken by Thornwood students.

The project started as an action research project involving a team of teachers working with Sandra Schecter (York University) and Jim Cummins (University of Toronto) to explore ways that the school could expand its partnerships with parents and the broader community. The school website (http://thornwood.peelschools.org/Dual/) describes the initial goals as follows:

The group is committed to forging a stronger home-school connection. We believe that reading in any language develops reading ability. We want to engage parents in reading with their children at home and to encourage discussion and the sharing of their experiences and realities. As a result, the group decided to create dual-language book bags, comprising dual-language books and multilingual audio tapes, for use at school and at home. Non-English speaking parents could enjoy reading the stories to their children in their own language and elaborating on the ideas, values, skills, and concepts introduced in this "expanded" home literacy program. Student/parent/

community volunteers would record the multi-lingual stories on audio cassettes.

In order to pursue this plan, the school ordered a range of commercial dual-language books. However, as Patricia recounts, "Difficulties with the acquisition of the dual language books necessitated an adjustment in our plans":

> Fortunately, my students were up to the challenge! During the first term, I usually take a low-key approach to promoting linguistic diversity (e.g., saying "hello" or "good morning" in other languages when taking attendance, singing songs in French, and asking students to share their bilingual skills when counting).... Delays in the delivery of the dual language books precipitated the creation of original, English/first language stories, written by my grade one students and translated by their parents or older ESL students in the school. By creating these books, with the help of teachers, friends, and family, the students had the opportunity to explore their languages, and English, in a developmentally appropriate way. I enjoyed the enthusiastic support of my students' parents.

At this point, a large number of student-created identity texts in multiple languages can be viewed and downloaded from the school website. Although the initial project involved grade 1 students writing stories in English and then working with various resource people to translate the stories into their L1s (because most students had not yet developed L1 literacy skills), the project evolved to encourage students who are literate in their L1 (e.g., newly arrived older students) to write in that language and then work with others to translate the stories into English. Students at all grade levels have become involved, and the creation of dual-language books has become a potent tool to support the integration of newcomer and ELL students. Students write initial drafts of stories in whichever language they choose, usually in their stronger language.

Thus, newcomer students can write in L1 and demonstrate not only their literacy skills but also their ideas, feelings, and imagination to teachers and other students. The image of newcomer students, in both their own eyes and the eyes of others, changes dramatically when they are enabled to express them*selves*. Newcomer students can also read books in their L1 written by other students or that form part of the school's extensive collection of commercial dual-language books. This communicates to students that their L1 talents are welcomed within the school and motivates them to write in their L1. Students can also take these books home from the classroom or school library for reading with their parents. Bilingual high school students have also become involved in helping students to compose and translate across languages.

Technology has added an important component to this project. Students' stories and illustrations are entered into the computer through word processing and scanning. The Dual Language Showcase website on which the stories are displayed enables students' bilingual stories to be shared with parents, relatives, or friends who have Internet access both in Canada and students' countries of origin. Teachers anywhere in the world can access and download these stories to use in their lessons, to assess students' L1 literacy skills, or to inspire their own students to create multilingual stories.

The Thornwood project has inspired other Toronto-area schools at multiple grade levels to use dual-language book creation as a tool to enable bilingual students to use their home languages and prior knowledge as potent tools to engage in learning. A number of these dual-language books are displayed on the Multiliteracies Project website (www.multiliteracies.ca). Kanta (grade 7 when she wrote *The New Country* with two friends) and Tomer (grade 6 when he wrote his stories), both students of Lisa Leoni in the York Region District School Board, testify eloquently to the power of both cognitive engagement and identity investment in fueling learning and academic participation:

Kanta:

My first language is Punjabi, my second language is Urdu, and my third language is English. When I came here in grade 4 the teachers didn't know what I was capable of. I was given a pack of crayons and a coloring book and told to color in it, and after that I felt so bad—like I'm capable of doing much more than just that. I have my own inner skills to show the world so when we started writing this book [*The New Country*], I could show the world that I am something more than just coloring. So that's how it helped me and it made me so proud of myself that I am actually capable of doing something and not just coloring, and I am so proud of myself that I am something.

Tomer:

I came here [Toronto] last year when I was in grade 6 and now I am in grade 7. With *Tom Goes to Kentucky* [Tomer's Hebrew-English book], it was easier to begin it in Hebrew and then translate it to English, and the other thing that made it easier was that I chose the topic. Because I love horses, when I'm writing about horses it makes me want to continue to do it, and do it faster. The name *Tom* came from my friend Tom who is still in Israel, the name *El General* [horse's name] is a name I knew from horse racing and the book is about a guy who wants to go on and be a better horseback [rider]. I felt great seeing my book on the Internet because everybody could see it and I don't need to show it to everybody, they can just click on my name in Google and go to the book. I told Tom to see it and all of my family saw it.

The Dual Language Showcase and Multiliteracies projects illustrate the *power of learning* when the interpersonal space of the classroom is expanded from an English-only to a multilingual zone and when technology is harnessed as a tool to amplify student voice. The students we have observed and have had the privilege to work with in these projects show high levels of literacy engagement and identity investment precisely because they are building on their preexisting knowledge, searching for deep understanding of issues and content, and taking ownership of the learning process.

RESOURCES

Cummins, J., Bismilla, V., Chow, P., Cohen, S., Giampapa, F., Leoni, L., Sandhu, P., & Sastri, P. (2005) Affirming identity in multilingual classrooms. *Educational Leadership*, 63(1), 38–43.

Schecter, S., & Cummins, J. (Eds.). (2003). *Multilingual education in practice: Using diversity as a resource*. Portsmouth, NH: Heinemann.

REFERENCES

Ada, A. F., & Campoy, F. I. (2004). *Authors in the classroom: A transformative education process.* Boston, MA: Pearson/Allyn and Bacon.

Allington, R. L. (2001). *What really matters for struggling readers: Designing research-based programs.* New York: Longman.

Allington, R. L. (2004). Setting the record straight. *Educational Leadership, 61*(6), 22–25.

American Educational Research Association (1999). *Standards for educational and psychological testing.* Washington, DC: Author.

Amrein, A. L. & Berliner, D. C. (2002, March 28). High-stakes testing, uncertainty, and student learning. *Education Policy Analysis Archives, 10*(18). Retrieved April 23, 2005, from http://epaa.asu.edu/epaa/v10n18/.

Angrist, J., & Levy, V. (2002). New evidence on classroom computers and pupil learning. *Economic Journal, 112,* 735–765.

Anyon, J. (2005). What "counts" as educational policy: Notes towards a new paradigm. *Harvard Educational Review, 75,* 65–88.

Armstrong, A., & Casement, C. (1998). *The child and the machine: Why computers may put our children's education at risk.* Toronto: Key Porter Books.

Attewell, P., & Battle, J. (1999). Home computers and school performance. *The Information Society, 15*(1), 1–10.

Au, K. H. (1998). Social constructivism and the school literacy learning of students of diverse backgrounds. *Journal of Literacy Research, 30*(2), 297–319.

August, D., & Shanahan, T. (Eds.). (2006). *Developing literacy in second-language learners: A Report of the National Literacy Panel on Language Minority Children and Youth.* Mahwah, NJ: Lawrence Erlbaum.

Balesse, L., & Freinet, C. (1973). *La lectura en la escuela por medio de la imprenta.* F. Beltran, trans. Barcelona: Editorial Laia. (Original work published 1961 as *La lecture par l'imprimerie a l'école* [Reading through printing in schools]).

Barndt, M., & McNally, J. (2001). The return to separate and unequal. *Rethinking Schools, 15*(3), 1–2.

Barton, D., Hamilton, M., & Ivanic, R. (Eds.). (2000). *Situated literacies.* London: Routledge.

Becker, W. (1977). Teaching reading and language to the disadvantaged: What we have learned from field research. *Harvard Educational Review, 47,* 518–543.

Becker, W., & Gersten, R. (1982). A follow-up of follow through: The later effects of the direct instruction model on children in the fifth and sixth grades. *Amercian Educational Research Journal, 19,* 75–92.

Béjoint, H. (2000). *Modern lexicography: An introduction.* Oxford: Oxford University Press.

Bennett, F. (2002). The future of computer technology in K–12 education. *Phi Delta Kappan, 83*(8), 621–625.

Bennett, R. (1987). *Cooperative learning with a computer in a native language class.* ERIC Document Reproduction Service, No. ED320709.

Bennett, R., et al. (1985). *Hupa Natural Resources Dictionary.* ERIC Document Reproduction Service, No. ED282698.

Berliner, D. C., & Biddle, B. J. (1995). *The manufactured crisis.* Reading, MA: Addison Wesley.

Bernhard, J. K. *The Early Authors Program.* Retrieved May 4, 2005, from www.ryerson.ca/~bernhard/early.html.

Bernhard, J. K., & Cummins, J. (2004, November 17–19). *Cognitive engagement and identity investment in literacy development among English Language Learners: Evidence from the Early Authors Program.* Paper presented at the English Language Learners Conference, National Center for Culturally Responsive Educational Systems, Scottsdale, AZ.

Bernhard, J. K., Cummins, J., Campoy, F. I., Ada, A. F., Winsler, A., & Bleiker, C. (in press). Identity texts and literacy development among preschool English language learners: Enhancing learning opportunities for children at risk of learning disabilities *Teachers College Record.*

Bernhard, J. K., Winsler, A., & Bleiker, C. (2004). *The Early Authors Program: A Miami-Dade early literacy initiative.* Final report submitted to the Child Care Bureau's Early Learning Opportunities Office.

Bernhard, J. K., Winsler, A., Bleiker, C., Ginieniewicz, J., & Madigan, A. (2005, April). *The early authors program: Implementing transformative literacy in early childhood education.* Paper presented at the American Educational Research Association, Montreal, Quebec.

Beykont, Z. F. (Ed.). (2002). *The power of culture: Teaching across language difference.* Cambridge, MA: Harvard Education Publishing Group.

Biddle, B. J., & Berliner, D. C. (2002). *What research says about unequal funding for schools in America.* Education Policy Studies Laboratory. Retrieved March 22, 2005, from www.asu.edu/educ/epsl/eprp.htm.

Bigelow, B., Christensen, L., Karp, S., Miner, B., & Peterson, B. (Eds.). (1994) *Rethinking our classrooms: Teaching for equity and justice.* Milwaukee, WI: Rethinking Schools.

Blok, H., Oostdam, R., Otter, M. E., & Overmaat, M. (2002). Computer-assisted instruction in support of beginning reading instruction: A review. *Review of Educational Research, 72,* 101–130.

Bracey, G. W. (1999, November 2). Poverty issues get short shrift in today's education debate. *USA Today,* p. 19A.

Bracey, G. W. (2003). *On the death of childhood and destruction of public schools: The folly of today's education policies and practices.* Portsmouth, NH: Heinemann.

Bransford, J. D., Brown, A. L, & Cocking, R. R. (2000). *How people learn: Brain, mind, experience, and school.* Washington, DC: National Academy Press.

Brown, K. (2000). Global learning networks: Heartbeats on the Internet. In J. V. Tinajero & R. A. DeVillar (Eds.), *The power of two languages 2000* (pp. 309–319). New York: McGraw-Hill School Division.

Brown, K., Cummins, J., Figueroa, E., & Sayers, D. (2002). Global learning networks: Gaining perspective on our lives with distance. In E. Lee, D. Menkart, & M. Okazawa-Rey (Eds.), *Beyond heroes and holidays: A practical guide to K–12 antiracist, multicultural education and staff development* (pp. 334–354). Washington, DC: Teaching for Change.

Burns, T. C., & Ungerleider, C. S. (2002/2003). Information and communication technologies in elementary and secondary education: A state of the art review. *International Journal of Educational Policy, Research, & Practice, 3*(4), 27–54.

Cain, C. J. (2005). (Re)writing inequality: Language of crisis implications in California educational reform. In T. L. McCarty (Ed.), *Language, literacy, and power in schooling.* (pp. 263–282). Mahwah, NJ: Lawrence Erlbaum.

Camilli, G., Vargas, S., & Yurecko, M. (2003). Teaching children to read: The fragile link between science and federal education policy. *Education Policy Analysis Archives, 11*(15). Retrieved May 4, 2005, from http://epaa.asu.edu/epaa/v11n15.

Camilli, G., & Wolfe, P. (2004). Research on reading: A cautionary tale. *Educational Leadership, 61*(6), 26–29.

Carnine, D. W., Silbert, J., & Kameenui, E. J. (1997). *Direct instruction reading.* (3rd ed.). Upper Saddle River, NJ: Merrill.

Carroll, S. J., Krop, C., Arkes, J., Morrison, P. A., & Flanagan, A. (2005). *California's K–12 public schools: How are they doing?* Santa Monica, CA: Rand Corporation.

Chall, J. S., Jacobs, V., & Baldwin, L. (1990). *The reading crisis: Why poor children fall behind.* Cambridge, MA: Harvard University Press.

Chall, J. S., & Snow, C. (1988, January). School influences on the reading development of low-income children. *The Harvard Education Letter, 4*(1), 1–4.

Chascas, S., & Cummins, J. (2005). *The e-Lective Language Learning Program.* Retrieved April 25, 2005, from www.e-Lective.net.

Chow, P., & Cummins, J. (2003). Valuing multilingual and multicultural approaches to learning. In S. R. Schecter & J. Cummins (Eds.), *Multilingual education in practice: Using diversity as a resource.* (pp. 32–61). Portsmouth, NH: Heinemann.

Clark, U. (2001). *War words: Language, history and the disciplining of English.* Oxford: Elsevier.

Cloud, N., Genesee, F., & Hamayan, E. (2000). *Dual language instruction: A handbook for enriched education.* Boston: Heinle & Heinle.

Coles, G. (2001). Reading taught to the tune of the "scientific" hickory stick. *Phi Delta Kappan, 83*(3), 205–212.

Coles, G. (2002). *Reading unmentionables: Damaging reading education while seeming to fix it.* Portsmouth, NH: Heinemann.

Coles, G. (2003). *Reading the naked truth: Literacy, legislation, and lies.* Portsmouth, NH: Heinemann.

Collier, V. P., & Thomas, W. P. (1999). Making U.S. schools effective for English language learners, Part 2. *TESOL Matters, 9*(5), 1, 6.

Cope, B., & Kalantzis, M. (2000). Multiliteracies: The beginnings of an idea. In B. Cope & M. Kalantzis (Eds.), *Multiliteracies: Literacy, learning and the design of social futures* (pp. 3–8). New York: Routledge.

Corson, D. (1997). The learning and use of academic English words. *Language Learning, 47*, 671–718.

Cuban, L. (2001). *Oversold and underused: Computers in the schools.* Cambridge, MA: Harvard University Press.

Cummins, J. (1981). Age on arrival and immigrant second language learning in Canada: A reassessment. *Applied Linguistics, 1,* 132–149.

Cummins, J. (1999). Alternative paradigms in bilingual education research: Does theory have a place? *Educational Researcher, 28*(7), 26–41.

Cummins, J. (2001). *Negotiating identities: Education for empowerment in a diverse society* (2nd ed.). Los Angeles: California Association for Bilingual Education.

Cummins, J. (2004). Multiliteracies pedagogy and the role of identity texts. In K. Leithwood, P. McAdie, N. Bascia, & A. Rodigue (Eds.), *Teaching for deep understanding: Towards the Ontario curriculum that we need* (pp. 68–74). Toronto: Ontario Institute for Studies in Education of the University of Toronto and the Elementary Federation of Teachers of Ontario.

Cummins, J., Bismilla, V., Chow, P., Cohen, S., Giampapa, F., Leoni, L., Sandhu, P., & Sastri, P. (2005). Affirming identity in multilingual classrooms. *Educational Leadership, 63*(1), 38–43.

Cummins, J., & Sayers, D. (1995). *Brave new schools: Challenging cultural illiteracy through global learning networks.* New York: St. Martin's Press.

Cunningham, A. (1990). Explicit versus implicit instruction in phonemic awareness. *Journal of Experimental Child Psychology, 50,* 429–444.

Cunningham, A. E., & Stanovich, K. E. (1997). Early reading acquisition and its relation to reading experience and ability 10 years later. *Developmental Psychology, 33*(6), 934–945.

Day, R. R., & Bamford, J. (1996). *Extensive reading in the second language classroom.* Cambridge: Cambridge University Press.

Dean, C. (1999, December 3). Poor results exposed by poverty analysis. *Times Educational Supplement.* Retrieved April 23, 2005, from www.tes.co.uk/search/story/?story_id=305619.

DeBell, M., & Chapman, C. (2003). *Computer and Internet use by children and adolescents in 2001* (NCES 2004-014). U.S. Department of Education. Washington, DC: National Center for Education Statistics.

DeFazio, A. J. (1997). Language awareness at the International High School. In L. Van Lier & D. Corson (Eds.), *Knowledge about language* (Vol. 6, pp. 99–107). Dordrecht, The Netherlands: Kluwer Academic Publishers.

de Klerk, G. (Ed.). (1998). *Virtual power: Technology, education, and community.* Long Beach, CA: Pacific Southwest Regional Technology in Education Consortium.

Delpit, L. (1995). *Other people's children: Cultural conflict in the classroom.* New York: The New Press.

DevTech Systems Inc. (1996). *A descriptive study of the ESEA Title VII educational services provided for secondary school limited English proficient students: Final report.* Washington, DC: National Clearinghouse for Bilingual Education.

Dewey, J. (1963). *Experience and education.* New York: Collier Books.

Dillon, S. (2005, April 26). Texas officials shrug off fine over Bush law. *The New York Times.* Retrieved April 26 from www.nytimes.com.

Donahue, P. L., Voelkl, K. E., Campbell, J. R., & Mazzeo, J. (1999). *The NAEP 1998 reading report card for the nation and the states.* Washington, DC: National Center for Education Statistics.

Donovan, M. S., & Bransford, J. D. (Eds.). (2005). *How students learn: History, mathematics, and science in the classroom.* Washington, DC: The National Academy Press.

Duncan, G. J., Brooks-Gunn, J., & Klebanov, P. K. (1994). Economic deprivation and early childhood development. *Child Development 65,* 296–318.

Durán, R. (2005). *Technology and literacy development of Latino youth.* Paper prepared as part of the Technology in Support of Young Second Language Learners Project at the University of California Office of the President, under a grant from the William and Flora Hewlett Foundation.

Durán, R., & Durán, J. (2001). Latino immigrant parents and children learning and publishing together in an after-school setting. *Journal of Education for Students Placed at Risk, 6*(1/2), 95–113.

Early, M., Cummins, J., & Willinsky, J. (2002). *From literacy to multiliteracies: Designing learning environments for knowledge generation within the new economy.* Proposal funded by the Social Sciences and Humanities Research Council of Canada, www.multiliteracies.ca.

Egan, K. (1986). *Teaching as story telling: An alternative approach to teaching and curriculum in the elementary school.* Chicago: The University of Chicago Press.

Egan, K. (1999). *Children's minds, talking rabbits & clockwork oranges: Essays on education.* New York: Teachers College Press.

Egan, K., & Nadaner, D. (Eds.). (1988). *Imagination and education.* New York: Teachers College Press.

Ehri, L. C., Nunes, S., Stahl, S., & Willows, D. (2001). Systematic phonics instruction helps students learn to read: Evidence from the National Reading Panel's meta-analysis. *Review of Educational Research, 71*(3), 393–447.

Elley, W. B. (1991). Acquiring literacy in a second language: The effect of book-based programs. *Language Learning, 41,* 375–411.

Elley, W. (1992). *How in the world do students read? The IEA study of reading literacy.* The Hague: International Association for Evaluation of Educational Achievement.

Elley, W. B., & Manghubai, F. (1983). The impact of reading on second language learning. *Reading Research Quarterly, 19,* 53–67.

Engelmann, S. (1969). *Conceptual learning.* San Rafael, CA: Dimensions Publishing.

European Commission. (2004). *A world of learning at your fingertips: Pilot projects under the eLearning Initiative.* Retrieved August 20, 2004, from http://europa.eu.int/comm/education/programmes/elearning/projects_en.html.

Evans, T. L. P. (1996). *I can read deze books: A quantitative comparison of the reading recovery program and a small-group intervention.* Unpublished doctoral dissertation, Auburn University, Auburn, AL.

Fellbaum, C. (Ed.). (1998). *WordNet: An electronic lexical database.* Cambridge, MA: MIT Press.

Fielding, L. G., & Pearson, P. D. (1994). Reading comprehension: What works. *Educational Leadership, 51*(5), 62–68.

Fitzgerald, J. (1995). English-as-a-second-language learners' cognitive reading processes: A review of research in the United States. *Review of Educational Research, 65,* 145–190.

Fletcher, J. D. (2003). Evidence for learning from technology-assisted instruction. In H. F. O'Neill Jr. & R. S. Perez (Eds.), *Technology applications in education: A learning view* (pp. 79–99). Mahwah, NJ: Lawrence Erlbaum.

Fordham, S. (1990). Racelessness as a factor in Black students' school success: Pragmatic strategy or Pyrrhic victory? In N. M. Hidalgo, C. L. McDowell, & E. V. Siddle (Eds.), *Facing racism in education* (Reprint series No. 21 ed., pp. 232–262), Cambridge, MA: Harvard Educational Review.

Foster, K. C., Erickson, G. C., Forster, D. F., Brinkman, D., & Torgesen, J. K. (1994). Computer administered instruction in phonological awareness: Evaluation of the DaisyQuest program. *The Journal of Research and Development in Education, 27,* 126–137.

Freebody, P., & Luke, A. (1990). Literacies' programs: Debates and demands in cultural contexts. *Prospect: A Journal of Australian TESOL, 11,* 7–16.

Freeman, R. D. (1998). *Bilingual education and social change.* Clevedon, England: Multilingual Matters.

Freeman, Y. S., & Freeman, D. E. (1992). *Whole language for second language learners.* Portsmouth, NH: Heinemann.

Freeman, Y. S., Freeman, D. E. & Mercuri, S. P. (2005). *Dual language essentials for teachers and administrators.* Portsmouth, NH: Heinemann.

Freinet, É. (1975). *Nacimiento de una pedagogía popular: Historia de una escuela moderna.* Pere Vilanova, trans. Barcelona: Editorial Laia. (Original work published 1969 as *Naissance d'une pedagogie populaire* [Birth of a popular pedagogy]).

Freire, P. (1970). *Pedagogy of the oppressed.* New York: Continuum.

Fuchs, T., & Woessmann, L. (2004). *Computers and student learning: Bivariate and multivariate evidence on the availability and use of computers at home and at school.* CESIFO Working Paper, No. 1321. Retrieved April 22, 2005, from www.cesifo-group.de/.

Gallagher, C. (2004, January). Turning the accountability tables: Ten progressive lessons from one "backward" state. *Phi Delta Kappan.* Retrieved April 22, 2005 from www.pdkintl.org/kappan/k0401gal.htm.

Garan, E. M. (2001). What does the report of the National Reading Panel really tell us about teaching phonics? *Language Arts, 79*(1), 61–70.

Garan, E. M. (2004). *In defense of our children: When politics, profit, and education collide.* Portsmouth, NH: Heinemann.

Gee, J. P. (1999). Reading and the new literacy studies: Reframing the National Academy of Sciences report on reading. *Journal of Literacy Research, 31,* 355–374.

Gee, J. P. (2000). The limits of reframing: A response to Professor Snow. *Journal of Literacy Research, 32,* 121–130.

Gee, J. P. (2001). Identity as an analytic lens for research in education. In W. G. Secada (Ed.), *Review of Research in Education, 25,* 99–126. Washington, DC: American Educational Research Association.

Genesee, F., Lindholm-Leary, K., Saunders, W. M., & Christian, D. (Eds.). (2006). *Educating English language learners: A synthesis of research evidence.* New York: Cambridge University Press.

Gensburger, A. (2005, February). Leaving the teacher behind. *No Child Left, 3*(2), Retrieved March 31, 2005, from www.nochildleft.com/2005/feb05departing.html.

Gervilliers, D., Berteloot, C., & Lemery, J. (1968/1977). *Las correspondencias escolares.* Barcelona: Editorial Laia.

Geva, E. (2000). Issues in the assessment of reading disabilities in L2 children— Beliefs and research evidence. *Dyslexia, 6,* 13–28.

Geva, E., & Clifton, S. (1993). The development of first and second language reading skills in Early French Immersion.

Canadian Modern Language Review, 50, 646–667.

Goddard, H. H. (1917). Mental tests and the immigrant. *Journal of Delinquency, 2,* 243–277.

Goodlad, J. I. (1984). *A place called school: Prospects for the future.* New York: McGraw-Hill.

Goodman, S. (2003) *Teaching youth media: A critical guide to literacy, video production, and social change.* New York: Teachers College Press

Goodnough, A. (2003, April 5). More intensive reading program is added for struggling pupils. *The New York Times,* pp. D1, D3.

Goolsbee, A., & Guryan, J. (2002). *The impact of Internet subsidies in public schools.* Chicago: National Bureau of Economic Research.

Graves, M. F., Juel, C., & Graves, B. B. (2001). *Teaching reading in the 21st century.* Boston: Allyn and Bacon.

Greaney, K., Tunmer, W., & Chapman, J. (1997). Effects of rime-based orthographic analogy training on the word recognition skills of children with reading disability. *Journal of Educational Psychology, 89,* 645–651.

Guthrie, J. T. (2004). Teaching for literacy engagement. *Journal of Literacy Research, 36,* 1–30.

Hakuta, K., Butler, Y. G., & Witt, D. (2000). *How long does it take English learners to attain proficiency?* Santa Barbara: University of California Linguistic Minority Research Institute.

Haney, W. (2002). Revealing illusions of educational progress: Texas high-stakes tests and minority student performance. In Z. F. Beykont (Ed.), *The power of culture: Teaching across language difference* (pp. 25–42). Cambridge, MA: Harvard Education Publishing Group.

Hatcher, P., Hulme, C., & Ellis, A. (1994). Ameliorating early reading failure by integrating the teaching of reading and phonological skills: The phonological linkage hypothesis. *Child Development, 65,* 41–57.

Healy, J. M. (1998). *Failure to connect: How computers affect our children's minds—and what we can do about it.* New York: Simon & Schuster.

Hoover, R. L. (2000). Forces and factors affecting Ohio Proficiency Test performance. Retrieved April 23, 2005, from www.cc.ysu.edu/~rlhoover/OPT/.

Hull, G., & Schultz, K. (2001). Literacy and learning out of school: A review of theory and research. *Review of Educational Research, 71,* 575–612.

Hull, G., & Schultz, K. (Eds.). (2002). *School's out! Bridging out-of-school literacies with classroom practice.* New York: Teachers College Press.

International Information and Communication Technologies (ICT) Literacy Panel. (2002). *Digital transformation: A framework for ICT Literacy.* Princeton, NJ: Educational Testing Services (ETS). Retrieved April 11, 2004, from www.ets.org/research/ictliteracy/ictreport.pdf.

Iran-Nejad, A., McKeachie, W., & Berliner, D. (1990). The multisource nature of learning: An introduction. *Review of Educational Research, 60,* 509–516.

Iversen, S. (1997). *Reading Recovery as a small group intervention.* Unpublished Doctoral dissertation, Massey University, Palmerston North, New Zealand.

Ivey, G., & Baker, M. (2004). Phonics instruction for older students? Just say no. *Educational Leadership, 61*(6), 35–39.

Jaeger, E. (2006). Silencing teachers in an era of scripted reading. *Rethinking Schools, 20*(3), 39–41.

Jhai Archives. (no date). Retrieved May 7, 2006, from http://splangy.com/cgi-bin/dada/mail.cgi?flavor-archive&id=20051229210059&list=jhaiupdates.

Jhai Foundation. *Formerly Project Hearts and Minds: Laos.* Retrieved May 8, 2005, from www.jhai.org/.

Jhai Foundation. *Good News Update from Jhai Foundation's Remote Village IT Project.* Retrieved May 8, 2005, from www.jhai.org/jhai_remote_launch_follow.htm.

Jhai Foundation. *Technology.* Retrieved May 8, 2005, from www.jhai.org/technology.htm.

Jhai Foundation. *The Jhai PC and Communication System.* Retrieved May 8, 2005, from www.jhai.org/jhai_remoteIT.htm.

Jonassen, D. H. (1996). *Computers in the classroom: Mindtools for critical thinking.* Englewood Cliffs, NJ: Prentice-Hall.

Jonassen, D. H. (1999). *Computers as mindtools for schools: Engaging critical thinking* (2nd ed.). Englewood Cliffs, NJ: Prentice-Hall.

Jonassen, D. H., Carr, C., & Yueh, H-P. (1998). Computers as mindtools for engaging learners in critical thinking. *TechTrends, 43*(2), 24–32.

Juel, C., & Minden-Cupp (2000). Learning to read words: Linguistic units and instructional strategies. *Reading Research Quarterly, 35*(4), 458–492.

Kamil, M. L., Intrator, S. M., & Kim, H. S. (2000). The effects of other technologies on literacy and literacy learning. In M. L. Kamil, P. B. Mosenthal, P. D. Pearson, & R. Barr (Eds.), *Handbook of reading research.* (Vol. III, pp. 771–788). Mahwah, NJ: Lawrence Erlbaum.

Klein, S. P., Hamilton, L. S., McCaffrey, D. F., & Stecher, B. M. (2000) What do test scores in Texas tell us?" *Education Policy Analysis Archives, 8*(49). Retrieved May 9, 2005, from http://epaa.asu.edu/epaa/v8n49/.

Kleiner, A., & Farris, E. (2002). *Internet access in U.S. public schools and classrooms: 1994–2001.* Washington, DC: National Center for Educational Statistics.

Kleiner, A., & Lewis, L. (2003). *Internet access in U.S. public schools and classrooms: 1994–2002* (NCES 2004–011). U.S. Department of Education. Washington, DC: National Center for Education Statistics.

Klesmer, H. (1994). Assessment and teacher perceptions of ESL student achievement. *English Quarterly, 26*(3), 8–11.

Kohn, A. (2000). *The case against standardized testing: Raising the scores, ruining the schools.* Portsmouth, NH: Heinemann.

Kourtis-Kazoullis V. (2002). *DiaLogos: Bilingualism and the teaching of second language learning on the Internet.* Unpublished doctoral dissertation, University of the Aegean, Primary Education Department, Rhodes, Greece.

Kozol, J. (1991). *Savage inequalities: Children in America's schools.* New York: Crown Publishers.

Kozol, J. (2005). *The shame of the nation: The restoration of apartheid schooling in America..* New York: Crown Publishers.

Krashen, S. D. (1999). *Three arguments against whole language & why they are wrong.* Portsmouth, NH: Heinemann.

Krashen, S. (2001). More smoke and mirrors: A critique of the National Reading Panel report on fluency. *Phi Delta Kappan, 83*(2), 119–123.

Krashen, S. D. (2004a). False claims about literacy development. *Educational Leadership, 61*(6), 18–21.

Krashen, S. D. (2004b). *The power of reading: Insights from the research.* (2nd ed.). Portsmouth, NH: Heinemann.

Kwan, A. B., & Willows, D. M. (1998, December). *Impact of early phonics instruction on children learning English as a second language.* Paper presented at the National Reading Conference, Austin, TX.

Ladson-Billings, G. (1995). Toward a theory of culturally relevant pedagogy. *American Educational Research Journal, 32,* 465–491.

Lambert, W. E., & Tucker, G. R. (1972). *Bilingual education of children: The St. Lambert experiment.* Rowley, MA: Newbury House.

Lave, J., & Wenger, E. (1991). *Situated learning: Legitimate peripheral participation.* Cambridge, England: Cambridge University Press.

Lee, E. (1998). Promoting equity at our school site. In K. Brown & E. Figueroa (Eds.), *Connecting math to our lives: Project announcement* (p. 2). Puerto Rico: De Orilla a Orilla.

Lee, E. (2002a). Anti-racist education: Pulling together to close the gaps. In E. Lee, D. Menkart, & M. Okazawa-Rey (Eds.), *Beyond heroes and holidays: A practical guide to K–12 anti-racist, multicultural education and staff development* (pp. 26–35). Washington DC: Teaching for Change.

Lee, E. (2002b). Looking through an anti-racist lens. In E. Lee, D. Menkart, & M. Okazawa-Rey (Eds.), *Beyond heroes and holidays: A practical guide to K–12 anti-racist, multicultural education and staff development.* (pp. 402–404). Washington DC: Teaching for Change.

Leithwood, K., McAdie, P., Bascia, N., Rodrigue, A., & Moore, S. (2004). The central purpose of Ontario's curriculum. In K. Leithwood, P. McAdie, N. Bascia, & A. Rodrigue (Eds.), *Teaching for deep understanding: Toward the Ontario curriculum that we need* (pp. 1–7). Toronto: OISE/UT and Elementary Teachers' Federation of Ontario.

LeLoup, J. W., & Ponterio, R. (2003, December). Second language acquisition and technology: A review of the research. *CAL Digest.* Washington, DC: Center for Applied Linguistics.

Leu, D. L., Jr., Castek, J., Coiro, J., Gort, M., Henry, L. A., & Lima, C. O. (2005). *Developing new literacies among multilingual learners in the elementary grades.* Paper prepared as part of the Technology in Support of Young Second Language Learners Project at the University of California Office of the President, under a grant from the William and Flora Hewlett Foundation.

Leu, D. J., Jr., & Kinzer, C. K. (2000). The convergence of literacy instruction and networked technologies for information and communication. *Reading Research Quarterly, 35,* 108–127.

Levine, A. (1996, October). America's reading crisis: Why the whole-language approach to teaching has failed millions of children. *Parents, 16,* 63–65, 68.

Lindholm-Leary, K. J. (2001). *Dual language education.* Clevedon, England: Multilingual Matters.

Linn, R. L. (2004). *Rethinking the No Child Left Behind Act accountability system.* Paper prepared for Center on Education Policy's Forum to Discuss Ideas to Improve the Accountability Provisions Under the No Child Left Behind Act. July 28, 2004, Washington, D.C. Retrieved April 23,

2005, from www.cep-dc.org/pubs/ Forum28July2004/.

Lloyd, S. (1993). *The phonics handbook*. Essex, UK: Jolly Learning.

Luke, A. (2002). What happens to literacies old and new when they're turned into policy? In D.E. Alverman (Ed.), *Adolescents and literacies in a digital world* (pp. 186–203). New York: Peter Lang.

Luke, A. (2006). Evidence-based state literacy policy: A critical alternative. In N. Bascia, A. Cumming, A. Datnow, K. Leithwood, & D. Livingstone (Eds.), *International handbook of educational policy*. Norwalk, MA: Springer.

Luke, A., Freebody, P., & Land, R. (2000). *Literate futures: The Queensland State literacy strategy*. Brisbane: Education Queensland.

Lynn, R. (2000, November 13) Oxnard teachers use parents' work in fields to grow students' minds. *The Desert Sun*. Retrieved December 11, 2000, from www.thedesertsun.com/news/stories/local/974080923.shtml.

Lyon, G. R., & Chhabra, V. (2004). The science of reading research. *Educational Leadership, 61*(6), 12–17.

Mathes, P. G., & Torgesen, J. K. (2000). A call for equity in reading instruction for all students: A response to Allington and Woodside-Jiron. *Educational Researcher, 29*(6), 4–14.

McAuley, A. (1998). Virtual teaching on the tundra. *Technos, 7*(3), 11–14.

McAuley, A. (2003). *Illiniqatigiit: Implementing a knowledge building environment in the Eastern Arctic*. Unpublished Ph.D. dissertation, The University of Toronto.

McAuley, S. (2001). Creating a community of learners: Computer support in the Eastern Arctic. *Education Canada, 40*(4), 8–11.

McCaleb, S. P. (1997). *Building communities of learners: A collaboration among teachers, students, families, and community*. Mahwah, NJ: Lawrence Erlbaum.

McCardle, P., & Chhabra, V. (Eds.). *The voice of evidence in reading research*. Baltimore: Paul H. Brookes.

McCarty, T. L. (1993, March). Language, literacy, and the image of the child in American Indian classrooms. *Language Arts, 70*, 182–192.

McCarty, T. L. (2002). *A place to be Navajo: Rough Rock and the struggle for self-determination in indigenous schooling*. Mahwah, NJ: Lawrence Erlbaum.

McCarty, T. L., & Romero, M. E. (2005, April 12). *Accountable to whom? NCLB, English-only, and Native American learners*. Paper Presented at the Annual Meeting of the American Educational Research Association Presidential Invited Session: Education in a Demographically Changing Society, Montreal, Canada.

McMillan, K., & Honey, M. (1993). *Year one of project pulse: Pupils using laptops in science and English* (Tech. Rep. 26). New York: Center for Technology in Education.

McNeill, L. M. (2000). *Contradictions of school reform: Educational costs of standardized testing*. New York: Routledge.

McQuillan, J. (1998). *The literacy crisis: False claims, real solutions*. Portsmouth, NH: Heinemann.

Media Lab Press Liaison, (2005). $100 Laptop. Retrieved May 8, 2005, from http://laptop.media.mit.edu/.

Mercer, J. R. (1973). *Labelling the mentally retarded*. Los Angeles: University of California Press.

Meskill, C., & Mossop, J. (2000). Electronic texts in ESOL classrooms. *TESOL Quarterly, 34*, 585–592.

Metcalf, S. (2002, January 28). Reading between the lines. *The Nation*. Retrieved February 22, 2003, from www.thenation.com/doc.mhtml?i= 20020128&s=metcalf.

Meyer, R. J. (2002). *Phonics exposed: Understanding and resisting systematic direct intense phonics instruction*. Mahwah, NJ: Lawrence Erlbaum.

Miller, C., & Swift. K. (1979). *Words and women*. Harmondsworth, UK: Penguin.

Miner, B. (2003, Spring). Keeping public schools public: Privatizers' Trojan Horse. *Rethinking Schools, 17*(3). Retrieved March 6, 2005, from www.rethinkingschools.org.

MIT News Office. (1997). MIT Media Lab, 2B1 Foundation seek "have-not" educators from Third World to break down economic barriers via computers. Retrieved May 8, 2005, from http://web.mit.edu/newsoffice/1997/2b1.html.

Morris, D. (1992). *Case studies in teaching beginning readers: The Howard Street tutoring manual*. Boone, NC: Fieldstream.

Morris, D., Shaw, B., & Perney, J. (1990). Helping low readers in grades 2 and 3: An after-school volunteer tutoring program. *Elementary School Journal, 91*, 133–150.

Moses, R. P. & Cobb, C. E., Jr. (2001). *Radical equations: Civil rights from Mississippi to the Algebra Project*. Boston: Beacon Press.

Nation, P., & Coady, J. (1988). Vocabulary and reading. In R. Carter & M. McCarthy (Eds.), *Vocabulary and language teaching* (pp. 97–110). London: Longman.

National Center for Education Statistics. (2003). *International comparisons in fourth-grade reading literacy: Findings from the Progress in International Reading Literacy Study (PIRLS) of 2001*. Washington DC: U.S. Department of Education.

National Center for Educational Statistics. (2004). *The Nation's report card: Reading highlights 2003*. Washington DC: U.S. Department of Education.

National Commission on Excellence in Education. (1983). *A nation at risk: The imperative for educational reform*. Washington, DC: U.S. Government Printing Office.

National Conference of State Legislatures. (2005). *Task Force on No Child Left Behind: Final report*. Denver, CO: National Conference of State Legislatures.

National Reading Panel. (2000). *Teaching children to read: An evidence-based assessment of the scientific research literature on reading and its implications for reading instruction*. Washington, DC: NICHD.

Negroponte, N. (1995). *Being digital*. New York: Alfred A. Knopf.

Neill, M., Guisbond, L., & Schaeffer, B., with Madden, J., & Legeros, L. (2004). *Failing our children: How "No Child Left Behind" undermines quality and equity in education*. Cambridge, MA: Fairtest: The National Center for Fair & Open Testing.

Neisser, U., Boodoo, G., Bouchard, T. J., Jr., Boykin, A. W., Brody, N., Ceci, S. J., Halpern, D. F., Loehlin, J. C., Perloff, R., Sternberg, R. J., & Urbina, S. (1996). Intelligence: Knowns and unknowns. *The American Psychologist 51*, 77–101.

Neuman, S. B. (1999). Books make a difference: A study of access to literacy. *Reading Research Quarterly, 34*(3), 286–311.

Neuman, S. B., & Celano, D. (2001). Access to print in low-income and middle-income communities: An ecological study of four neighborhoods. *Reading Research Quarterly, 36*, 8–26.

New London Group. (1996). A pedagogy of multiliteracies: Designing social futures. *Harvard Educational Review, 66*, 60–92.

Newkirk, T. (2002, April 24). Reading and the limits of science. *Education Week*.

Newman, D., Griffin, P., & Cole, M. (1989). *The construction zone: Working for cognitive change in school*. Cambridge: Cambridge University Press.

Norton, B. (2000). *Identity and language learning: Gender, ethnicity and educational change*. London: Longman.

Ogbu, J. U. (1992). Understanding cultural diversity and learning. *Educational Researcher, 21*(8), 5–14, 24.

Oppenheimer, T. (1997). The computer delusion. *The Atlantic Monthly, 280*(1), 45–62.

Oppenheimer, T. (2003). *The flickering mind: The false promise of technology in the classroom, and how learning can be saved*. New York: Syndetic Solutions.

Organization for Economic Cooperation and Development. (2001). *Knowledge and skills for life: First results from PISA 2000.* Paris: Organization for Economic Cooperation and Development.

Organization for Economic Cooperation and Development. (2004a). *Learning for tomorrow's world: First results from PISA 2003.* Paris: Organization for Economic Cooperation and Development.

Organization for Economic Cooperation and Development. (2004b). *Messages from PISA 2000.* Paris: Organization for Economic Cooperation and Development.

Pahl, K., & Rowsell, J. (2005). *Understanding literacy education: Using new literacy studies in the classroom.* San Francisco: Sage.

Papert, S. (1980). *Mindstorms: Children, computers, and powerful ideas.* New York: Basic Books.

Parker, L. L. (2005). *Language development technologies for young English learners.* Paper prepared as part of the Technology in Support of Young Second Language Learners Project at the University of California Office of the President, under a grant from the William and Flora Hewlett Foundation.

Parsad, B., & Jones, J. (2005) *Internet access in U.S. public schools and classrooms: 1994–2003.* Washington, DC: National Center for Educational Statistics. Retrieved April 24, 2005, from http://nces.ed.gov/pubsearch/pubsinfo.asp?pubid=2005015.

Payne, K. J., & Biddle, B. J. (1999). Poor school funding, child poverty, and mathematics achievement. *Educational Researcher, 28*(6), 4–13.

Pavlenko, A., & Norton, B. (2006). Imagined communities, identity, and English language learning. In J. Cummins & C. Davison (Eds.), *International handbook of English language teaching.* Norwell, MA: Springer.

Peirce, B. (1995). Social identity, investment, and language learning. *TESOL Quarterly, 29*, 9–31.

Pérez, A., & Singer, M. Retrieved August 10, 2005, from the Project FRESA website: http://www.orillas.org/fresa.

Perry, T., and Delpit, L. (Eds.). (2001). *The real Ebonics debate: Power, language, and the education of African-American children.* Boston: Beacon Press.

Peterson, B. (2001). Teaching math across the curriculum. In B. Bigelow, L. Christensen, S. Karp, B. Miner, & B. Peterson (Eds.), *Rethinking our classrooms: Teaching for equity and justice* (Vol. 2, pp. 84–88). Milwaukee, WI: Rethinking Schools.

Piaget, J. (1929). *The child's conception of the world.* New York: Harcourt, Brace, Jovanovich.

Pinnell, G. S., Lyons, C. A., Deford, D. E., Bryk, A. S., & Sletzer, M. (1994). Comparing instructional models for the literacy education of high-rish first graders. *Reading Research Quarterly, 29*, 8–39.

Pittway, D. S. (2004). Investment and second language acquisition. *Critical Inquiry in Language Studies: An International Journal, 1*(4), 203–218.

Popham, W. J. (2004, July 28). *Ruminations regarding NCLB's most malignant provision: Adequate yearly progress.* Paper prepared for Center on Education Policy's Forum to Discuss Ideas to Improve the Accountability Provisions Under the No Child Left Behind Act. Washington, DC. Retrieved April 22, 2005, from www.cep-dc.org/pubs/Forum28July2004/.

Popham, W. J. (2005, April/May). F for assessment. *Edutopia*, pp. 38–45.

Postlethwaite, T. N., & Ross, K. N. (1992). *Effective schools in reading: Implications for educational planners. An exploratory study.* The Hague: The International Association for the Evaluation of Educational Achievement.

Pressley, M., Duke, N. K., & Boling, E. C. (2004). The educational science and scientifically-based instruction we need: Lessons from reading research and policy making. *Harvard Educational Review, 74*, 30–61.

Ramírez, J. D. (1992). Executive summary. *Bilingual Research Journal, 16*, 1–62.

RAND Education. (2004). *Meeting literacy goals set by No Child Left Behind: A long uphill road.* Research Brief, RAND Corporation. Retrieved March 12, 2005, from www.edteck.com/read/pdf/RAND_RB9081.pdf.

Rand Reading Study Group. (2002). *Reading for understanding: Toward an R&D program in reading comprehension.* Santa Monica, CA: RAND Corporation.

Ravitch, D. (March 15, 2005). Failing the wrong grades. *New York Times.* Op-Ed.

Reyes, M. L. (2001). Unleashing possibilities: Biliteracy in the primary grades. In M. L. Reyes & J. Halcón (Eds.), *The best for our children: Critical perspectives on literacy for Latino students* (pp. 96–121). New York: Teachers College Press.

Rose, D., & Dalton, B. (2002). The brain and reading comprehension. In M. Pressley, L. Gambrell, & C. C. Block (Eds.), *Comprehension instruction: Building on the past and improving instruction for today's students.* San Francisco: Jossey Bass.

Rossell, C. H., & Baker, K. (1996). The effectiveness of bilingual education. *Research in the Teaching of English, 30*, 7–74.

Rothstein, R. (2002). *Out of balance: Our understanding of how schools affect society and how society affects schools.* Thirtieth Anniversary Essay. Chicago: The Spencer Foundation.

Rouse, C. E., Krueger, A. B., & Markman, L. (2004, February). *Putting computerized instruction to the test: A randomized evaluation of a "scientifically-based" reading program.* NBER Working Paper No. W10315.

Russell, M., & Haney, W. (2000, January). The gap between testing and technology in schools. *NBETPP Statements, 1*(2), 1–8. Retrieved May 10, 2005, from www.softwaresecure.com/pdf/V1N2.pdf

Russell, M., & Plati, T. (2000). *Mode of administration effects on MCAS Composition performance for grades four, eight and ten.* A report submitted to the Massachusetts Department of Education by the National Board on Educational Testing and Public Policy.

Russell, M., & Plati, T. (2001, January 21). Mode of administration effects on composition performance for grades eight and ten. *Teachers College Record.* Retrieved May 10, 2005, from www.tcrecord.org/Content.asp?ContentID=10709.

Sacks, P. (1999). *Standardized minds: The high price of America's testing culture and what we can do to change it.* Cambridge, MA: Perseus.

Santa, C. M., & Hoien, T. (1999). An assessment of Early Steps: A program for early intervention of reading problems. *Reading Research Quarterly, 34*(1), 54–79.

Schecter, S., & Cummins, J. (Eds.). (2003). *Multilingual education in practice: Using diversity as a resource.* Portsmouth, NH: Heinemann.

Schlesinger, A., Jr. (1991). *The disuniting of America.* New York: W. W. Norton.

Schultz, L. H. (no date). A validation study of WiggleWorks, the Scholastic Beginning Literacy System. Retrieved, September 2, 2004, from http://teacher.scholastic.com/products/wiggleworks/pdfs/WWValid.Study.pdf.

Shanahan, T. (2001). Response to Elaine Garan. *Language Arts, 79*(1), 70–71.

Shanahan, T. (2004). Critiques of the National Reading Panel Report: Their implications for research, policy, and practice. In P. McCardle & V. Chhabra (Eds.), *The voice of evidence in reading research* (pp. 235–265). Baltimore: Paul H. Brookes.

Share, D., & Stanovich, K. (1995). Cognitive processes in early reading development: Accommodating individual differences into a model of acquisition. *Issues in Education: Contributions from Educational Psychology, 1*(1), 1–57.

Shohamy, E., Levine, T., Spolsky, B., Kere-Levy, M., Inbar, O., & Shemesh, M. (2002). *The academic achievements of immigrant children from the former USSR and Ethiopia.* Report (in Hebrew) submitted to the Ministry of Education, Israel.

Sirotnik, K. A. (1983). What you see is what you get—Consistency, persistency, and mediocrity in classrooms. *Harvard Educational Review, 53,* 16–31.

Skourtou, E., Kourtis-Kazoullis, V., & Cummins, J. (2006). Designing virtual learning environments for academic language development. In J. Weiss, J. Nolan, & P. Trifonas (Eds.), *International handbook of virtual learning environments* (pp. 443–469). Norwell, MA: Springer.

Snow, C. E., Burns, M. S., & Griffin, P. (Eds.). (1998). *Preventing reading difficulties in young children.* Washington, DC: National Academy Press.

Stanovich, K. E., & Stanovich, P. J. (1998). Ending the reading wars. *Orbit, 28*(4), 49–55.

Stefanakis, E. H. (2002). *Multiple intelligences and portfolios: A window into the learner's mind.* Portsmouth, NH: Heinemann.

Stotsky, S. (1999). *Losing our language: How multicultural classroom instruction is undermining our children's ability to read, write, and reason.* New York: The Free Press.

Thomas, W. P., & Collier, V. (1997). *School effectiveness for language minority students.* Washington, DC: National Clearinghouse for Bilingual Education.

Thomas, W. P., & Collier, V. P. (2002). *A national study of school effectiveness for language minority students' long-term academic achievement.* Santa Cruz, CA: Center for Research on Education, Diversity and Excellence, University of California–Santa Cruz. www.crede.ucsc.edu.

Tizard, J., Schofield, W. N., & Hewison, J. (1982). Collaboration between teachers and parents in assisting children's reading. *British Journal of Educational Psychology, 52,* 1–15.

Tonucci, F. (1981). *Viaje alrededor de "El Mundo": Un diario de clase de Mario Lodi y sus alumnos.* M. Vassallo, trans. Barcelona: Editorial Laia. (Original work published 1980 as Un giornalino di classe [A classroom newspaper]. Roma Bari: Guis, Laterza and Figli Spa.)

Toohey, K., Manyak, P., & Day, E. (2006). ESL learners in the early school years: Identity and mediated classroom practices. In J. Cummins & C. Davison (Eds.), *International handbook of English language teaching.* Norwell, MA: Springer.

21st Century Literacy Summit. (2002). *21st century literacy in a convergent media world* [White paper]. Berlin, Germany: Author. Retrieved April 14, 2003, from www.21stcenturyliteracy.org/white/WhitePaperEnglish.pdf.

Uriarte, M. (2002). The high stakes of high-stakes testing. In Z. F. Beykont (Ed.), *The power of culture: Teaching across language difference* (pp. 3–24). Cambridge, MA: Harvard Education Publishing Group.

Valdés, G., & Figueroa, R. A. (1994). *Bilingualism and testing: A special case of bias.* Norwood, NJ: Ablex.

Van Herrin, C. (2005, November 23). *LapTopical: The laptops' weblog.* Retrieved May 7, 2006, from www.laptopical.com/annan-unveils-cheap-laptop.html.

Vellutino, F. R., Scanlon, D. M., Sipay, E. R., Small, S. G., Pratt, A., Chen, R., & Denckla, M. B. (1996). Cognitive profiles of difficult-to-remediate and readily remediated poor readers: Early intervention as a vehicle for distinguishing between cognitive and experiential deficits as basic causes of specific reading disability. *Journal of Educational Psychology, 88,* 601–638.

Venezky, R. L. (1998). An alternative perspective on Success for All. *Advances in Educational Policy, 4,* 145–165.

Verhoeven, L. (2000). Components in early second language reading and spelling. *Scientific Studies of Reading, 4*(4), 313–330.

Vincent, C. (1996). *Singing to a star: The school meanings of second generation Salvadorean students.* Doctoral dissertation, George Mason University, Fairfax, VA.

von Zastrow, C. (2004). *Academic atrophy. The condition of the liberal arts in America's public schools.* Washington, DC: Council for Basic Education.

Vygotsky, L. S. (1978). *Mind in society: The development of higher psychological processes.* Cambridge, MA: Harvard University Press.

Warschauer, M., Grant, D., Del Real, G., & Rousseau, M. (2004). Promoting academic literacy with technology: Successful laptop programs in K–12 schools. *System, 32,* 525–537.

Warschauer, M., Knobel, M., & Stone, M. (2004). Technology and equity in schooling: Deconstructing the digital divide. *Educational Policy 18*(4), 562–588.

Wenglinsky, H. (1998). *Does it compute?: The relationship between educational technology and student achievement in mathematics* (Policy Information Report). Princeton, NJ: Educational Testing Service.

Wilhelm, T., Carmen, D., & Reynolds, M. (2002, June). *Connecting kids to technology: Challenges and opportunities. Kids Count Snapshot.* The Anne E. Casey Foundation. Retrieved August 23, 2004, from www.aecf.org/publications/data/snapshot_june2002.pdf.

Willis, J. (2003). Instructional technologies in schools: Are we there yet? *Computers in the Schools, 20*(1/2), 11–33.

Winerip, M. (2003, May 28). The changes unwelcome, a model teacher moves on. *The New York Times.* Retrieved May, 28 2003, from www.nytimes.com.

Winkley, C. (2005, May) *Teachers' perspectives on authorship as a pedagogical tool to develop voice: A participatory study.* Unpublished doctoral dissertation, University of San Francisco.

Wong Fillmore, L. (1991). When learning a second language means losing the first. *Early Childhood Research Quarterly, 6,* 323–346.

Wood, J. (2001). Can software support children's vocabulary development? *Language Learning & Technology, 5*(1), 166–201.

Worswick, C. (2001). *School performance of the children of immigrants in Canada, 1994–98* (No. 178; ISBN: 0–662–31229–5). Ottawa: Statistics Canada.

Wrigley, T. (2003). *Schools of hope: A new agenda for school improvement.* Stoke on Trent, UK: Trentham Books.

Yatvin, J. (2002). Babes in the woods: The wanderings of the National Reading Panel. *Phi Delta Kappan, 83*(5), 364–369.

Zinn, H. (1995). *A people's history of the United States, 1492–present.* New York: Harper Perennial.

INDEX